"FOURTH QUARTER" FIRST

How Today's Family Business Pioneers Are Achieving Incredible Lasting Results

Nick Niemann

FAMILY
BUSINESS
PIONEER
INSTITUTE

"Begin with the end in mind."

Stephen Covey
Author, "The 7 Habits of Highly
Effective People"

"If a man knows not to which port he sails, no wind is favorable."

Ancient philosopher Seneca

"Start with the end outcome and work backwards to make your dream possible."

Author Dr. Wayne W. Dyer

"If you don't change the direction you are going, then you're likely to end up where you're heading."

John C. Maxwell
World's #1 Leadership Expert

"A dream written down with a date becomes a goal. A goal broken down into steps becomes a plan. A plan backed by action makes your dreams come true."

Greg S. Reid
Founder and CEO of Secret Knock

"Control your own destiny or someone else will."

Jack Welch
Former CEO of General Electric

"Never run away from anything. Never."

Winston Churchill

"What does it avail an archer to know how to hit the outer parts of the target, if he does not know how to hit the center?"

St. Louis de Montfort

Preface

Hundreds of Family Business Leaders/Pioneers over the course of 37 years have trusted us to "look into the future" with them for a very specific reason. Whether they are a startup or already well into many years with their business, they want to achieve remarkable success in all four quarters of their life as a business leader and owner. And they don't want to let down those who depend on them.

In each case, we've found that the best approach for achieving incredible results, as author Stephen Covey reminds us, is to "Begin with the end in mind." Applied to the success of Family Business Leaders, this means to begin everything by understanding the whole picture by seeing and starting with your personal "Fourth Quarter First."

By deciding early on what you want your Fourth Quarter to look like, you can set the right course in your first three quarters to be on target when your personal Fourth Quarter arrives. Too many business owners have had a great First, Second and Third Quarter, but have lost the game in their Fourth Quarter. What's the point of doing that!

None of us want to let down those who depend on us. We all want to keep the promises we have made to ourselves, to our families, to our colleagues, to our stakeholders, to our customers and to our communities.

The Family Business Leaders we work with deploy a Pioneer Mindset. You are eager to explore and create new opportunities. You look for new ways to advance the lives of your colleagues, customers and family. You begin with a specific, thoughtful end in mind in everything you do. And you set a course for winning all of your Four Quarters.

You know your plan may not be perfect and that it is subject to change. But for now, you proceed every day with your end objectives in mind. You understand where you want to head, how to get there, and who you won't let down.

Nick Niemann, JD
Family Business Continuity Attorney
www.FourthQuarterFirst.com

To check Nick's availability to work on a "Fourth Quarter" Game Plan with you, your spouse, your CEO, your President, your partner, your colleague, your mentor, your parent or your client, please contact him at 402-633-1489 or email him at nniemann@McGrathNorth.com.

Introduction

I first met Nick Niemann when I brought the Vistage International CEO Peer Group program to Nebraska several years ago. I interviewed Nick to decide if I wanted him to serve as the Legal Counsel on our Trusted Advisor Board. I came expecting to hear typical lawyer talk. Instead, what I quickly saw was a new breed of attorney. Nick was soon also interviewing me. He wanted to know how Vistage could enhance the business and personal lives of its CEO members, how it could vastly improve the companies which joined it and how big I planned to grow our Nebraska presence.

I quickly learned Nick was working with business strategists from 45 countries to co-create what would become known as Business Model Generation. This international initiative would introduce the world to the Business Model Canvas -- a powerful new technique for creating, re-designing, improving and pivoting a company's Business Model to achieve greater success. Nick was soon being asked to personally teach this profit system to over 850 Vistage CEOs and Key Executives throughout the U.S. and Canada. This remarkably versatile system is now being used by over 5,000,000 entrepreneurs and strategic thinkers around the world.

As a former CEO of an international company, I've worked with many attorneys. But never one like Nick Niemann. He is a business profit strategist first, who happens to also have an incisive legal mind.

So, I wasn't surprised when organizations like Secret Knock, one of the country's top programs for entrepreneurs, asked him to speak to their business leaders. Nor was I surprised when Inc. Magazine asked him to become part of their Launch! program for startup entrepreneurs. And I wasn't surprised when the founder of CEO Space International personally asked Nick to join their program.

Nick has that pioneer mindset which tirelessly explores ways to bring greater success to the business leaders he works with every day. As I have told him: "I know the work that goes into mastering something --- and you are a master!"

Cathy Fitzhenry
Omaha Chair - Vistage International, the world's leading CEO peer group organization

"FOURTH QUARTER" FIRST

Your "Fourth Quarter" First
The Essential Mindshift For Family Business Pioneer Success

Your Profit Playbook
Profitable Growth For Your Business

Your Protection Playbook
Wealth Protection For What You're Building

Your Estate Playbook
Lifestyle Continuity For You And Your Family

Your Succession Playbook
Personal Freedom On Your Terms

Your "Fourth Quarter" Game Plan
Putting It All Together

Information And Background

Index

Your "Fourth Quarter" First

The Essential Mindshift For Family Business Pioneer Success

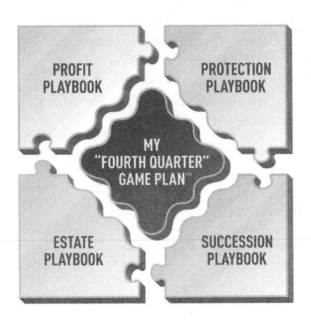

CHAPTER
1

Today's Family Business Pioneers

"We are almost there", said my Dad. "Just a little further ahead." It was 1968 and my Dad and Mother had brought the family to Kentucky for vacation. My Dad had wanted us to see the Kentucky horse farms he was always talking to us about. I had asked if we could also include a visit to the burial site of Daniel Boone.

All of a sudden we were there, next to the American Pioneer who had fascinated me from the first time I had read about his daring exploits and his courage in the face of daunting odds.

Daniel Boone was the first American Pioneer I learned about. My Dad was the first Family Business Pioneer I learned from.

Today's Family Business Pioneers

The term "Business Pioneer" is often limited to well known business leaders like Thomas Edison, JP Morgan, Henry Ford, Ray Kroc, Warren Buffett, Bill Gates, Jeff Bezos, Sam Walton and Steve Jobs. The global business publication, Financial Times, adds some insights, by naming the "50 Leading Business Pioneers" in a variety of business sectors.

However, I think those of us in business meet Business Pioneers every day. Every family business leader who lives to explore and create new opportunities and to find new ways to advance the lives of their colleagues, customers and family are Business Pioneers in my book.

The reality today and into the future we all face is that if you and your leadership team are not Business Pioneers, the likelihood of continuing success is becoming extremely remote.

Over the past several years I've had the opportunity to meet (and learn from) today's Business Pioneers from practically every business sector throughout the U.S. and Canada. My work with McGrath North, Vistage International, CEO Space International, Secret Knock, The John Maxwell Company, Family Firm Institute, Business Enterprise Institute, Strategyzer, James Malinchak International and Inc. Magazine has introduced me to business owners, CEOs and key executives who are leading the way for the next great future for our American society, either as the leaders of startup companies or as the leaders of existing or longstanding companies.

The Family Business Pioneers I've worked with and learned from have a very definite mindset which sets them apart. They love to take on and solve new opportunities from a startup perspective. They have a high degree of passion to reach their goals by overcoming the challenges and failures they face. That is to say, they have grit. They are willing to take calculated risks and will "boldly go where no one has gone before".

And the approach they invariably take is to first decide on the end result they want and then work backwards to figure out the steps needed to get there.

As an entrepreneur and business leader, my Dad was a great example of the explorer mindset of America's Family Business Pioneers. He saw his responsibility in keeping his businesses going as not only a responsibility to his own family, but also to those dependent on him and his companies for the jobs that supported their families. As someone who spent the early part of his career playing minor league baseball in the 110 degree heat throughout small towns in southern Texas, and then spent a tour of duty facing enemy lines during the Korean War, he realized that "you change the conditions that can be changed, and you figure out how to overcome those you can't." He exemplified the Business Pioneer spirit we see in so many business successes today.

Where Are We Headed?

Somehow, today, despite all of the progress, growth, innovation and success that our country has experienced over the past many years, many seem to be asking whether this "Land of Opportunity" is now coming to a close. Have we as a country reached a stall point? Have we as a country peaked out? Will our children have decent jobs? Does college still make economic sense? Do couples still believe they can afford to have all of the children God wishes to bless them with? Is retirement at a reasonable age still a reality?

A lot of demographic, economic and fiscal statistics seem to shed a negative response to these questions. As I write this book, tremendous attempts are being made by our new President Trump to bring companies and investment back to the United States – to again unleash the full power of American ingenuity.

For many years, we have seen intense, unnecessary over-regulation of business. We have seen job gains remaining tough to come by, and many of those which we see are part-time at moderate pay. College graduates have been finding that jobs in their fields are harder to come by. Young adults are living longer with their parents due to financial reasons. Young couples are delaying marriage and delaying the start of their families.

The disruptive impact, and opportunities from, technology, robotics and AI, are being felt and explored. Many companies are struggling to adjust to new, fast paced change. Many fail. But many succeed.

The U.S. is not alone. My travels in Canada and Europe and interviews with business leaders abroad show the same is occurring there – both as to companies and families.

Speaking to 25,000 attendees at a recent conference, long time Cisco CEO John Chambers predicted that more than a third of businesses today will not survive the next ten years. He warned companies that they must not "miss a market transition or Business Model" or "underestimate your competitor of the future." He made it clear that "Either we disrupt or we get disrupted."

Many blame government policies and programs. Many blame the impact of new technology. Many blame globalization. Many hope each new national leader will finally make a real, positive difference. Perhaps this time we are finally seeing this.

However, these are all simply the conditions of the playing field and the rules of the game – for small, middle market and big business. While we can advocate mightily for better playing conditions and more productive rules, as we all should, life and opportunities don't wait for perfect conditions.

As my Dad would say in the face of tough times, "Amen and Glory Be." That was his way of saying that we are responsible for going after our own outcomes, despite the playing conditions.

> ## *Pioneer Mindset*
> ☑ *What You Don't See.* *Constantly seek and destroy your personal and business blind spots – otherwise, they will hurt you.*

We have all heard the statistics on how few family businesses make it to the second or third generation and how many implode in the first generation. Thirty-four percent of businesses fail in their first two years. Less than 50% are still operating after six years.

Of those that make it past the new business childhood phase, only 30% to 35% survive to the second generation. Only 12% to 15% make it to the third generation, while 3% make it to the fourth generation.

These statistics, whether correct or not, have been widely reported, such as by USA Today and the Small Business Administration.

So, how can this be addressed? Clearly we all see new thriving businesses being created across the business landscape every day. At the same time, we watch with dismay as many businesses fail or stall and jobs and personal wealth and opportunities and dreams and careers and retirements are lost.

What are we not learning in our business schools or our business association conferences or our business lives. Or what are we learning but not putting into practice? Are there some fundamental ingredients which, if put into place and practiced, would produce better results?

I believe there are. And if we just listen to the Family Business Pioneers we meet every day, the ingredients become clear.

Building on yesterday's and today's Family Business Pioneers we are living in an exciting time for incredible business opportunities.

As my Dad would say – "Now don't blow it."

The Pioneers In Our Midst

Who exactly are the Business Pioneers I've been speaking of for many years and throughout this book.

The Business Chemistry Program has also been seeing this. Its March 2017 report titled "Business Chemistry® in the C-Suite" described the 4 primary types of leaders it saw: Pioneers ("who value possibilities and spark creativity", Drivers ("who value challenge and generate momentum"), Guardians ("who value stability and bring order and rigor") and Integrators ("who value connection and draw teams together"). It concluded that each leader is a composite of all 4 of these work styles, but most leaders' behavior and thinking are more closely aligned towards one or two. It found that as to CEOs, 51% of them are primarily Pioneers. It further described Pioneers this way: "Pioneers value possibilities, and they spark energy and imagination on their teams. They believe risks are worth taking and that it's fine to go with your gut. Their focus is big-picture. They're drawn to bold new ideas and creative approaches."

It seems to me this is a good practical summary of the mindset which I've seen in successful Family Business Pioneers around the country.

The Family Business Pioneer Mindset

Yet, there is so much more to how the Family Business Pioneer thinks and acts. Over the course of the past 37 years, I've been engaged by hundreds of Family Business Pioneer CEOs to work together with them to grow, protect and pass on their companies. In every engagement, each CEO has also taught me something about the mindset they deploy to achieve incredibly successful, profitable and fulfilling organizations.

The answer isn't a single secret. <u>The answer is a mindset that consists of the many specific ways they think and act.</u>

Throughout this book, in addition to covering the actions they are taking, I'll share much of these aspects of the Pioneer Mindset which I've learned from Family Business Pioneer CEOs from around the world.

> ## *Pioneer Mindset*
>
> ☑ *Developing Others.*   The pioneer mindset can be *developed and learned. Or not. Your call.*

CHAPTER
2

What Happens When . . . ?

How do today's Family Business Pioneers achieve lasting success? Whether instinctively or methodically, I see them asking and answering some version of essentially the following two key questions time and time again:

- "What will be the probable, almost certain, future outcome of our present course, if left unchanged?"

- "What's missing, the presence of which will make a substantial difference in producing a better future outcome?"

Or, in short – they first look into the future, to their personal Fourth Quarter, and ask "What Happens When …?"

In studying these questions, in the context of the reasons why businesses succeed and fail, I believe there are certain key ingredients which are present in long term successful companies, and which are practiced by great Business Pioneers, which are deficient or missing from those companies and business owners who falter, stall or fail.

For those companies, the presence of these ingredients will produce a better future outcome.

It Starts With "What Happens When. . .?

This all begins with companies and their leadership being prepared for both the expected and unexpected by being able to address

"What Happens When. . .?" in the variety of situations that impact the life of business owners and the companies they lead.

> ### *Pioneer Mindset*
> ☑ *Circle of Options. Your options are not limited to the two points at the ends of a line, but instead extend to every point on a circle that connects those two points.*

Some examples* from our experience of working with family business owners from around the world help to illustrate the importance of continually asking (and answering) this question – and <u>the results if you don't</u> do this. These follow.

Bob's Business Model Countdown: Understanding How "Transferable Value" Impacts Your Game Plan

Bob had come to us with high expectations as to the price he thought his Company would sell for as he approached his expected retirement date. He was certain of this because he had seen other "similar" companies sell in the past for a 1.2X multiple of gross revenue. He figured his Company would easily sell for the same.

However, what Bob had failed to understand was that buyers are only partly interested in top line revenue. More important to a company's selling price is the future net cash flow the company can reasonably be expected to produce. If you can predict what the company's cash flow will be, when it will occur, and whether a buyer can achieve this when it buys the company, then you can reasonably estimate the company's "transferable value".

Bob's gross margin and bottom line failed to live up to industry standards, which meant he wasn't likely to achieve the price or retirement he had envisioned. Most importantly, however, was that our study of his industry told us his Business Model was likely dying. Unless he invested in some new directions, he could soon be driving his Company into the ditch.

---

*   <u>While these examples are</u> real, I've changed the actual names, types of businesses and other details so that no specific person or business can be identified.

Bob had been focusing on the smooth ride he had been enjoying. However, like Blockbuster when faced with Netflix, the bridge was washing out up ahead, and he was driving with his headlights turned off. Bob's retirement would be delayed.

What happens when you misunderstand value and haven't been constantly challenging your Business Model's design? What was missing for Bob that would have produced a better outcome?

Pioneer Mindset

☑ **Direction.** *Snapshots are good. But your best friend is seeing the opportunities and threats nestled in trends.*

Dave's "Mulligan" Game Plan: May I Please Have A Do-Over?

Dave's assistant plant manager didn't have a lot of good news to report to Dave's wife, Jennie. The explosions which had rocked Dave's chemical plant in New Elm City, and the resulting chemical fires, had killed Dave, the plant manager and two plant inspectors. They also seriously injured a dozen other employees and forced the evacuation of residents within a 5-mile radius of the plant, many of whom were checking into local hospitals with complaints of lung irritation.

Dave had just told Jennie that morning he was concerned he may have deferred the maintenance program for too long. He had lined up an inspection for that day.

Fusion Blend Chemical Corporation blended oilfield production chemicals and then distributed them through several distribution sites in the United States and Middle East. Dave had worked for the Company for twenty years before purchasing it ten years ago. He had paid off the purchase price in four years, had doubled the Company's size and was looking forward to his and Jennie's retirement in 5 years, when he planned to put Fusion Blend on the market.

Besides the tragic loss of her beloved husband, Jennie was about to face the effects of Dave's "Mulligan" Game Plan – which had been based on his assumption that he'd always have a second shot at overcoming whatever befell him and his Company. However, there would be no do-over for Dave or Jennie, especially as the business and personal lawsuits started lining up.

What happens when you have failed to put asset protection strategies in place in advance? What was missing for Dave and Jennie that would have produced a better outcome?

The Impact of Frank's Family - On His Personal Wealth

Frank was visibly upset when he came in to see us in the Fall of 2011. He had been planning to retire in three years by age 60, based on the combined value of his personal investments and his Company. This was now on hold for an indefinite period of time. Like many, he had suffered a significant hit in the 2008 – 2009 stock market declines and the recession's impact on his business. But this wasn't what was bothering him. He had resolved the financial spending issues he had had with his wife and put his business back on solid footing.

Frank was starting to understand that business owner Business Continuity and Succession Planning is not just about the business. During his tenure as the founder and owner of Zuppo Building Components in Sioux Falls, South Dakota, he had enjoyed a healthy bottom line. While it took years to achieve this level of success, he was happy to be able to share the fruits of his labors with his children. For his Estate Planning and Asset Protection reasons, he had gifted 48% of his stock to his and his wife Fione's four adult married children and their spouses. As a Subchapter "S" corporation, he was also able to easily distribute dividends to himself, to Fione and to their children's families.

The recent call by their son, Lou, is what prompted the referral of Frank to me.

Frank had no idea that Lou and his wife had pledged their Zuppo stock as collateral for both an unnecessary home remodeling project and to help secure financing for Lou's Fort Lauderdale real estate development business. The Florida real estate market had zapped both the equity in his home and the viability of his business.

The bank was calling and was ready to either demand a high price for the stock or plan to remain a shareholder in Zuppo for a long time (also possibly threatening its Subchapter "S" status).

Frank's local corporate and estate planning attorneys had handled the stock gifts but never suggested that he have his children and their spouses sign a Family Buy-Sell Agreement. They were family, after all.

What happens when you have enabled your family to become owners in your business, but you didn't put a Buy-Sell Agreement in place because you thought that was just for non-family owners? What was missing for Frank, Fione and Lou that would have produced a better outcome?

Pioneer Mindset

☑ *Course Correction.* *Be quick to fully recognize when the situation has changed.*

Sally's Game Plan – Up in Smoke With Her Perishable Business Model

I had just returned from presenting my Business Model Profit program to three CEO groups in Winnipeg Canada when Sally came to visit with me. She had just been referred to me by her Insurance Advisor. Fifteen years earlier she had gone "all in" by converting her commercial real estate business and becoming one of Blockbuster Video's landlords. She had established a very efficient operation by building and leasing Blockbuster Video stores to Blockbuster, Inc. throughout the Midwest.

Sally thought she had the ideal Game Plan. She viewed her big bet as a certain long-term annuity. After all, the public demand for movies was not expected to subside.

Unfortunately, Sally's risky "Flea Flicker" Game Plan promised either a big gain or getting sacked. On September 23, 2010, Blockbuster filed for Chapter 11 bankruptcy protection. Dish Network eventually won the auction to buy Blockbuster for a fraction of its previous value.

In April 2011, Blockbuster's landlords objected to Dish's assumption of leases, claiming they did not have adequate assurance the new owner would honor the leases. In the end, Dish announced it would only keep 500 Blockbuster stores open. At its peak, Blockbuster had more than 4,000 stores nationwide.

Sally had been sacked for a major loss.

Just like Carl Icahn, who called Blockbuster "the worst investment I ever made" (Harvard Business Review, April 2011), Sally had also failed to understand why Blockbuster's Business Model, like the Business Models of all companies, had a limited life. All Business Models are perishable. Sally failed to understand that her own Business Model suffered from the same fate.

For Sally, her loss was substantial and her exit outlook considerably bleaker than what she had foreseen 15 years earlier.

What happens when you don't recognize that all Business Models, including yours, are perishable? What was missing for Sally that would have produced a better outcome?

Harry's Game Plan – Misunderstanding The "X Factor" In Succession Planning

Harry couldn't understand what had gone wrong. He thought he had groomed the perfect team to take the reins of his biotechnology company – ready to step in and march the Company forward just like he had done for the past 35 years.

However, ever since he returned from his three week vacation, his team was a bit jittery, which only seemed to get worse when he was around. Harry had worked with a variety of consultants and experts over a period of time and tried to implement the various suggestions they had given him. But in the end, all he had was a "Junk Drawer" Game Plan and an apparently frustrated team that couldn't understand the direction he was setting.

Baby boomer Harry had failed to understand the X Factor in Succession Planning. In a world of Facebook, LinkedIn, Instagram, Groupon, GoNabit, BRIC, Twournal, Nowism, Flash Sales, Foursquare and Off And Away, Harry was having a hard time even carrying on a conversation with his team, much less deciding who among them could best take over leadership.

As Baby Boomer business owners come to grips with the notion of passing their Company forward to the next generation of leaders, it becomes important to understand Generation X and Millennials – their belief systems and world views. By examining the presumptions that Gen

X and Millennials have about life, relationships and responsibility, Boomer executives can attract and keep the right team members and select the right successor, as well as prepare themselves for the organizational changes that will likely occur as the succession process unfolds.

This is not a warning, exactly. It is more like the opening of a window that has been closed for a long time. If the succession with Gen X and Millennials unfolds optimally, a new view of future possibilities will emerge. Your Company's product line may become more relevant and competitive. A new sensitivity to environmental responsibility, community and technology may surface. Your Business Model may change and develop. And this is just the beginning.

Harry thought he had two or three key employees who could succeed him. How could he know how to choose the right successor? And how could he be sure they stuck with him?

What happens when you don't apply next generation thinking to your Business Continuity and Succession Planning? What was missing for Harry that would have produced a better outcome?

Pioneer Mindset

☑ **Mistakes.** *Share your mistakes so your team can learn from them.*

Timeout For Janet – Facing Down The Double-Double Exit Tax

Janet had recently been referred to meet with us because the sale of her business wasn't working out as she had hoped. She had worked hard for 20 years to build a successful human resource firm and was looking forward to being able to sell it now at top price.

However, the buyer (like most buyers) was insisting that, for tax purposes, it wanted this to be an asset purchase rather than a stock purchase. Janet was distressed to learn that this meant a double Federal income tax. Because Janet had chosen to be taxed as a "C" corporation rather than as an "S" corporation, this meant the corporation would pay the first tax on its gain and she'd pay the second tax when she distributed the sales proceeds from the Company.

Unfortunately, since Janet owned 100% of the stock of her Company, the State of Nebraska would also impose a double tax on the sale. Janet was facing the double-double tax.

A national survey by the Exit Planning Institute a few years ago found that 75% of those owners who had already exited from their companies were not satisfied with the results. The reason was that their lack of advance planning resulted in a failure to understand their options.

Janet was about to find herself in the same situation with tax planning choices that needed to be put into action well ahead of a sale to be effective.

What happens when you miss out on using tax reduction strategies because you didn't act soon enough? What was missing for Janet that would have produced a better outcome?

Oops! Time To Hit The Reset Button

Kyle was in a much different mood than when he had first come to see me two years earlier. He had been referred in by Financial Advisor who I knew from Illinois. He hadn't been sure back then that he needed to come in, but his financial advisor had insisted. He didn't engage us then on what turned out to be his first retirement.

Over the course of 26 years, Kyle had founded and built a very successful consumer product distribution business. He had built a very effective distribution network which was producing a $2 million per year EBITDA and growing at a 5 year average annual rate of about 10% in top line revenue and about 12% in bottom line EBITDA. When he came in 2 years ago, he had been ready to finally sell the business to his key employee Ralph. Ralph had been with Kyle for 15 years. Kyle was sure that Ralph was the guy to succeed him. He had visited with Ralph off and on for a couple of years and felt that Ralph was both interested and very capable and would be able to take the business to the next level. He had already talked to Ralph about the key terms and how he would seller-finance 30% of the transaction with a bank of Ralph's choosing to finance 70% of the purchase price.

I explained to Kyle back then that we had a specific process for accomplishing a successful sale to an inside key employee. This involves specific steps which, if followed, would produce a high likelihood of completing a successful transition and exit.

Kyle thought otherwise. He had already determined what the terms would be and that his regular corporate attorney was prepared to draw up the documents so that Kyle could promptly get on with his well-earned retirement.

That was 2 years earlier. Kyle was here now to report to me that indeed the sale to Ralph had proceeded. As it turned out, the bank wasn't willing to finance any part of the transaction, so Kyle needed to seller-finance 100% of it. At the time, he decided that was no problem. He had full confidence that this was going to work out just fine.

Unfortunately, rather than spending his retirement years at his Wisconsin cabin with his wife, he was now back owning and running the business. Within six months, Ralph had defaulted on the seller-financing and, after a four month attempt to restructure and work things out, Kyle finally realized that Ralph just wasn't cut out to be an entrepreneur, a leader, a CEO or a business owner. While Ralph had been a strong operational manager, he just wasn't ready, and never would have been ready, to own, lead and execute what was needed to take the business forward successfully.

Ralph had moved on. Kyle was now stuck with a business which was now producing an EBITDA that had fallen to $1.5 million per year, had lost certain other key personnel, and was showing a negative trend to top line revenue.

What happens when you haven't taken the time to develop your successor correctly and when you pick the wrong buyer and the wrong transaction terms in selling your Company? What was missing for Kyle and Ralph that would have produced a better outcome?

Larry, Jr./Larry, Sr. – A Certain Simple Plan

It was supposed to be a simple plan. However, as Larry, Jr.. explained it, he described a scenario that was all too familiar to me. His father, Larry, Sr., had founded a very successful business-to-business service company thirty years earlier that had been extremely successful during his father's lifetime. Larry, Sr. was an extremely effective innovator as well as a strong leader and motivator. He was the driving force behind his Company.

Larry, Sr. had always expected Larry, Jr. would step in upon his death. However, Larry Sr. had unexpectedly died a few months earlier.

Larry, Jr. was now finding the Company was slipping away from him. He admitted he lacked his father's talents and drive and that he had really never felt comfortable taking over the Company (but he couldn't tell his father that). Since his father hadn't developed a strong leadership team, Larry, Jr. was concerned the Company wasn't going to be worth even the estate taxes still due on it, much less provide the income he needed.

He was now ready to take his chips off the table and sell the Company. He was willing to stay active in the Company for a couple years but he was running out of steam, and his family wanted to see him more. His business was producing consistently strong cash flow at a level that is normally very attractive to most private equity group buyers. Yet he and his M & A intermediary found that none would touch him. When he came to see me about this, it became clear he had made six of the common mistakes business owners and their advisors commonly overlook. And he was running out of time for a course correction if he was going to have a Company built to sell.

What happens when you haven't designed your Company or your leadership team to line up with the features your likely Company buyer wants to see? What was missing for Larry, Sr. and Larry, Jr. that would have produced a better outcome?

Pioneer Mindset

☑ *Want To Be Innovative?* *Forever question and examine yourself and the world around you with curiosity, confidence and courage.*

Seeing The Heart and Soul

What drives the passion of today's Family Business Pioneers? That really is where we must start when beginning with the end in mind.

Into The Future

Peter Drucker is regarded as the founder of modern management. He once summarized the essence of his approach by saying: "I don't predict the future. I look at what has happened already and point out the inevitable result."

Knowing the probable, almost certain future outcome of your present course is the first step for Family Business Pioneers. Knowing what's missing which could produce a better future outcome is the critical next step.

This happens if and when business owners begin with the end in mind, i.e. with their "Fourth Quarter" First.

Pioneer Mindset

☑ *Step Back.* *Always step back away from the detail to make sure you are catching the big picture, the big issues and the big opportunities.*

CHAPTER

3

Beginning With Your "Fourth Quarter" In Mind

My Dad could see that I was getting frustrated.   He had introduced me to puzzles at a young age.   He always liked to work out how the pieces needed to fit together.

Working on a book of mazes, I kept making the wrong turns and hitting dead ends.   "The secret to solving maze puzzles", he said, "is to start at the end and work backwards."   Little did I realize as a young boy how this well known "secret" drove my Dad's approach to his life and business.   Or how it would drive my future approach to working with Family Business Pioneers.

Reaching The Results You Want

As author Stephen Covey has reminded us, "Begin with the end in mind."   For Family Business Pioneers, this means "Begin with your Fourth Quarter First."

This is the key to success which I've seen time and again put into practice by successful Family Business Pioneers and it is the mindset they've asked us to deploy with them.

Eventually, every business owner will reach the Fourth Quarter of their time as a business owner.   At that time, every owner wants to accomplish certain personal, financial, business and estate planning goals. Yet, way too many fail to do so.   They went through the first three quarters of their life as a business owner without fully considering what would be needed to successfully win their Fourth Quarter too. Our team is working to change that.

Efforts by business owners to be fully satisfied with their eventual success have been, on average, less than satisfying. For example, some studies show that over 75% of former business owners regretted the decision to sell their Company because the sale did not accomplish their personal or business objectives. What was the reason the business owners gave? They did not understand all of their options, so they didn't make informed decisions.

Create Opportunities Now So You Have Options Later

Over the years, we have worked with hundreds of business owners from around the U.S. to help them overcome these odds and achieve a successful outcome for the time and capital they have invested in their businesses. This book is intended to help you to see more of a Business Continuity and Succession Planning process which will help you to create and understand your options and will provide the active steps which we suggest you look at taking today so you can successfully retire from, pass on, sell or exit from your Company someday tomorrow.

Pioneer Mindset

☑ *Create Options.* *Plant a lot of seeds. Fertilize. Water.* *Nurture. Harvest. Repeat.*

What Will Be Your "Fourth Quarter" Outcome?

What do you hope will be the future outcome of the time and financial investment you are making or planning to make in your business? Based on over 37 years of working with owners of small, middle-market and large closely held or family businesses in practically every business sector, I've found the answers to this question tend to be very similar. Most owners of closely held or family businesses have some or all of the following hopes or wishes:

• That your income from the business will continue to grow and provide an increasing standard of living for you, your family and your colleagues.

- That your business will help you accumulate sufficient financial resources for a comfortable retirement.

- That your business will not suffer or be lost through the negative influence of either internal or external adversities or claims.

- That both your business and your family can financially survive your unexpected, premature disability or death.

- That you can retire upon your own terms, while leaving your business in the good hands of successor leadership which you have selected and groomed.

- That ultimately you can either pass on a successful and valuable business to your family, or sell your business to your fellow owners, management or an outside buyer of your choice at a full and fair price, while minimizing potential federal and state taxes.

- That you can accomplish all of this with minimal shareholder, management and family squabbles.

- That your advisors will work together with you on understanding your options to help you make informed decisions.

These tend to be common business owner wishes, whether you own all or part of your business, whether your business is small or large, whether you are in the business of selling products or services, and whether you started the business yourself or inherited or bought it from someone else.

The Present Atmosphere

This is no small matter for business owners and their families in our country. Fortune Magazine has reported that the largest intergenerational transfer of wealth in history is now underway, totaling $45 trillion, which it says will be transferred over a 55-year period through 2052. It says about one third of this will pass to baby boomers, while the rest will go mainly to baby boomer children. Cornell University economist and demographic expert Robert Avery has predicted that baby boomers themselves will transfer $10 trillion to later generations. The Exit Planning Institute reports that the vast majority of this wealth is stock in more than 12 million closely held companies and that over the course of ten to fifteen years more than 70% of these businesses are expected to be transferred. A study by Boston College has projected that over the next 50 years $41 trillion of American wealth will transfer from the current generation to the next generation.

A recent survey of business owners by the Business Enterprise Institute found that 69% plan to exit in the next 10 years. Most of these business owners were in the 50 to 75 age range.

How Do You Achieve The Future Outcome You Want?

Almost all of the Business Pioneers who we have worked with over the years are very good at what they do. They also all realize that a business is not successful or profitable simply because they might wish it to be so. It's a basic and well understood principle of business – to be profitable and successful, you need to actively take the steps needed to efficiently provide, at a competitive price, products or services that a significant segment of the consumer or business public needs or wants.

You know you can not simply wish or hope this will happen on its own. The successful family business requires years of hard work, planning, dedication, and good business decisions. Likewise, you can't simply wish for your future Fourth Quarter to be successful and then expect it to be. You need to actively cause your Fourth Quarter to be successful – by starting very early on.

Over the years, I've had the opportunity to work with my own family in a number of their business operations, which have included restaurants, supermarkets, ranching, farming, retail merchandising, construction and real estate. They have provided good examples of the "entrepreneur's work ethic," not just by working hard in their businesses, but also by working hard on their businesses.

I've also had the opportunity to get to know many business owners. Most business owners whom we've worked with tend to realize, some sooner than others, that the future outcome they want for their business (and family) will be realized only if they apply the same skills to work ON their business as they have applied to working IN their business.

How is this done? It's done by realizing that your business should not rule your life. It's done by realizing that you need to take the steps necessary to rule one of the most important but too frequently overlooked aspects of being a business owner – the proactive, successful future transition and future exit process. It's done by asking the two fundamental questions mentioned earlier and then taking decisive action based on the answers.

Question 1: What Will Be The Probable, Almost Certain, Future Outcome Of Our Present Course, If Left Unchanged?

I encourage business owners to take some time to answer this. What will be the outcome of your present course? The probable almost certain future outcome of a business owner's investment of time and capital depends on how well you understand this.

What we do through Business Continuity and Succession Planning is to work with you ON your business through various Business Continuity and Succession Planning tools and techniques which have a proven track record of producing a better outcome for those who utilize them.

Learn From The Past And Create Your Future

So, where do we begin? The first step is to understand the "probable, almost certain, future outcome of your present course, if left unchanged." Will you be able to sell your business? Will your business be in a position to be sold at top dollar and minimized taxes when you are ready to depart. Will you have a capable successor, whether amongst your family or key employees or recruitable from outside the company? Are you prepared for the unexpected?

Understand What Is Right. Deal With What Is Wrong

We begin this review by making certain, as advisors, that we both have a solid understanding of your business and personal situation. A good physician will not make a diagnosis or recommendation without first doing a thorough "Patient History and Physical" (known in the medical field as an "H and P"). Likewise, a good Business Continuity and Succession Planning advisor first needs to do a brief "History and Physical." Like a medical History and Physical, this typically reveals the areas of most concern which need to be addressed.

What we have found over the years is that to the extent this reveals that certain tools are missing, the probable almost certain future outcome for your business investment will be less than that hoped for. This "History and Physical" leads to the next question.

Question 2:   What's Missing, The Presence Of Which Will Make A Substantial Difference In Producing A Better Future Outcome?

There are many different Business Continuity and Succession Planning tools and techniques from which we select for business owners to successfully provide the missing components, the presence of which equips you and your business for achieving a substantially better present and future for your business.

These tools and techniques can help assure that you can successfully enhance and protect your current and future business profits and value during your First, Second and Third Quarters, as well as successfully pass on or sell your business when you reach your Fourth Quarter – whether that is due to your retirement, disability or death – or just a desire to do something else.

Stop, Look Both Ways, Proceed With Care

My purpose, as a Business Continuity and Succession Planning advisor, is to help you determine which of these tools and strategies can best assist you. Based on your particular needs as a business owner, this process requires a certain amount of detailed discussions and planning over a period of time with one or more other professionals working together.

I'll Wait Until…

"I'll wait until… the economy bounces back… or until we reach our next revenue milestone… or until my family pushes a bit harder about my plans…" or until this, that or the next thing. This is what we call the "Wait and See" Game Plan. It is a recipe for failure.

Don't Overdo It or Underdo It

Don't overdo it by spending so much time planning for your future that you neglect the continuing needs of running your Company. Likewise, don't underdo it by neglecting to determine and take the actions needed to be successful in protecting, transitioning and exiting from your Company. What good is it to reach the Fourth Quarter only to realize you only had a "Third Quarter Game Plan" and now find yourself without the game plan needed to actually win the game.

Triage

A medical professional will, after an assessment of the situation, prioritize the most immediate and secondary needs of the patient and then address the most critical needs first. Likewise, we find that in the Business Continuity process (what we call Fourth Quarter Planning), a similar triage is almost always necessary or appropriate. While we advocate the need to address all of the actions described in this book, this does not mean they need to be addressed in the same order described in this book.

Avoiding Fourth Quarter Train Wrecks

Family Business Leaders/Pioneers tell us they most want to avoid Train Wrecks. Throughout this book we will identify the 24 avoidable Train Wrecks that Business Leaders/Pioneers face during their Fourth Quarter.

The Key To Success

Our firm has helped plan ahead for, design, negotiate and implement the purchase, sale or transfer of hundreds of businesses with values ranging from a few hundred thousand dollars to several hundred million dollars. Each transaction presents unique objectives, hurdles and opportunities. And each business owner's success was dependent on the focus on Business Continuity which occurred well in advance of the sale or transfer of the business.

The key to success is to get started well in advance - to become engaged early in the Business Continuity process. The best results are achieved when the business owner "begins with the Fourth Quarter First", whether you are presently in your First Quarter, Second Quarter, Third Quarter or Fourth Quarter.

Pioneer Mindset

☑ *The Lighthouse Effect.* Determine the probable, almost certain, future outcome of your present course if left unchanged. Then find what's missing, the presence of which will produce a substantially better outcome.

Chapter

4

Am I In Or Near My "Fourth Quarter" Yet?

Beginning with the "Fourth Quarter" First does not mean that you must carve in stone a departure date from your business or the terms and conditions of your departure. If you are like most business owners, you have played, and will continue to play, one of the most crucial roles in establishing the past success and future potential for your Company.

Address The Possibilities

Fourth Quarter Planning recognizes the fact that you will actually exit your business eventually. Perhaps you plan to lead your business until your death or disability. Perhaps you plan to retire before your death or disability, but intend to own your Company until your death or disability. Your plans or situation might also include one or more of the following:

- **Ready. Just In Case.** You plan to keep working on growing your Company for some time yet, but you are seeing it needs to be better structured for your unexpected death, disability or other unexpected exit or opportunity.

- **Retirement. Yeah. Maybe.** You are seeing retirement at some point even though you intend to own your Company until your death or disability.

- **Partner Options**. You are seeing the need for you and your partners to agree (or revise your agreement) on future ownership buy-sell options.

- **Business Model Heading South.** You are seeing or feeling (or being told of) the need to change, fix or improve your Business Model, but you just won't act on it like you used to.

- **Get Ready. Get Set. Go.** You want to work towards achieving a certain level of success quickly because you want to be able to exit soon.

- **Just In Case.** You aren't ready to exit yet, but you are seeing the need to have a plan in place.

- **Get Successor Ready.** You would like to still run your Company for a while, but want to start developing a successor so you can spend more time doing something else, such as traveling with your spouse and family.

- **Did It. Next.** You've achieved your goals as a business owner and would like to leave when and if the best opportunity comes up.

- **Ready To Coach.** You would like to give an adult child or key employee the opportunity to start leading the Company (and perhaps be able to coach them for a while).

- **Will Team Stick?** You are wondering whether your key colleagues or possible successor will stick with you.

- **Slow It Down.** You are ready to retire or slow down as soon as feasible.

- **They Grow Up Fast.** You would like to spend more time with your children or grandchildren.

- **Spouse Actually Loves You.** Your spouse would like you to retire or slow down.

- **So Do Your Children.** Your children would like you to retire or slow down.

- **But Stay Invested. Ok?** You would like to retire from most active duties, but remain as owner for a while.

- **New Stuff! Really?!?** You are not sure whether you are able or willing to keep up or catch up with the new technologies or Business Models demanded in your industry.

- **Thinking. Thinking.** You are spending more time thinking about what your Company is worth than how to grow it.

- **It's The Economy. Again!?!** You are not sure you want to fight another economic down cycle.

- **Window Closing.** You may recognize that valuation multiples or business sector consolidation today may present a temporary window of opportunity for your exit.

- **Find Out.** You want to take some time to test the market for the sale of your Company.

- **Not Investing More.** Taking your Company to the next level will require a new level of debt or equity investment which may not be desired or feasible.

- **Time To Diversify.** As you've reached this point in your life, you have a decreasing tolerance for risk and a desire to remove some financial chips from the table.

- **Customers Thinking.** You realize that some customers may start wondering whether you have a capable successor to continue your great service for them.

- **Enough.** Fatigue and boredom may be starting to set in.

- **Turn The Page.** You can start to see getting ready to start a new chapter in your life or have just lost the "fire in the belly" to continue pursuing your business.

- **Someone Is Stepping Up.** You never thought you would sell, but someone is offering you the right price and the right terms.

- **Anyone? Anyone?** You are wondering whether anyone will be interested in buying your Company at the price and terms you want.

- **Keeping Healthy.** You or your spouse or other family member are starting to encounter some health concerns or you want to take some steps to head off the development of health concerns.

- **Staying Step Ahead.** You realize your banker and surety may start wondering if your Fourth Quarter will impact their comfort level with your Company.

- **You Groomed Them.** You have some adult children or key colleagues who are starting to insist on leadership or ownership if they are to remain with the Company.

- **Want To Help Others.** You have community or charitable ventures you would like to spend more time pursuing.

- **Next Game.** You want to exit your Company and invest in a new venture.

- **Won't Wait Till Too Late.** You realize waiting for the "two minute warning" won't be the best route for anyone impacted by your decisions.

- **You're Cashin Out.** You are ready to sell your Company and cash out now.

- **DIY? No.** You realize your expertise is in running your Company, not in do-it-yourself succession and exit planning.

- **Gotta Protect Others As Well.** You know you are in or approaching your "Fourth Quarter" and you don't want your Company, family, colleagues, or customers to be at risk from the changing personal, business and financial dynamics that will hit in your personal "Fourth Quarter".

- **Best Course.** You have come to realize that the best course for your family, your long term colleagues, and your valued customers, is for you to lay in the ground work and the planning for your exit, whether your exit occurs sooner or later, so that you have best provided for the well being of your family, the continuity of your business, the continuity of employment for your valued colleagues and the continuity of products and services for your valued customers.

The "Plays" in the Fourth Quarter Game Plan Playbooks get the most attention during a Business Leader's personal "Fourth Quarter". However, most of them should be deployed throughout the life of a Business Leader.

Am I In Time For Avoiding Fourth Quarter Train Wrecks?

Achieving incredible Fourth Quarter results requires that actions be taken years ahead of time to avoid "Fourth Quarter" Train Wrecks. Some examples include the following (some with more specific pre-exit time estimates):

- **Business Model.** Ongoing Business Model design and innovation (always).

- **Profit.** Develop and use a Profit Strategy Team (always).

- **Culture.** A company culture which creates incredible loyalty with your colleagues and customers (always).

- **Income Taxes.** Elect Subchapter "S" tax status to avoid double tax on sale of business (5 years) and to build tax basis to reduce taxable gain (ongoing).

- **Financials.** Utilize credible, buyer-acceptable, reviewed or audited financial statements (3-5 years).

- **Cash.** Bridge the gap between your "cash-in-pocket" freedom needs and your company's net realizable value (5-10+ years).

- **Team.** Build a dynamic leadership team depth chart (always).

- **Successor.** Identify and develop specific capable successors (5-10 years).

- **Funding.** Acquire adequate financial gap contingency funding (such as the build up in life insurance) while in good health and insurable, to fun life's "capital calls" (always).

- **Estate Taxes.** Implement Estate Tax reduction program (10-20 years).

- **Key Owners.** Determine and implement key employee buy-in (5-10 years).

- **Retention.** Determine and utilize key employee retention incentive (always).

- **Industry.** Bring Company up to industry level financial and business benchmarks to be profitably growing today and to help attain desired Fourth Quarter pricing (always).

- **Structure.** Implement pre-exit business entity restructuring (2-5 years).

- **Guidance.** Develop outside Board of Director members to help guide the Company today and in the event of your unexpected death or disability (always).

- **Buyer.** Find acceptable outside buyer at the right time in the business and economic cycle (2-5 years).

- **Protection.** Take the actions to protect what you are building (always).

- **Options.** Business owner Buy-Sell and Business Continuity Agreements (always).

- **Advisors.** Put the right team of outside advisors around you who have specific capabilities and experience in Fourth Quarter issues, strategies and planning (always).

Regardless of your present plans or intentions, putting the proper cornerstones into place now – well ahead of your Fourth Quarter – is critical to achieving profitable success in all Four Quarters. This includes a future transition and future exit, whether your transition or exit occurs according to your timetable or is prompted by unexpected circumstances.

Pioneer Mindset

☑ *Unlearn.* *Face the need to unlearn much of what you learned that just isn't so (or is no longer so).*

Chapter

5

The Elephant In The Room

An "elephant in the room" is, of course, any situation which is very obvious to a group of persons but which is not being openly discussed. The "elephant in the room" in many closely held businesses is the question of what will happen to the business when its present key owner or owners move on, whether planned or unplanned. This concern exists regardless of whether you are in your First, Second, Third or Fourth Quarter.

Regardless of the extent to which this topic is discussed, it is nevertheless on the minds of the many persons impacted by the success of you and your business. These persons typically include yourself, your spouse, your children, your other key employees, most of those you employ (your colleagues), your franchisor (for franchisees), your banker, your bonding company (for contractors), your main customers or clients, your key suppliers, your key advisors, and your local community.

How well you have dealt with, planned for, openly discussed and specifically addressed the various concerns of these persons regarding your future expected or unexpected exit has significant direct impact not only on yourself and your immediate family, but also on your business today and into the future. This is due to the differentiated concerns each of these persons consciously or subconsciously bring into your business.

The Exit Factor

We refer to the collective seen and unseen impact of the exit concern on how these persons deal with your business and with you as the "Exit Factor". Just as the saying goes "all politics are local," it is equally true that "all business is personal." Each of these persons have their own personal reasons for their concern with your Fourth Quarter.

This does not mean they are concerned only with themselves, but simply that they will have an interest in your business that will reflect their unique circumstance.

For example, your spouse may be interested, among other things, in the impact of the business on your continuing good health, on your ability to spend time together, on the future role of one or more of your children in the business, as well as a salary continuation or other economic impact regarding your expected or unexpected exit. Your children may be interested, among other things, on who will run the Company and the impact this would have on other members of your family, as well as the financial impact of the business to them.

A key employee may be interested, among other things, on whether he or she will have the opportunity to reach full potential for leadership in your Company or whether he or she might be passed over in favor of a less competent family member – whether with regard to being able to manage the Company or to being an owner in the Company. The failure to deal with this can, of course, lead to the loss of key employees to other competing companies who are more willing to address this. Your other employees will often be concerned, among other things, with the continuation of the success of the Company (and therefore, their employment potential), as well as the potential for a change in Company culture upon your exit.

If you are a franchise business, your franchisor will be concerned with the continued viability of your franchise upon your planned or unexpected exit. This impacts not only the franchisor's income, but as importantly, the integrity and reputation of its franchise system.

Your banker or other business lender, surety or bonding company will, among other things, be concerned both personally with the loss of a close personal relationship that a good banker, lender, surety or bonding company will have developed with you, as well as a concern for the viability and balance sheet of the business if your Fourth Quarter possibilities are not properly handled.

Your co-owners, in addition to the loss of a personal business colleague, will be concerned with whether they, you, or a third party will ultimately own the business in a planned exit, or with their ability to work with your family through a transition upon your unexpected exit.

And so on.

Your concerns as a key owner will typically span all of these interests, which is fine, because you are the one who has the best opportunity to deal with the Exit Factor.

Pioneer Mindset

☑ *Stop The Rocking Chair.* *Actually get somewhere by converting worries into your next fun challenge.*

Collaboration vs. Uncoordinated Actions

One of the problems which business owners tell us they have faced in the past is that it is very difficult to find professional advice or a professional approach which addresses and prioritizes all of the steps and considerations which need to be dealt with to look ahead to their Fourth Quarter.

As a result, many business owners have tended to take uncoordinated actions over the course of several years, based on the isolated advice of advisors who have dealt only with their specific field of expertise. Perhaps an advisor has talked about some tax planning. Maybe an advisor has talked about a buy-sell agreement to deal with certain contingencies. Perhaps an advisor has talked about your retirement goals. Perhaps an advisor has placed you in some financial products. Perhaps an advisor has talked about a living trust or a "succession plan." Perhaps you have met with an advisor about selling your business.

All of these steps with your advisors have likely been perfectly appropriate great steps at the time. Or not. If these steps have been isolated, uncoordinated efforts between you and your advisors, you likely have started and stopped, and probably started and stopped several times since, in attempting to think through some plan for your future. You might now have a "Junk Drawer" Game Plan and have become frustrated with the process because you instinctively know that you have not solved the puzzle that needs to be put together for a successful Fourth Quarter.

Pioneer Mindset

☑ *Sanity Check.* *Make sure you have a capable someone to sanity-check your "great" ideas.*

The Necessary Expertise

A large reason for these unsatisfactory results amongst the efforts of business owners is because planning for a business owner's Fourth Quarter is outside the expertise for most business owners, and it is something that most professional advisors only deal with certain facets of.

By and large, most professional organizations still fail to address the full range of business owner Fourth Quarter planning needs.

The result is a general lack of the in depth Business Continuity and Succession Planning services needed by business owners in planning ahead for their Fourth Quarter.

Many advisors we are honored to work with have seen the need for better results for their business owner clients. These advisors see the incredible impact of collaborating to magnify the combined results of working together.

The Fourth Quarter Game Plan Program

This is why I've developed the Fourth Quarter System. Using this program, a Fourth Quarter Game Plan can be designed, prepared and tailored for business owners. Each plan is the result of a review of the Fourth Quarter process. Each plan consists of a carefully selected number of the Plays detailed in this book. And each plan is the result of the proper coordination and collaboration between the trusted advisors on your team.

Pioneer Mindset

☑ *Take It On.* *If a courageous conversation is what's needed, then go have a courageous conversation. Now.*

Chapter

6

12 Reasons For Incredible "Fourth Quarter" Results

Over the past several years, I have spoken with business owners around the country who had decided they had reached the point of being ready to leave their businesses. However, no one was stepping up to provide them the Fourth Quarter advice, guidance or results they wanted. These business owners had spent all of their time aggressively working in their business, but had spent little time aggressively working on how they would eventually transition from or exit from their business.

They found themselves late in the game with few options to achieve their Fourth Quarter objectives. Simply put, they hadn't put their "Fourth Quarter" First. They were too late. They were in their personal Two Minute Warning or Overtime.

On the other hand, we've worked with many Family Business Pioneers early on to coach them on achieving incredible results.

What follows are 12 of the top reasons I've seen for why Family Business Pioneer Fourth Quarters succeed with incredible results. Each of these reasons impacts the Company's ongoing profitability as well as an owner's future success.

- **Sustainable Business Growth.** Your Company has a profit strategy program for continuing Business Model design and defense and for sustaining continued product and service innovation, brand recognition, customer engagement, business growth and profitability, all of which impacts your Company's present growth and survival, and therefore your future Fourth Quarter results.

- **Capable Leadership and Successors.** A process for replacing you and other key management or leadership (either internally or externally) has been identified and developed, and you have properly developed, incented and retained key personnel.

- **Co-Owner Issues and Disputes Avoided Up Front.** You have utilized a Buy-Sell Agreement and a Business Continuity Agreement to pre-decide how ownership will be bought and sold (and funded) between partners upon death, disability, divorce, disputes, and retirement and how to avoid or resolve co-owner disputes due to future disagreements.

- **Well Designed Company Structure and Key Asset Protection.** Your Company is properly structured to protect assets and to deal with contingencies, and you have identified your key intangible assets and adopted the legal safeguards to protect your key intangible assets (such as your key employees and intellectual property rights).

- **Clear and Consistent Owner Objectives.** Your business, financial, personal, transition and exit objectives are determined in advance and do not conflict with each other (or with the objectives of your partners, key employees, spouse or other family members).

- **Cash Flow Impact On Company Price Is Understood.** You understand your overall Fourth Quarter result is dependent upon an inside buyer's or third-party buyer's expectations and needs regarding your Company's future cash flow and you have uncovered or understood how your Company's exit-appropriate buyer-specific valuation is to be determined.

- **Management of Personal Wealth.** You have properly managed your personal (non-company) wealth, avoiding the need to draw on Company resources or to disrupt your transition timing and your successor's expectations.

- **Business Owner Estate Plan.** You have realized the difference between a regular Estate Plan and a business owner Estate Plan, and you have adequately protected your family and have addressed your family's needs and desires relative to your business.

- **Keeping the Business Always Ready for Sale.** You realize your Company should always be ready to be sold. This impacts present earnings. And the future can quickly change (for the better or worse) your presently expected business transition and Fourth Quarter timing.

- **Pre-Exit Tax Tools.** Pre-Exit tax minimization steps have been taken in time.

- **Capable Inside Buyer Exists.** You have groomed a capable inside buyer (such as a partner, key employee or family member) to be ready to buy when you're ready to sell, and you have designed an economically and financially feasible, mutually beneficial, tax efficient sale structure to an inside buyer.

- **Understanding the M & A Market.** You are able to sell to a third party because you understand, have addressed, and manage toward the expectations of the mergers and acquisition market for your Company in your industry.

The critical Main Plays identified in this book were developed to specifically achieve these principal reasons for why so many Family Business Pioneers have been achieving incredible Fourth Quarter results.

The purpose of Fourth Quarter Planning is to lay out a systematic approach which helps assure that you timely and thoroughly take the steps needed to achieve success in accomplishing your personal, financial, transition and exit objectives before and during your personal Fourth Quarter.

The Fourth Quarter Planning process provides a means for business owners to help see the status of their own future transition and exit situation and will show you the steps needed to actively do something about it. This is not a plan to read and then put on the shelf. It's a plan that is intended to help business owners address the call-to-action every business owner needs to undertake.

A Fourth Quarter Game Plan can address the above 12 opportunity areas, amongst others, and will help you avoid pitfalls and mistakes. This plan provides you with a tailored roadmap for how you will achieve your Fourth Quarter successfully, on your terms and on your timetable.

Pioneer Mindset

☑ *Your Choice. The future you want won't happen on its own. Cause what you want or accept what others impose on you.*

Chapter

7

What Is "Fourth Quarter" Planning?

Most of us would never invest in a publicly held company on the stock market if no process existed for seeing that investment grow, for fairly valuing that investment and for being able to exit that investment at fair value at a time of your choosing. What's more, most of us would never continue to pour more and more money and effort into that investment, year after year, never knowing what the company is worth and never knowing how you could eventually cash out from it or pass it along to your family. Most of us would view investing and operating under that scenario as insanity.

Yet, this is exactly the situation in which business owners often find themselves. They have spent years investing time, money and effort into their closely held company, only to be stymied and frustrated as they begin to think about how they can eventually retire from, pass on or exit their business.

The SBA reports that up to 90% of the net worth of small business owners is tied up in their business. Most business owners want their exit to result in the continuation and success of the business, while at the same time, they want this net worth to obtain financial security and freedom for themselves and their families.

What Is Fourth Quarter Planning?

Fourth Quarter Planning first of all is a mindshift which Family Business Pioneers have been asking us to deploy with them. It is a belief in the need to "begin with the end in mind" if you really intend to be successful. It is more than just strategic, continuity, succession, estate or exit planning. It is the deliberate, adaptable and customized process for working with business owners and their families and colleagues to continue to profitably build their business while at the same time working towards a successful future transition and eventual exit from their Company, while also addressing how to protect what you're building and how to take control of your legacy.

Ideally, a business owner's future Fourth Quarter will occur on the business owner's terms and timetable. However, sometimes unforeseen events (such as the owner's unexpected death or disability or the loss of key employees) will frustrate the best laid plans. For this reason, Fourth Quarter Planning addresses not only your planned, foreseeable growth and future exit, but also provides back up plans in the event of an unexpected owner, partner or key employee death, disability, departure, dispute, divorce or business downturn.

Fourth Quarter Planning helps you to avoid the "entrepreneur's curse" of being in "wealth prison". It helps you to convert your business equity into liquid investments to help achieve the "freedom" element of financial freedom.

The Essence Of Fourth Quarter Planning

Fourth Quarter Planning, in its essence, is designed to work with the business owner to achieve the following:

- Peace of mind rather than confusion

- Maintaining control rather than being out of control

- Charting your own route (with backup routes) rather than going where the wind blows you

- Reaching for the stars rather than being amongst the fallen stars

- Family accord rather than family discord

- Accomplishing hopes and dreams rather than living through a nightmare

- Creating leaders to succeed you rather than simply creating managers who will run the train off the tracks

- Achieving future financial security rather than ending up in financial uncertainty

- Leaving a legacy rather than leaving a mess

- Navigating your specific, charted course rather than running blindly through a maze of dead ends

- Creating your own seller's market for your business rather than settling for whatever comes along

- Overcoming your transition and exit roadblocks rather than being steamrolled.

"Boy. I Never Saw That One Coming."

Many business owners have heard me say that my job is to "look into the future" with you. And then work together on what is needed to avoid foreseeable pitfalls and to achieve the outcome you want. That is the essence of Fourth Quarter Planning. To look ahead. To see it coming. To plan accordingly.

> ## *Pioneer Mindset*
> ☑ *"Fourth Quarter" First. Begin all thinking with the end in mind.*

Your Fourth Quarter Needs Versatility

Fourth Quarter Planning is intended to enable the business owner to have the option to move in several directions, depending on future events and circumstances.

This is similar to the Chess Board piece of the Knight. The Knight is the most versatile piece on the Chess Board. Unlike all other Chess Board pieces, the Knight can move in eight different directions and can 'jump over' all other chess pieces (of either player) to reach its destination.

Fourth Quarter Planning, when fully designed and implemented, likewise will provide the business owner with several alternatives for achieving his or her goal and with the ability to 'jump over' what may be roadblocks for others.

Due to its versatility, a Knight in Chess should always be close to where the action is. This piece is generally more powerful when placed near the center of the board where its flexibility is the greatest.

The Knight is also the only piece that can move at the beginning of the game before a pawn or any other piece. It also is the only piece that can be in a position to attack a king, queen, bishop or rook without being reciprocally attacked by that piece.

Likewise, a Fourth Quarter Game Plan provides a business owner with a versatile and effective plan which can be used throughout the course of a business owner's next moves during his or her First, Second, Third and Fourth Quarters.

> ### *Pioneer Mindset*
>
> ☑ *Disruption. Massive disruption is now an ongoing reality in every business sector. The only question is whether you will help cause it or be a "victim" of it.*

Fourth Quarter Planning Dynamics

Fourth Quarter Planning needs to deal with the interaction of three key dynamics involved with the closely held family business. This is the intersection where the company's business dynamics meet the family's personal dynamics and the owner's financial dynamics. Unless all three are addressed, a successful Fourth Quarter is less than likely.

I have often found it necessary or helpful to act in a mediator's role in helping the family members or other partners decide how they will work together in the future. Fourth Quarter Planning truly presents a situation where the intersection of the business, family and ownership dynamics needs to be carefully, thoughtfully and skillfully addressed.

Fourth Quarter Planning

Profit Planning	+	Protection Planning	+	Estate Planning	+	Succession Planning

Chapter

8

Who Is Impacted By Your "Fourth Quarter"?

Everyone's financial and family well-being depends to a large degree on how well our economy performs, i.e. on how well the economy produces and sustains good jobs for the 150 million Americans who want a job outside the home or for the three billion people worldwide who want to work. However, the economy is no better than the performance of those hundreds of thousands of companies which comprise our vast economic ecosystem. And every small business and middle-market company is impacted by whether its business owners have or have not "begun with their Fourth Quarter in mind."

So who is personally impacted and who can (or should) be doing something about this?

The Family

The financial well-being and health of personal relationships is often highly vested in the success of the Company, which in all cases is dependent on the critical actions to be taken before and in the Fourth Quarter.

The Business Owners

Often much or most of the business owner's wealth, legacy and overall activities in life are tied up in the Company which he or she created, built, bought or inherited. The business owner is in the primary position to want and to cause a successful Fourth Quarter.

The Board of Directors

The Board of Directors has the fiduciary responsibility, as the top management within an organization, to see to its short-term, mid-term and long-term success. The board is in the position to recognize the need for, and it has the platform to urge the owners to address, a Fourth Quarter Game Plan.

The CEO/President

The CEO or President may or may not own (or yet own) the Company. He or she is charged with leading the organization to short-term, mid-term and long-term success. He or she is in a position to recognize the need for, and to urge the owners to develop, a Fourth Quarter Game Plan.

The Key Executive

The key executive's role includes the responsibility to bring to the CEO/president the concerns and solutions for impacting the organization's success. Their careers, and the careers of those who depend on the key executive team, are dependent on how well the business owner has understood the principles of the Fourth Quarter system.

Key executives usually realize they are not responsible simply for their own silo. An understanding by each team member of how the key parts of the organization fit together is vital to any organization's success and an important role in the actions of each key executive.

The Profit Strategy Team

Those organizations which engage in deliberate strategic planning often do so through some form of an Advisory Board, which is what I call a Profit Strategy Team. This group becomes largely responsible for the future success or failure of the organization, based on the approach taken.

Most strategic plans which I have reviewed are not strategic at all. They tend to focus on tactical and operational changes rather than reviewing and critically adjusting or creating the three key ingredients necessary for powerful long-term success for the organization (business model, leadership and culture). Fourth Quarter planning provides a powerful program to plug into any existing strategic planning program to actually make it strategic.

The Front Line

Every employee or associate within an organization has the capability to become innovators and problem solvers in setting new and alternative directions to grow their organizations with Fourth Quarter thinking.

The Investor

Three quarters of venture-backed firms in the U.S. don't return investors' capital, according to the Wall Street Journal. Think about how those statistics could be reversed if investors fully applied the ingredients in the Fourth Quarter system.

The Lender and Bonding Company

All lenders and bonding companies have faced defaults or lost opportunities that could have been better addressed had they and their customers applied the thinking behind the Fourth Quarter system to take care of the balance sheet and the Company's long term prospects.

The "Capital Call" Funder

Life in business presents what we refer to as "capital call events". Death or disability of an owner or other key person or family member are examples. A capital infusion from your early investment in the right portfolio of life insurance, disability insurance and long term care insurance is key to a successful Fourth Quarter.

The Outside CPA

An active role in, and a sharp understanding of, a client's Fourth Quarter Planning is critical to every assurance/audit, tax and consulting engagement.

The Financial Advisor

The business owner's Financial Advisor needs to play a key role in where the owner is heading, which Fourth Quarter thinking provides.

The Strategic Planning Advisor

True strategic planning is the decision of which Business Model to use, not the tactical actions to operate it. These principles are taught in the Fourth Quarter system.

The Human Resources Director

By managing the hiring, training and promotion criteria, you are vital to an organization's Root Force Culture and Dynamic Leadership Core, key components to Fourth Quarter planning.

The Industry Association or Professional Association

Member companies and firms are anxious for their industry and professional conferences to bring programs critical to the short and long term success of their organizations. The Fourth Quarter system does exactly that.

The Business Buyer and the Business Seller

As *The New M & A Playbook* by Harvard Business Review makes clear, the best way to achieve success in an acquisition is to think of the target in terms of its Business Model. An understanding of the concepts covered in the Fourth Quarter system is critical to buyers, sellers and their advisors.

The Corporate Attorney

Critical to correct legal advice is a solid understanding of how and why the organization's Business Model actually works and how this fits into Fourth Quarter success.

The Estate Planning Attorney

Trusted with helping clients to preserve their business and investment wealth, the ingredients in the Fourth Quarter system are critical to estate and succession planning advice and Company valuation.

The Company Appraiser

A deeper dive into the Business Model of the Company and its long term Fourth Quarter mindset is critical to better valuation insights and accuracy.

The ESOP Trustee

The fiduciary responsibility to act with care, skill, prudence and diligence necessitates an understanding of Fourth Quarter principles.

The Business Coach

Imagine bringing not just tactical and operating insights, but also true strategic (Business Model) thinking, to your business clients as part of their Fourth Quarter program.

The Startup Company

Less than 50% of you survive for 5 years. What if you had better understood how to design and energize your Company with Fourth Quarter thinking.

The Executive Peer Group Organization

An understanding of Fourth Quarter design features is key to implementing all of the other business topics covered by your peer groups.

The Chamber of Commerce and Department of Economic Development

When your employers stall or fail, jobs are lost and your community suffers. Bringing a solid understanding of Fourth Quarter design to your members is key to community growth and to retaining companies in your community.

The Franchisor and the Franchisee

Each needs to think and act in terms of continuous design and improvement to your franchise Business Model, as well as business protection and succession, each of which are highlighted in the Fourth Quarter system.

The Succession and Exit Planning Advisor

What good is the "perfect" Succession Plan or Exit Plan if you don't apply all of the Fourth Quarter ingredients for keeping your clients' companies intact and fully performing.

It's Your Move

In presenting these topics at international, national and regional conferences for business and professional associations, and at Executive Briefings and Boot Camps for individual companies and organizations, I've found that business and community leaders are eager for new truly "strategic thinking" on how to build the long term success of their organizations and communities.

Fourth Quarter thinking will continue to prompt the moves within companies and organizations which are critical to supporting the jobs, families, dreams and aspirations of those who depend on you.

Pioneer Mindset

☑ ***Bring It.*** *Relish, learn from and take on the competition through focus, commitment, persistence, execution and sheer will. Let your passionate, positive optimism be contagious.*

Chapter
9

Overcoming The Big "Fourth Quarter" Roadblocks

Every business owner faces a number of roadblocks when thinking about, planning for and eventually exiting his or her business. These roadblocks exist whether your Fourth Quarter is nearby or far off, anticipated or unexpected.

These roadblocks can collectively create a bottleneck which delays, diminishes or dooms planning for your successful Fourth Quarter. These roadblocks prevent the vast majority of Fourth Quarters from being successful or from accomplishing the results that business owners want to see.   A Fourth Quarter roadblock is any obstruction which prevents or delays the freedom you always wanted to achieve by being a business owner.

16 Common Fourth Quarter Roadblocks

The essence of Fourth Quarter Planning includes overcoming the roadblocks to achieve your full freedom. Some of these are from internal forces. Some are from external forces.

By knowing in advance that these are common Fourth Quarter roadblocks, we are able to plan ahead early on to avoid them.   Fifteen common roadblocks are:

- **Hanging On Too Long.** You will or may simply want to keep owning and/or working too long for personal, non-economic reasons. You won't be ready to retire or you won't be ready to move on to a new venture.   You may have accomplished all of your economic goals and all of your other roadblocks to a successful exit have all been dealt with. However, you simply want to keep working and you won't be ready to pass on ownership. This may be fine. Or it may become destructive, either to your health, your family well-being, and the goals and objectives of your key employees (who may decide to move out to a company with leadership opportunities). Or it might cause you to miss a selling opportunity that won't be there later. Not understanding how to move on and how to take on new personal and family objectives post-exit, i.e. "hanging on too long", can become a roadblock to a successful Fourth Quarter that ought to be occurring sooner rather than later.

- **Tax Hit.** If you haven't planned at least five to ten years ahead of your exit to address the tax issues that you will face upon your lifetime exit or your death exit, then your Fourth Quarter is unlikely to be as successful as you'd like because of the "tax hit" roadblock.

- **Price Mis-Expectation.** If you don't know or can't achieve a reasonable, realistic value for your business, then "price mis-expectation" becomes a roadblock that will bottleneck your Fourth Quarter and not provide the walk away or retirement funds you intended.

- **Leadership Void**. If you haven't worked on grooming one or more potential leaders (not simply managers) or if you don't have the likelihood for recruiting a successful leader from the outside upon your exit, "leadership void" in your depth chart is a roadblock to a successful Fourth Quarter.

> ## *Pioneer Mindset*
> ☑ *Truth*. *Radically embrace every aspect of transparent truth.*

- **Objectives Chaos.** If your personal, financial and prime business owner objectives conflict with each other, then "objectives chaos" is a roadblock to your successful Fourth Quarter.

- **The Missing Buyer.** If your business or Business Model in its present or likely future make-up is not marketable (or is not marketable at a fair price) to an insider or outside third party, then "the missing buyer" is a Fourth Quarter roadblock.

- **Business Model Decline.** You haven't kept your Company in a growing, profitable Business Model.

- **Asset Loss.** You have lost much of what you've built because you failed to protect your assets from outside exposures or family issues.

- **Financing Gap**. Insufficient or unwilling outside bank or other third party lender financing can create a "financing gap" roadblock which means you need to carry back part of the sale price.

- **Financial Dependence.** If your Company's outside third party ongoing operations financing requires your ongoing, post-exit personal guarantee or other financial support, then "financial dependence" is a roadblock to your successful Fourth Quarter.

- **Third Party Consents.** If outside consents (e.g. from a lender, franchisor, or licensor) are needed and will be difficult to obtain, then "third party consents" can delay and sometimes sidetrack your Fourth Quarter.

- **Co-Owner Disputes.** If co-owner disputes can't be resolved (resulting in the loss of business value), or if you can't require other owners to sell or to buy (when you are ready to exit), then "co-owner disputes" can become a roadblock to your Fourth Quarter.

- **Family Disputes.** Family disputes (usually over money, shares of ownership or leadership roles) tend to doom many businesses and owner Fourth Quarters.

Pioneer Mindset

☑ *Sandwich It. Wrap critique in praise.*

- **Insufficient Cash Flow.** If your business doesn't generate sufficient, predictable cash flow, then "insufficient cash flow" will mean neither a sale to an insider nor to an outsider will likely meet your objectives.

- **Non-Credible Accounting.** A "non-credible accounting" system which can't be relied on by a potential inside or outside buyer, can delay or prevent a successful Fourth Quarter indefinitely.

- **Unexpected Adversity.** An "unexpected adversity", such as a downturn in your business or the loss of key employees (including yourself), can delay or prevent a successful Fourth Quarter.

> ### *Pioneer Mindset*
> ☑ *Whose Side. Don't ask if God is on your side. Ask if you are on God's side.*

Overcome The Biggest Roadblock – Optimism Bias

The biggest roadblock in Fourth Quarter Planning is actually a mental decision. It is the reliance on a misplaced belief that everything will just be ok without any real effort to make it so. However, that's not the world we live in. Just as in your business operations, you need to make it happen if you want to be successful in your Fourth Quarter.

Being optimistic is a tremendous frame of mind. However, we are all at risk of being overly optimistic, something psychologists refer to as "optimism bias" (also known as unrealistic optimism). This is a cognitive bias that causes a person to believe they are less likely to experience a negative event compared to others. The risk here is we don't see the need to take specific actions to achieve specific Fourth Quarter outcomes.

> ### *Pioneer Mindset*
> ☑ *Optimism. Be the optimist, but beware of "optimism bias".*

Do Something Today To Make It Happen

This book is intended to help Business Pioneers learn how to move and how to recognize and overcome your Fourth Quarter roadblocks and bottlenecks. You will learn specifically what you need to do today to help make your Fourth Quarter successful tomorrow.

> ### *Pioneer Mindset*
> ☑ *Capture The Essence. Don't expect the person you are serving to try to decipher what you mean. Make your point immediately easy and clear.*

Chapter
10

Know What Port You Are Sailing To

As the Roman statesman and philosopher Seneca wisely observed: "If a man knows not to which port he sails, no wind is favorable."

Put slightly differently, French philosopher Michel de Montaigne suggests: "A man who does not have a picture of the whole in his head cannot possibly arrange the pieces."

Or, as St. Louis de Montfort stated: "What does it avail an archer to know how to hit the outer parts of the target, if he does not know how to hit the center?"

The first step listed in a famous rabbit stew recipe is "Catch rabbit". Likewise, as you and your advisors begin the Fourth Quarter Planning process, we don't want to overlook the obvious. Every business owner must begin the Fourth Quarter Planning process by reviewing his or her primary personal, business and financial objectives. Once established, your objectives become the final destination towards which your Fourth Quarter Game Plan needs to advance.

The Fourth Quarter Planning process, whether you intend to sell the business to an outside party or to transfer it internally to a family member or an employee, cannot proceed until the owner's objectives are thoroughly analyzed, understood and internally consistent.

Where Are You And The Business Going?

Often the startup entrepreneur is more focused on this than the business owner who has owned the Company for many years. Many startup entrepreneurs have a clear plan when they begin as to how big they want to grow the Company and how soon they want to trigger their exit.

Are You A Golf Ball On Your Way To Becoming A Basketball?

Think of it this way – no matter which quarter you are in. If we could think of your Company as a ball, are you a golf ball with plans to remain a golf ball, or are you aiming to become a baseball then a softball, then a soccer ball and then a basketball? Are you positioning yourself to grow a little or to grow a lot. It's important that we all understand this up front.

Pioneer Mindset

☑ *Growth.* *Decide if your business is a golf ball with plans to become a baseball, softball, soccer ball and basketball or just stay a golf ball.*

Define Your Universe

This review of the owner's objectives needs to be thorough, specific and forthright. A successful Fourth Quarter will involve help from a number of advisors. If these advisors don't understand the mission, they won't be working in a coordinated effort. If the team quarterback isn't clear if the play is a run to the left or a pass to the right, the likelihood of successfully scoring is remote.

Before addressing your primary objectives as a business owner, the Fourth Quarter Planning process needs to begin with an understanding of your personal, business and financial objectives.

This review of your objectives is the time to consider what you want to do post-exit and to address the type of legacy you want to leave to your family, your business and your community.

Pioneer Mindset

☑ *Telescope It.* *You can't build or invest in a future for anyone if you can't see past today. Always be looking into the future to anticipate the ripple impact of today's actions on tomorrow's possibilities.*

Prime Fourth Quarter Objectives

In the Fourth Quarter Planning process, your Fourth Quarter Game Plan and the various planning tools are dependent on six prime objectives. These in effect represent different forks in the road. While a good Fourth Quarter Game Plan includes fall back plans, it is critical that you and your advisors begin by having a keen understanding of the following six prime business owner objectives:

1. **Who** – Who do you presently believe you will want to eventually transfer your business and duties to?

2. **What** – What part of the business (or businesses) do you presently believe you will eventually want to transfer or keep?

3. **Where** – Where are you taking your business to and then where will your next personal or business adventure be?

4. **When** – When do you presently believe you want to eventually exit or slow down from active duty and/or ownership?

5. **Why** – Why are you a business owner in the first place?

6. **How Much** – How much net cash-in-pocket do you presently believe you need or want to have when you eventually exit your business and how close are you to this goal?

First, it's necessary to start to identify your primary and fallback plans. For example, if we were to discuss your ownership, your options normally include a sale to outside third parties, or sale to inside key employees, a sale or transfer to family members, or a sale to your partners.

Second, its necessary to know what part of your business or businesses you intend to transfer or keep. This can entail a review of personal, business, investment and tax objectives.

The third prime objective is to determine where you are taking your business to and where you want your next personal or business adventure to be. In other words, what will you "retire" <u>to</u>. And, if you are considering a move to another State upon your retirement and if you presently are a resident in a State which will tax the gain on the sale of your business, then you should consider whether a move to a State which doesn't impose a tax should be considered before your sale. Certain actions are needed ahead of your sale to establish your new legal residency in another State.

The fourth prime objective is to determine approximately when you want to exit your business. This addresses not simply your desire to transfer ownership, but also the time you desire to reduce or retire from your active leadership.

The fifth prime objective considers why you went into the business in the first place. This drives everything. This will help us all to address what's missing and what's still needed.

The sixth prime objective is to determine your "Cash-In-Pocket Target." If the "Cash Needed From Sale of Business Today" is more than the net cash which can be realized from selling your business today, then your Objectives need to be coordinated accordingly.

Family Bootcamps

Fourth Quarter Planning needs to address the interaction of business dynamics, family dynamics and financial dynamics. As you begin to consider your personal, business and financial objectives, we typically work with our clients to address one or more family bootcamps or conferences where we can discuss, evaluate and consider your objectives in light of the wishes and expectations of your loved ones.

> ## *Pioneer Mindset*
> ☑ *The Decision Makers. Know the trigger impact of your careful choice of words and the ROI to every decision maker and influencer in the decision pathway.*

Chapter
11

Create An Advisor Team Which Collaborates

One of my favorite TV shows as a young boy was Mission Impossible. The show always began with Jim Phelps deciding to accept the mission and then selecting the team needed for that specific mission from his Impossible Mission Force portfolio. Fourth Quarter Planning happens in much the same way.

Choosing Your Trusted Advisor Team

Depending on the degree of complexity of your situation, the design and implementation of your successful Fourth Quarter Game Plan requires the collaboration of your Advisor Team deploying several key areas of advisor knowledge and experience. Some individuals may possess more than one of these areas.

As a Business Continuity Attorney, I've designed the Fourth Quarter System in such a way as to enable you, as well as your other trusted advisors, to collaborate on the design and implementation process using your business knowledge and their regular expertise, regardless of their actual Fourth Quarter Planning experience.

For example, a CPA who has little experience in Fourth Quarter Planning nevertheless is critical to obtaining incredible results due to his or her knowledge of you, your family and your Company and of the tax planning, cash flow projections, and accounting systems issues which impact Fourth Quarter Planning.

The best financial and insurance advisors are committed to developing specialized knowledge in areas which directly impact Fourth Quarter Planning. Many of these advisors are very good at collaborating and at working hard with business owners in addressing their specific Fourth Quarter Planning needs.

Pioneer Mindset

☑ **Serve.** *Always Be Serving (ABS) customers and prospects by looking for new ways to eliminate persistent pain points, achieve incredible gain and get their job done.*

If you have a regular corporate attorney and a regular estate planning attorney, we likewise want them on the Fourth Quarter Planning team. They provide their professional and personal insights regarding you, your family and your Company, often gained over the course of several years, which enable me as a Business Continuity and Succession Planning Attorney to more quickly and accurately pinpoint the best planning tools and techniques to utilize. Attorneys from different law firms routinely work together today, each bringing their particular area of expertise to bear on the project to be accomplished.

If you regularly work with your Company banker to help grow your business (which we normally suggest you should be doing), we want your banker to work with the Planning team. The Fourth Quarter Planning process needs to be conducted within the reality of your current banking relationship and future financing options, which is best accomplished when your banker is involved in the process. In addition, your banker brings a number of planning tools and services to the table which can be critical to success.

You may or may not have ever utilized a Mergers & Acquisitions Market Analyst, a Business Appraiser, or a Business Strategy Advisor. We often want to utilize a Business Appraiser to help address business valuation. We often want the M&A Market Analyst to assist in determining the outside market for selling your business and to assist in implementing an outside sale. We bring one or more Business Strategy Advisors to the process, depending on your particular needs.

Our collaboration approach has been designed to enable your regular or new advisors to "plug into" this Fourth Quarter Planning process to assist in designing the right Fourth Quarter Game Plan for you.

Pioneer Mindset

☑ **Value.** *Always give more than you receive.*

So What Now? - Working On Your Business

If you stayed with me up to this point in the book, hopefully I have provided you with a little information that you didn't have and have answered a few questions that you did have, as well as perhaps provided a little motivation and direction for taking the steps needed to "always being ready to exit."

At this point in the book, you have a simple decision to make. From here forward, your main objective shouldn't be to just learn additional information about Fourth Quarter Planning. I've covered the beginning of what I think business owners need to know in order to be effective and successful in accomplishing their own personal Fourth Quarter.

Put A Stake In The Ground

The balance of this book is now focused specifically on the actions you very likely need to take if you want to actually put this knowledge to effective use for you, your spouse, your family and your business colleagues.

To be successful with your Fourth Quarter, it's up to you to do something to actually cause this success. The first step is for you to decide that you are going to cause a given result to occur. The second step is to take the actions that will help you make this happen.

Coaching For The Fourth Quarter

To employ a sports analogy, the 2017 Super Bowl is a great example of not planning ahead to play all 4 Quarters. The Atlanta Falcons had built a seemingly impossible to lose third quarter lead of 28 – 3. However, the New England Patriots Coach Belichick and Quarterback

Tom Brady had begun the game with all Fourth Quarters in mind and engineered an epic 34-28 comeback win.

Whether you are just beginning or have already gotten through your personal First, Second or Third Quarter, you still won't win the game until you successfully finish your Fourth Quarter. The Fourth Quarter Planning process serves as a coach, helping you to decide when and how to successfully play and finish the game.

> ### *Pioneer Mindset*
> ☑ *Sandbox.*   *Play well together in the sandbox.   Be collaborative, give praise to others, remember who gave you that great idea and be appreciative towards those who help you.*

Chapter

12

Achieving Incredible "Fourth Quarter" Results While Avoiding "Train Wrecks"

The Family Business Pioneers we've worked with have told us they want Four Essential Results. Our Fourth Quarter Game Plan System has been designed to work with Business Pioneers and your trusted advisors as a team to achieve these <u>Four Essential Results</u> while facing the following realities <u>before, during</u> and <u>in</u> your personal Fourth Quarter:

First Result = Profitable Growth for your business.

The reality being faced to accomplish this is that the speed and the force with which Business Models are changing and being created (or dying) is unprecedented.   This rapidly accelerating "perfect storm" is affecting the life of all companies today. This impacts all business owners at all times, but especially impacts Fourth Quarter business owners when many won't invest in, take on, look for or see the changes necessary to keep profitably growing.   True strategic planning at the Business Model level is needed today to remain profitable and to improve the lives of those you seek to impact.

Second Result = Wealth Protection for what you're building.

The reality today is that in our litigious, competitive society others will often try (legally or illegally) to take the assets or wealth you have built or the key personnel you have developed. You can take certain steps, before troubles arise, to properly and legally minimize these risks and help protect what you're building. You don't want to have to start over or try to recover anytime – especially in your Fourth Quarter - if the unexpected (but often very predictable) happens to you.

Third Result = Lifestyle Continuity for you and your family.

Estate Planning should actually be lifestyle continuity planning through controls you put into place now while you are alive and well. This should provide you with peace-of-mind today that the controls you have adopted will enable your family to navigate the twists and turns they will face. Business owners need to address several, often overlooked, Estate Planning techniques, funding and control issues that are unique to business owners.

Fourth Result = Personal Freedom on your terms.

You've been or expect to be successful in building and operating your Company. Will you be successful in transitioning, retiring and exiting from your Company in the future - at your option, on your terms and on your timetable? Specific actions are needed to achieve a successful transition and future exit, retirement or time off (from ownership, active duty or both). The time to be taking these actions is well beforehand.

The Fourth Quarter Planning Process.

We have seen too many half-way attempts at succession, transition or exit planning. These attempts have the same thing in common — they seek to apply a narrow specialty to a situation that demands multiple areas of knowledge.

Building, growing and exiting a closely held or family business successfully has never been quick or easy. Given the many unforeseen events which can occur before you exit, we have found that a successful Fourth Quarter needs to rest on a specific design process that begins when you begin as a business owner. This is an experience-based, proven step-by-step process that has been leading Family Business Pioneers to their ultimate success — the achievement, through professional collaboration, of the above Four Essential Results.

Pioneer Mindset

☑ *Think and Show.* *Overcome your so-called left or right brain dominance and learn to think and express logically, laterally and visually. Put the dots on the page. Connect the dots.*

The Main Plays In The Fourth Quarter Planning Process

The next sections in this book describe the Main Plays which we are teaming with Business Pioneers to deploy for achieving these results and for avoiding the 24 Fourth Quarter Train Wrecks.

The 24 Avoidable Fourth Quarter Train Wrecks

Train Wrecks Which Derail Profitable Growth

- Your leadership team doesn't effectively deal with business innovation roadblocks
- A "fear of change" mindset is overtaken by today's massive Business Model disruptions
- Your Business Model misfires, declines or fails
- Poor Company culture deflates your team performance and customer loyalty
- External forces (competitors, insurgents, economy, technology, government) start to beat you
- Business expansion opportunities start to be lost or ignored

Train Wrecks Which Derail Wealth Protection

- Business disputes and litigation losses deplete your business resources
- Company ownership is not correctly controlled or funded with the right buy-sell-hold options
- Avoidable co-owner disputes crush you
- Leadership team members leave to find better opportunities elsewhere
- Company hits the skids if CEO/President is lost unexpectedly by illness, accident or death
- Personal risk exposures deplete your personal resources

Train Wrecks Which Derail Lifestyle Continuity

- Inadequate Estate Plan controls damage your Company and deplete family wealth
- Bloodline wealth opportunities wasted
- Wrong family members become Company owners or receive control
- Business and estate disputes damage your family
- Wrong family members remain Company owners or remain in control
- Estate tax hit

Train Wrecks Which Derail Personal Freedom

- Insufficient cash-in-pocket to meet your business and personal needs or objectives
- Wrong successor, no successor, or great successor leaves (to go help your competition)
- Company not always in prime condition to be operated, transferred or sold
- Income tax hit
- No effective inside route exit
- No effective outside route exit

Are You Serious About This? Then Put It In The Budget

Those things in your business which you are serious about you put into the budget – your time budget and your financial budget. You are serious about having customers ("Customer Segments" to use the Business Model language we discuss later), so you budget for marketing, advertising and fulfillment ("Customer Channels") and customer retention ("Customer Relationships"). You are serious about having great products or services to sell to them ("Value Proposition"), so you budget for product and service development, production and fulfillment costs ("Key Activities"). You are serious about having great facilities and great colleagues to lead and perform for you ("Key Resources"), so you budget for your investment in facility and personnel costs.

If you are serious about having an incredibly successful life as a business owner, we are finding that those Family Business Pioneers who budget for the time and investment you will make in working with your inside Profit Strategy Team and your outside Advisor Team ("Key Partners") leads to incredible Fourth Quarter results.

Fourth Quarter Progress Report

How prepared are you already? For a quick "Fourth Quarter" Fitness Checkup, go to the Information and Background section at the end of this book.

Pioneer Mindset

☑ *Kobayashi Maru. You can win only if you first figure out what it takes to win. If you need to change the rules or situation or setting or premise or scope or players to win, then figure out the fastest way and do it (as long as your change is in all ways legal, ethical and moral).*

Your Profit Playbook

Profitable Growth For Your Business

Your Profit Playbook

Profitable Growth For Your Business

Goodnight Irene: Not the Result She Had Expected

Irene* had inherited a great import/export business which had been started by her grandfather over fifty years ago. In fact, she had turned this into a small fortune. However, as the old joke goes, the problem was she had started with a large fortune which was becoming a small fortune. What had at one time been a leading edge business was now wilting into irrelevance.

Irene had always expected this would never happen to her. She had what we call the "Wishes Are Horses" Game Plan. As the saying goes, "If wishes were horses, then beggars would ride." In fact, a successful retirement (or company sale) won't occur just by wishing it to be so.

Irene didn't see the deterioration occurring in her customer base, the lack of systems for addressing product and Business Model innovation, the changes needed to her customer channels, or the impact of the failure to bring in new key partners. She wished it was otherwise. However, the likelihood of a profitable outlook or a successful sale anytime soon was remote.

What happens when you let yourself get stuck in a Business Model that will no longer be profitable?

This section of the book addresses the Main Plays which Family Business Pioneers are taking now "with their Fourth Quarter in mind" to achieve lasting "Profitable Growth For Your Business."

---

*   While this example is real, we've changed the actual names, type of business and other details so that no specific person or business can be identified.

Chapter
13

Dynamic Leadership Core Deployed

Incredible Result: "Our Leadership Team never answers a question by saying: 'Because that's how we've always done it.'"

Avoidable Train Wreck: Your leadership team doesn't effectively deal with business innovation roadblocks.

Main Play: The Profit Strategy Team

What This Is: You have developed and deployed a Profit Strategy Team (aka Advisory Board) of dynamic leaders, who have been fully briefed on the internationally acclaimed Business Model Canvas profit system. The team is empowered to continuously find the full profit impact of Business Model trends, patterns, disruptive forces and innovations and to implement rapid Business Model improvements.

The tears in my Dad's eyes told me everything I needed to know. It was March 2, 1969 and my Dad was walking up the driveway from my Grandfather's home where he lived on the side of the lake on our farm.

The doctor had arrived a few minutes earlier and announced the bad news. Apparently a phlebitis in my Grandfather's leg had thrown a blood clot to his lungs. He had died during his sleep.

The trauma which every family goes through upon the sudden loss of a loved one is compounded when the loved one is also the founder and head of the family business.

The little corner grocery store business which my Grandfather had founded in 1917, and grown to several other corner grocery stores throughout the area, before converting to supermarkets, had grown into a small chain of five supermarkets by 1969.   My Grandfather had successfully navigated the major Business Model shift from the corner grocery store to the supermarket in the 1930s and 1940s. He and my Dad and my Uncle had successfully adjusted the supermarket Business Model many times since, while most of their competitors had fallen by the wayside.

And clearly, my Grandfather, my Dad and my Uncle had established what I call a very successful Root Force Culture (discussed later) within and throughout their entire organization, which was largely responsible for their success.

Now, however, the strength of their leadership team, what I call a Dynamic Leadership Core, would be tested. How solid was the Dynamic Leadership Core which they had or had not put into place prior to my Grandfather's unexpected sudden death.

These were no small issues in the mind of a 13 year old. By this time in 1969, my Grandfather and my Dad and my Uncle were involved not only in the ownership and management of the supermarket business, but also farming, ranching, restaurants, real estate, and retail merchandising.

> ## *Pioneer Mindset*
> ☑ ***Presence.***   *Your demeanor impacts trust, respect and influence. Be self-aware.*

Business Continuity and Succession Planning

Fortunately, the impact of their Root Force Culture had been at play in the thinking and actions of my Grandfather, my Dad and my Uncle as they built their Core. They had conscientiously planned for these types of contingencies. My Dad and my Uncle were already part owners and leaders in the businesses with my Grandfather. And, my Grandfather had an ownership plan in place for them to acquire full ownership from his estate upon his death.

They had also already agreed to overall Company leadership in the event of this type of contingency. My Uncle would become president of the supermarket chain (with my Dad as vice president), while my Dad would become president of the other business interests. Ownership Plan – Check. Leadership Development – check. Succession Plan – check. Buy-Sell and Business Continuity Agreements – check.

And, lastly, my Grandfather had an Estate Plan in place which assured a smooth transition with regard to the balance of his estate amongst my Dad, my Uncle and their two sisters. Business Owner Estate Plan – check.

Three main constituencies exist with virtually all organizations. These are: owners, leaders and family. The mishandling of either can have an extremely disruptive impact on the organization, not only in good times, but especially in bad times.

Times change. People change. Needs change. Desires change. Wants change. Ambitions change. Expected events happen. Unexpected events happen.

If the organization's leadership has not put the right ingredients into place to address these dynamic realities, the organization will stall, falter or fail. It is just a matter of time.

By contrast, where these dynamics have been anticipated and dealt with, the organization is able to live and thrive in a more secure, comfortable environment because all three constituencies (as well as others who rely on the organization, such as employees, customers, and suppliers), will realize that the organization has been designed and built on a platform which will adjust to these changing events.

Pioneer Mindset

☑ *Lifetime Value.* *Know the lifetime value (or cost) of each relationship and decision.*

Dynamic Leadership Core

In order to build an organization which will endure, a strong Business Model Command (discussed later) is simply not enough. And a strong Root Force Culture (discussed later) is not enough. The Business Model itself must rest on a strong platform, your Dynamic Leadership Core, which provides it with the business, financial and leadership support which it needs in order to thrive, adapt, persist, grow and change as the future confronts it.

Business owners, leaders and family, your Dynamic Leadership Core, must continually ask and answer the two key questions which we discuss frequently:

- What will be the probable, almost certain, future outcome of our present course, if left unchanged?

- What's missing, the presence of which will make a substantial difference in producing a better future outcome?

Larry Bossidy and Ram Charan in their book *Confronting Reality – Doing What Matters To Get Things Right*, concluded "You have to make your organization more capable of changing." They found that "it stands to reason, then, that the more change your organization can handle, the more freedom you have in adjusting your Business Model." They found that you "have to build in the flexibility you will increasingly need by making your organization change – ready."

Recognizing the change which is facing all organizations today, Dave Gray, in his book *The Connected Company* alluded to the need to have a strong Dynamic Leadership Core on which to build. He concluded "the time to change is now, while you still have the financial resources to change assertively and proactively." He recognized that the "time to change is not some day in the future, when you have reached a crisis of GM, Kodak or Greek proportions."

In order for all organizations to have the type of Dynamic Leadership Core necessary to enable it to address and deal with internal and external change, the organization needs to think in terms of these three principal constituencies – family, leaders and owners – because they each affect the guidance, management and operations of every organization.

Too often organization structure planning is centered around various topical areas which fail to properly address the needs, wants, desires, capabilities, motivations, strengths and weaknesses of each of these three key constituencies. By instead designing the organization's management and operational platform around these three constituencies, the organization is in a better position to address the concerns and to develop the strengths of each.

Often, of course, the same person or persons might wear all three hats. However, if they confuse the fact that they each wear one, two or all three of these hats, then chaos will often prevail within an organization.

Let's take a look at the principal motivations of each of these three groups.

First, the owners have either created, invested in, been given or purchased the organization (or membership in it). In either case, they have made a significant capital investment and/or sweat equity investment. For business owners, their main financial objective is to own and operate a profitable Company, which will provide income over time and eventually provide an opportunity to either cash out or to transfer their ownership to other family members or to other members of the team. They may also have non-financial objectives which may relate to goals for their families, trusted employees, valued customers and the community.

The leaders within an organization are responsible for the management and overall direction of the organization. They will typically, of course, be motivated by a variety of factors ranging from various career and financial objectives to an interest in simply being involved as part of an organization striving to achieve important business, cultural and societal objectives.

The family members of the owners, leaders and other personnel have their own personal, financial and career objectives. Whether or not they are personally involved as owners or leaders within the organization, their financial wellbeing is generally largely dependent on the success of the organization. Family members not currently in the organization may have career objectives which involve future employment with the organization.

Pioneer Mindset

☑ *Title Only. Always be earning the right to your title. Title may mean you're a manager, but title alone doesn't make you a leader.*

The Dynamic Leadership Core Actions To Be Taken

Each of these three key constituencies in organizations which endure are normally organized and operate through three distinct groups:

- The owners normally act through a Board of Directors.

- The leaders normally guide the organization through an executive team or a strategic planning team, which I call a Profit Strategy Team.

- The family normally acts through a Family Council (whether informally or formally).

The Board of Directors

The Board of Directors in lasting, successful organizations normally handle three key actions:

- Financial Protection – To handle accounting, legal, tax, risk management, organizational structure, asset protection and organization funding.

- Leadership Development – To handle appointment of officers, development of leadership bench strength and organizational chart (which should all be designed in light of your Business Model instead of according to traditional positions).

- Ownership Continuity – To handle continuity of ownership and business decisions through Buy-Sell and Business Continuity Agreements, an employee ownership protocol, and ownership Succession and Exit Planning.

The Profit Strategy Team

The Profit Strategy Team (often also called an Advisory Board) in lasting, successful organizations normally takes care of three key actions:

- Business Model Design - To activate the creative steps needed to continually research, develop and test their Business Model Portfolio so they can effectively preserve, eliminate and create (just like a company will research, develop and test future product and service offerings, the long term organization will research, develop and test various Business Model alternatives to create a portfolio of present and future Business Model possibilities).

- Organization Culture Design - To develop the protocols to see that the essential practices of a Root Force Culture are present, prevalent and actively deployed by the right leadership team.

- Business Model Execution - To make the tactical decisions on how to best execute, and optimize the value from, their Business Model(s).

The Family Council

The Family Council (whether formally created or informally acting) in lasting, successful organizations normally takes care of three key actions:

- Family Career Plans - To establish a family employment policy early on so that the children of the organization's leaders and owners have a clear understanding of the prerequisites to employment in the business and understand that employment there is not an entitlement.

- Family Financial Plans - To establish sanity in each family member's understanding and stewardship with regard to wealth and spending.

- Family Estate Plans - To establish the responsibility of each adult family member to do advance planning to take care of your family if you should die or become disabled.

Pioneer Mindset

☑ *Spider Web It. Seek every opportunity from each venture BDA (Before, During and After) the venture.*

Actually Putting This Into Practice

The gunpowder in your fireworks celebration will not ignite without charcoal. The ingredients of saltpeter and sulfur are not enough. Yet time and again I've seen organizations become underachievers because they won't take the steps to put these elements of their Dynamic Leadership Core into place. This isn't rocket science. If the family, leaders and owners are fueled by a Root Force Culture, they will easily realize the "probable, almost certain future outcome of our present course, if left unchanged" and will put these elements of a Dynamic Leadership Core into practice towards "producing a better future outcome."

The long term, successful organization wants to look at and address the ingredients to build the right platform to achieve both the near term and long term needs, desires and aspirations of the owners, the leaders and the family, all in the context of a clear understanding of the Company's Business Model and Culture.

The Dynamic Leadership Core is necessary to support, direct and change the Business Model Command. By addressing the needs, desires and aspirations, and utilizing the talents, of the owners, the leaders and the family, the long term organization has the opportunity to build a core which will produce successors and which will withstand the destructive forces which have shortened the achievements, lives or profitability of so many companies.

> ### *Pioneer Mindset*
> ☑ *Left/Right and Ahead.* *Compete against your vision of the future, not just against your competition.*

This Works

And it works. For example, my Dad successfully transitioned his ownership to my Uncle upon his retirement because my Uncle's family had children in the business who had become the third generation leaders. This is how our Dynamic Leadership Core worked in our Company. And it supported a Business Model Command which has currently developed and is operating across three main types of grocery store Business Models throughout the central Midwest – Cub Foods, County Market and Save-A-Lot, all from its relationship with its Key Partner, SuperValu.

> ### *Pioneer Mindset*
> ☑ *Relationship.* *You can't lead a person if you don't really know that person.*

Baseball

In my Dad's language as a former professional baseball player, this means knowing when the starting pitcher should call it a day so you can bring in the reliever.

My Grandfather, my Dad and my Uncle knew that leadership needs to be dynamic – you need to know how to develop bench strength and you need to know when to bring in the relievers. By doing it right, they created and developed Niemann Foods, which is now starting its second 100 years in business.

Pioneer Mindset

☑ *Leadership Team. If you are a Walt, find your Roy (and vice versa).*

Chapter

14

The Pioneer Mindset Deployed

Incredible Result: "In this battle of now constant, massive disruption and new horizons, our Company is built to explore new possibilities, to endure and adapt, and to profitably grow."

Avoidable Train Wreck: A "fear of change" mindset is overtaken by today's massive Business Model disruptions.

Main Play: The "Pioneer Mindset" Initiative

What This Is: This program, taught to your Company's leadership and aspiring leaders, builds the Pioneer Mindset into the culture of your Company. This system of leadership recognizes that a pioneer mindset is necessary for success today. This program is designed to overcome the External and Internal Forces which destroy or hold back business growth and profitability.

I loved the pony business and I loved growing up on our little pony farm in Quincy, Illinois. As a young boy, I figured it would last forever. But by 1969 it was a mere shadow of itself.

And by 1971, my family's Shoppers Village retail store had closed. My family's Colonial Inn Restaurant wasn't far behind, to be later followed by the closing of our Pronto Restaurant and then the S & H Greenstamp redemption store. The Niemann Bros. warehouse distribution business was shuttered by the late 1970's, as well as our Westgate Fireworks business and later our Burger Chef Restaurant franchise. After having been in business for decades, they all seemed to have run their course.

What the heck was going on? While our family just pivoted to other opportunities, these had been great family businesses.

As I approached high school, I began to notice many other companies coming and going on the Quincy, Illinois landscape. My travels to and from college in Omaha showed me more of the same. Companies which at least appeared to be pretty successful were seemingly, all of a sudden just gone.

The Life And Death Of Companies

Corporations, of course, have a history which in the western world have been around for only about 500 years. During that time, they collectively have had huge success and have produced goods and services and created wealth which has enabled world population to explode and standards of living to soar.

However, when looked at individually, most commercial corporations have been, as Arie De Geus states in his book, *The Living Company*, "dramatic failures – or, at best, underachievers." As he points out, "They develop and exploit only a fraction of their potential. For proof, you need only consider their high mortality rate."

De Geus points out that the "average life expectancy of a multinational corporation – Fortune 500 or its equivalent – is between 40 and 50 years." De Geus goes on to demonstrate that that figure, "short though it seems, represents the life expectancy of companies of a considerable size. These companies have already survived their first 10 years, a period of high corporate 'infant mortality.' In some countries, 40 percent of all newly created companies last less than 10 years."

Pioneer Mindset

☑ *Second Chances.* *Fumbles are inevitable. The ability to recover is priceless.*

De Geus cites a study by the Stratix Group in Amsterdam which indicates that the average life expectancy of all firms, regardless of size, measured in Japan and much of Europe, is only 12.5 years. He says he knows "of no reason to believe that the situation in the United States is materially better."

Indeed!   According to the U.S. Small Business Administration, only 50% of new businesses survive five years. Only 33% reach 10 years and only 25% last 15 years or more.

Didn't someone have a formula or something for avoiding what had to be heartbreak upon heartbreak to families and to their hopes and dreams?

Apparently not. And the problem isn't just disappearing.

While this is occurring in small businesses and family businesses, we can see this in just a sampling of large well-known companies that have completely or essentially failed:

- A & P Supermarkets
- MySpace
- TWA
- Polaroid
- Smarter Image
- BlackBerry

- Blockbuster Video
- Comdisco
- Kodak
- Woolworth
- Atkins Nutritionals
- FAO Schwarz

- Borders
- Montgomery Ward
- Bethlehem Steel
- Radio Shack
- Sears
- Howard Johnson's

They all had a recognizable brand. They were all fairly large companies, most of them being publically held. In other words, these were not small start-up or middle market companies which failed to materialize.

However, what they failed to do is profitably innovate, i.e. they apparently didn't have what it takes to effectively move when one should move. They did not have an "Always A Startup" mindset. They stuck to a static Business Model, and they all failed.

The reality is that "Business Models are living much shorter lives these days." (Fortune Magazine, October 2, 2006).

As Saul Kaplan, author of *The Business Model Innovation Factory* has observed: "Business Models just don't last as long as they used to." Kaplan goes on to say: "During the industrial era, Business Models rarely changed and were handed down from generation to generation. ... Those days are over. The industrial era is not coming back."

Many other organizations self-destruct not due to static Business Models but due to organization cultures and leadership which enable, condone or promote greed, corruption, fraud, poor management or other questionable or nondesirable conditions or practices which develop improper Business Models or which destroy otherwise good Business Models.

Well known examples include:

- Arthur Andersen
- MCI Worldcom
- Standard Oil
- Enron
- Bear Stearns
- Adelphia
- E.F. Hutton
- TWA
- Drexel Burnham

Are organizations (and the Business Models and cultures on which they are based) simply perishable? Are almost all organizations (whether large or small), in the words of De Geus, destined to be "underachievers"?

"I'm Ok. You're Not"

"What does it matter? Our Company is ok. It's the other person's Company or sector we are talking about. Right? I'm ok. You're not."

Therein lies the problem and the start of what I call the "Business Model Myth". This problem is overcome by having a Pioneer Mindset. In the now constant disruptive conditions we are in, the likelihood of surviving without a Pioneer Mindset will be very slim.

The Business Model Myth

Will the probable, almost certain, future outcome of the present course of your Company be that of lasting success? The Business Model Myth is the unwarranted belief that your Business Model will, through natural market forces, evolve on its own to replicate (or improve) today's outcome indefinitely. Many either believe it or at least act as if it is truth.

The reality is just the opposite. A mindshift is needed. Without a proactive, creative hand, a Company's Business Model, the leadership which supports it, and the culture which fuels it, will mutate and disintegrate into an unrecognizable, unprofitable organization which will linger or perish. The only question is how soon and who will it take down with it.

As Forbes Magazine has found, it's "up to each of us as leaders to build a culture that inspires innovative brilliance in our own teams and organizations." ("Why A Startup Mentality Is Key To Your Success." January 28, 2016).

The belief that your Company's past success and endurance is proof that your Company will endure into the future has become foolhardy.

The Business Model Myth is believing everything is fine. Never is everything fine. It is believing your present Business Model will last. Never will any Business Model last. It is believing your Business Model will profitably evolve on its own. It won't. It is believing you can go it alone. You can't do it alone.

The seven hidden, destructive internal forces which infect the culture of many companies (described in this book) are destroying or holding back companies and the financial freedom of the families, leaders and owners who depend on them.

All business leaders (and those they lead) run the risk of believing that their Business Model will continue to perform as well for them as it has in the past. The fact that most believe this is proven by the following fact. Most business leaders devote substantial time and resources to product research, development and testing. Yet most devote little time or resources to Business Model research, development and testing. This is now changing – due to the Business Model Generation (discussed below).

Sudden Impact - The 4 Relentless External Forces

However, just as products and services have a limited life, so too do Business Models. Every Business Model has four epicenters which center around our Resources, our Offers, our Customers and our Finances:

Business Model Epicenters

Resources	Offers	Customers
Finances		

We all face the impact of four Relentless External Forces on these four Business Model Epicenters – which will have a positive or negative impact on your business, depending on the culture and leadership of your Company. These are the following:

- Offer Forces – These are the external forces which impact the nature and efficacy of the products, services and experiences which we offer. These forces include technology, insurgents, competitors and the needs and wants of those who we serve.

- Customer Forces – These are the external forces which impact our existing and potential future customers. These forces include society, demographics, products/services and customer makeup.

- Resource Forces – These are the external forces which impact the availability and pricing of the resources necessary for our business. These forces include value chain, infrastructure, assets and transformative issues.

- Finance Forces – These are the external forces which impact our revenue and cost systems. These forces include regulatory actions, market changes, price points and capital supply.

This absolutely necessitates the need for continual research, development and testing into revised and new Business Model designs for our organizations. This is true, at least, if you intend to drive an organization which has the promise of being optimally profitable and optimally durable.

While many business leaders are fortunate to see some accidental, profitable Business Model micro-evolution occurring (e.g. in response to random personnel, customer or supplier suggestions), those organizations which have endured long term have realized that intentional, creative Business Model design, and a leadership core that is on the move and a positive culture to enable it, to support it and to fuel it, are necessary if an organization is to stay highly profitable now and is to endure over the long haul. In short, to endure, an "Always A Startup" Mindset is vital.

Pioneer Mindset

☑ *Always A Startup. Center your culture around ingenuity and blank slate reinventive thinking with the curiosity, courage, confidence and persistence to reinvent, repurpose and rid the status quo … but only if you want your business to endure.*

Overcoming The 4 Relentless External Forces With The Pioneer Mindset

While most organizations let themselves succumb to a life well short of their potential, many have navigated these Relentless External Forces, and overcome the internal opposition, to successfully change or move from one Business Model to others. Let's look at just two examples – one a very old Company and another relatively new.

Hudson's Bay Company (HBC), founded in 1670, is North America's longest continually operated Company. Beginning as a fur trading company it diversified or transformed its Business Model over the many years into liquor, canned salmon, coffee, tea, tobacco, real estate, shipping and natural resources. Today it focuses principally on retail, operating Hudson's Bay, Canada's largest department store, and Home Outfitters, Canada's largest home specialty superstore.

This need to be able to intentionally adjust or move to new Business Models has not been lost on Jeff Bezos of Amazon. Since its beginning in 1995, Amazon has fundamentally changed its Business Model several times. It was initially set up as a "sell all, carry few" Business Model, relying on the fulfillment capabilities of many book wholesalers and publishers. Through its drop-shipping model, it could offer over a million books while stocking only about 2,000. However, as online retailing matured, Amazon couldn't rely just on its vast product selection, as other Internet retailers began to also offer a wide array of stockless products through various drop-shipping models.

These Relentless External Forces led Amazon to move to a "sell all, carry more" Business Model, for which it greatly expanded its own warehouse fulfillment capabilities, with a focus on quick, efficient and excellent delivery. In 2006, it further reinvented its Business Model by beginning the Fulfillment by Amazon program, enabling independent sellers to use Amazon's warehouse network to fill their orders. Through its fulfillment-for-hire Business Model, Amazon's key value proposition and competitive strength became fulfillment, the very task it had outsourced in its early years. And on and on it goes for Amazon.

In both of these examples, had these companies been hampered by the internal human forces which destroy the ability to properly change, their Company culture would not have come up with, much less enabled, these necessary shifts, adjustments and transformations to their Business

Models to have occurred in response to the four Relentless External Forces.

Again, the insights of Arie De Geus are instructive: "Companies die because their managers focus on the economic activity of producing goods and services, and they forget that their organizations' true nature is that of a community of humans. The legal establishment, business educators, and the financial community all join them in this mistake."

In other words, a focus by the organization's leaders simply on executing your Business Model is not sufficient to sustain an organization. The uniquely human community aspect of culture must be an ingredient (which we call your Root Force Culture) in a viable formula which seeks, finds and implements Business Model change.

> ### *Pioneer Mindset*
> ☑ *Attitude. Why not us. Why not right now. Hurry!*

The Pioneer Success Formula

Based on my experience and research with hundreds of organizations throughout the world, we can achieve lasting success for any organization through the three ingredients (discussed in the next chapters) in the following formula:

The Pioneer Success Formula

$$
\begin{bmatrix} \text{Business} \\ \text{Model} \\ \text{Command} \end{bmatrix} + \begin{bmatrix} \text{Dynamic} \\ \text{Leadership} \\ \text{Core} \end{bmatrix} + \begin{bmatrix} \text{Root} \\ \text{Force} \\ \text{Culture} \end{bmatrix} = \begin{bmatrix} \text{Lasting} \\ \text{Success} \end{bmatrix}
$$

Critical to the success is the presence of all three of these ingredients. For example, the best Business Model Command combined with a great Culture may survive for a short while, but it will fail to endure without a strong Leadership Core. Likewise, a great Leadership Core and a great Culture will fail if the Business Model Command doesn't work.

This Formula for overcoming the Business Model Myth and the Relentless External Forces and for achieving lasting success is the right mix of the ingredients needed to assure that we live up to our responsibilities to each other to create the jobs and to keep our business growing, which will support our families, our colleagues, our customers and our communities.

Pioneer Mindset

☑ ***Boston Legal.*** *Express at least three separate winning reasons for your proposition, each stronger than the previous. If you don't have three winning reasons, why are you pushing it.*

The "Pioneer Mindset" Initiative

Fast paced disruption is the common denominator today. Innovation displaces existing companies, Business Models, products, services and ideas. Those business owners who endure are those who are always seeking to be a disruptor rather than being disrupted.

They always have a startup mindset and always begin with the end in mind.

They begin with their "Fourth Quarter" First. And, just like America's pioneers before them, they are going for it – and winning big!

This is exactly the mindset of the startup Company. You seek change. You seek innovation. You seek discomfort. You seek new. You seek different. You seek new ways to collaborate. You seek breaks from the past. You are not bound by preconceived notions or past methods. You focus on what customers and potential customers want or need or might need. You look to disrupt others. You have the constant attitude of an insurgent. You have a belief that much that is new and untested is entirely possible. You don't fear failure – you seek to learn from it.

This, of course, is easier said than done. However, unless your leadership team is willing to plant and water and nourish and grow the seeds of this startup mindset throughout your culture, the odds are you'll never reach the level of First, Second, Third and Fourth Quarter success and endurance you and your colleagues and your family are seeking.

John Maxwell has been voted by Inc. Magazine as the #1 leadership and management expert in the world. Such well known leadership experts also ranked by Inc. Magazine were Jack Welch (#3), Dale Carnegie (#7), Richard Branson (#9), Michael Porter (#10), Tom Peters (#12), Stephen R. Covey (#13), Brian Tracy (#25), Peter Drucker (#29), and Jim Collins (#48).

Based on my study directly with John Maxwell and earning his leadership certification as a John Maxwell Certified Speaker and Coach, we have developed the Pioneer Mindset Initiative Program which we are deploying with Business Pioneers (and their teams) for building a leadership team and for considering and developing potential successors. This enables us to work closely with business owners in considering the important decision on who should be the owner's successor, as well as how to further develop their successor's leadership skills.

Pioneer Mindset

☑ *What If?* *Think and explore the possibilities of the opposite.*

Chapter
15

Business Model Command Deployed

Incredible Result: "We are keeping the leaders of other companies awake at night."

Avoidable Train Wreck: Your Business Model misfires, declines or fails.

Main Play: The "Business Model Command" Initiative

What This Is: This program, taught to your Profit Strategy Team, shows how to keep your Company in command of a highly profitable Business Model by knowing precisely: "What" business you are really in, "Why" your Business Model (still) works (and when it won't any longer), and "How" your Business Model creates, captures and delivers unique, profitable value.

Standing in the middle of a smelly pony stall, wearing boots that were three sizes too big, with a pitchfork in hand, shoveling pony manure into a trailer attached to my Dad's 1948 Willy's Jeep, might be an unlikely setting for someone to start to understand exactly how business works. But that is exactly where I found myself as an eight year old working on my Dad's farm on a hot summer day in 1964. For some reason, my Dad felt this would be a good way for me to start to understand business.

My Grandfather had taught my Dad well, and he was determined to teach me. Both were entrepreneurs who had worked hard at scratching out a living in various types of businesses in my home town of Quincy, Illinois. Amidst their great successes had come a fair share of business failures, known to us in our family as excellent learning opportunities. My

Dad and Mother were determined that I and my six siblings would understand and appreciate what it took to be successful in business.

"You and your brother figure out how to spread the load in the south pasture. It will help the grass grow," said my Dad. So my brother Ferd (then ten years old) and I figured it out. Since the Willy's Jeep wasn't exactly designed to be driven by eight and ten year olds, we just rigged a feed box behind our back in the driver's seat, shifted the Jeep to first gear and "figured it out".

We had a pretty small, forty acre pony farm which, in the early 1960's, was actually a pretty decent business. A lot of kids still lived in the country and the minibike hadn't yet become a sensation. The pony market had some good traction. At the time we had a breeding herd of about 100 Shetland ponies. My brother and I soon became involved in the annual process of weaning the colts and getting them ready for either a quick sale or training.

What Is A Business Model?

Some interesting things for an eight year old to see living in the midst of a business. Though I didn't understand the fancy terminology at the time, I could see that my Dad provided a pretty good offer to his customers ("Value Proposition"). He and a hired hand would break the ponies for riding. He also sold pony saddles, bridles, halters and lead straps. As I saw him walk potential customers (generally other dads) around the pasture with their son or daughter in tow ("Customer Segments"), I could hear his sales pitch. This one-stop shop approach for setting up a parent to have a rideable pony for his or her child from day one was a complete offer which made the direct, onsite sales presentation (his "Customer Channel") much easier. And his promise to take the pony back and refund the price certainly helped to build a strong bond with his customers ("Customer Relationship") as well as go a long ways towards knocking down much of the customer's potential objections to purchasing.

But I couldn't understand how my Dad could offer a complete package (pony, saddle, bridle, halter and lead strap) for a package price which was less than the sum of the parts if bought separately. Yet, that was simply my Dad's strategic thinking in developing the method to be used for his pricing ("Revenue Stream"). He had clearly figured out the interaction of his costs ("Cost Structure") and, even when throwing in free delivery (ahead of his time!), he was able to operate the pony business at a profit.

Now, I noticed that my Dad, his hired hand, and my brother and I seemed to be the only persons doing all of the work on this farm. As some of the main assets of the business ("Key Resources"), we each had certain assigned jobs ("Key Activities") for which we were responsible. Cleaning out the pony stalls would never have been necessary at all if my brother and I hadn't done the chores to feed and water the ponies before and after school every day.

But we still couldn't do this by ourselves. My Dad clearly had a system for how he would buy ponies at the right price from local farmers or sales auctions. And our 40 acres didn't generate enough grass or hay to feed the herd. My Dad had developed strong relationships with a couple of local hay farmers to provide us the raw materials needed to grow our herd. And, every now and then, I would see the local veterinarian pay us a visit to treat a sick pony or two. And I was constantly tagging along as my Dad gave a tour of the pony farm to local grade school classes and boy scout and girl scout troops, the leaders of which were referral relationships which my Dad had cultivated. All of these persons outside our business who helped make it work ("Key Partners") were clearly also important to the operation of the farm itself as well as to getting the word out about the joys of owning a pony.

And there you have it. At eight years old, I was seeing through my Dad's little pony business what Dr. Alexander Osterwalder of Switzerland would 40 years later define and detail as the nine Building Blocks that make up every Business Model of every business and organization, regardless of size, age or business sector, throughout the world.

> ## *Pioneer Mindset*
> ☑ *Breaking Rocks Or Building A Church.* *Start by knowing what business you are really in.*

The "Business Model Command" Initiative

To build and grow a successful business during all Four Quarters of a Business Pioneer's time in action, it's necessary to always be in command of your Business Model (which itself is the command center for your Company's ability to be profitable). In The Business Model Command Initiative we teach Profit Strategy Teams the three essential features in the design and evaluation of our Business Models which must continually be addressed and revised. These are:

1. **What:** What business are we really in?

2. **Why:** Why does (or will) our Business Model (still) work (if it does)?

3. **How:** How does our Business Model profitably create, deliver and capture unique value?

Misunderstanding What Business We're Really In.

My life starting as an eight year old in a family of entrepreneurs was full of many opportunities to "build character", as my Dad referred to all of these jobs which he had for us.

"If you are done with your break time," said my Dad, "let's get back in the truck. I've got some jobs to be done over at the Pronto."

The Pronto Restaurant was another of our family's business ventures. To my Dad though, he wasn't in the "restaurant" business. He was in the business of "creating family memories". Simply put, that's what he did when he took our family out to dinner. And he wanted the same experience for those who came to his family restaurant.

The Goldilocks Principle

In deciding "What business are we really in?", it's necessary to apply the "Goldilocks Principle" to achieve the "Goldilocks Effect". If we define our business too narrowly, we pass up opportunities because they are not in our perceived line of business. On the other hand, if we define our business too broadly, we'll lose focus of our goals, our capabilities, our market and our customers.

Instead, by defining our business "just right" we will see and capture the right opportunities, achieving what is known as the Goldilocks Effect.

For example, at the turn of the last century, almost all of those who decided that they were in the "buggy whip" business closed their doors upon the advent of the automobile. Instead, as Harvard Business

School professor Theodore Levitt pointed out in his well-known 1960 Harvard Business Review article, "Marketing Myopia", had buggy whip makers viewed themselves as being in the "transportation business", providing a stimulant or catalyst to an energy source, they may have found opportunities to adapt to a way that could serve the emerging automobile marketplace.

The buggy whip analogy may have some historical problems. However, the horse carriage parts makers provide a great example. If they thought they were in the "horse carriage" business, then they saw no opportunity when the automobile came along.   There were 13,000 businesses in the wagon and carriage industry in 1890, according to Thomas A. Kinney, author of *The Carriage Trade: Making Horse-Drawn Vehicles In America*. The people "who made the most successful transition were not the carriage makers, but the carriage parts makers," he said. They realized they were in the transportation parts business, not the horse carriage parts business. One such company still in business is the giant Timken Company. Its roller bearings were first used in 1899 in wagon wheels.   According to Mr. Kinney, Timken easily adapted to the automobile because roller bearings could be applied "to nearly anything that moved."

The key is to think in terms of customer satisfaction, solutions and benefits rather than products and services.   As we teach in our Business Model Profit programs, business entrepreneurs need to focus on the benefit of the feature (not just the feature). For example, someone who happens to sell office equipment could view their business as "business workflow improvement". A hairdresser might view his or her business as "image enhancement". A company selling film and cameras would probably have been better served to view itself as in the business of "storytelling" or "imaging".

Pioneer Mindset

☑ *Close The Sale.* *Alleviate the risk of buying while being very clear how your solution substantially helps the buyer.*

"Marketing Myopia"

Professor Levitt focused on this back in his 1960 "Marketing Myopia" article. He addressed one of the major challenges which most organizations still face today. He explained that: "Every major industry was once a growth industry. But some that are now riding a wave of growth enthusiasm are very much in the shadow of decline. Others which are thought of as seasoned growth industries have actually stopped growing."

In every case, the reason growth was threatened, slowed or stopped was not because the market was saturated. It was "because there has been a failure of management." He explained that this failure is caused by what he called "marketing myopia." This is what occurs when Company leaders define their business too narrowly, which is a form of nearsightedness or shortsightedness.

Levitt described a few examples:

Industry	Myopic Purpose	Broader Purpose
Railroads	Train Travel	Transportation
Hollywood	Movies	Entertainment
Oil Companies	Petroleum	Energy

Levitt cites, by contrast, companies such as DuPont and Kaiser and Reynolds, which have thrived for centuries by remaining extremely customer focused and which evolved – in terms of the products and services they offered – as the needs of their customers changed.

Maria Ferrante–Schepis (*Flirting With The Uninterested*) gives us another example. As she points out, insurance companies are not really in the protection business. They are in the "lifestyle continuity business", by keeping the lives of individuals, businesses and families intact when the unexpected happens.

What Is Our Real Purpose?

We can get the answer to this question right if we stop thinking about what we sell and start thinking about who buys (or could buy) from us. Who are the people we can help? What do they (and what will they) really need from us? What job do they really need done? What are we really fundamentally accomplishing?

Harvard Business School professor Ted Levitt gets us started in the right direction: "People don't want a quarter-inch drill – they want a quarter-inch hole."

So, how can we adjust our Business Model and culture to provide it?

Starbucks CEO Howard Schultz faced this question before he built Starbucks into the business it is today. On a buying trip to Milan, Italy, for Starbucks he found that the coffee bars not only served excellent espresso, they also served as nesting places or public squares. They were a big part of the glue of Italy's society (in a country that had 200,000 of them).

So, when he returned from Italy he had a vision that Starbucks was not about the coffee. Instead it was about providing a welcoming place for people – a form of refuge between home and work – where they could meet with associates and friends. Coffee was integral. But Starbucks would be "in the people business serving coffee, not the coffee business serving people."

A simple story from Peter W. Schutz, former CEO of Porsche and the author of *The Driving Force – Extraordinary Results With Ordinary People* illustrates this perfectly. Peter, now a fellow Vistage National Resource Speaker, and I had the opportunity to visit when he was in Omaha for a Vistage CEO Board meeting. Peter related an "old story" about the importance of being part of something bigger and better; in other words, of knowing "what business we're really in." Three men were working on a construction site. All three were performing exactly the same task. A passerby asked the first one "What are you doing here?" He answered, "I am busting rocks." The passerby asked the second man the same question. The answer was, "I am earning my living." He then asked the same question of the third man, but got a very different answer, "I am helping my colleagues build a church." The third man understood the real purpose of the business he was in.

I still have fond memories of the family nite out. My Dad had it right when he designed the Pronto Restaurant as being in the business of "creating family memories", not the business of serving food.

While not sufficient by itself to keep you in business forever, he clearly understood the business he was really in. He understood the real purpose of his business. Many do not.

> ## *Pioneer Mindset*
> ☑ *"It's [Not] The Economy Stupid".* Constantly ask *"why, why, why" each part of your Business Model works – so you can act based on why it actually does and recognize when the "why" has changed.*

Misunderstanding Why Our Business Model (Still) Works

My fun as an eight year old didn't stop with cleaning out smelly pony stalls or getting up at 5:30 in the morning to feed the ponies in zero degree weather before going to school. My Dad had just backed his pickup truck up to the loading dock, so my brother Ferd and I knew what was coming. "If you're done with your break, turn off Petticoat Junction and load the truck," my Dad said. "We are heading to Food Center."

If we were old enough to drive a Willy's Jeep around the farm, we were certainly old enough to work at our Food Center Supermarkets.

My brother and I of course needed to spend the fifty cents we had just earned. So we invariably ended up walking through the aisles of one of our family's supermarkets. To an eight year old, the supermarket seemed always to be huge and to have just about every product known to man. I had just assumed that is the way grocery stores had always been. Little did I realize then what had occurred 34 years earlier in a little town of 11,000 people called Herrin, Illinois, some 150 miles to the southeast of us.

What I learned from my Dad (whose name was also Ferd) he had learned from my Grandfather (whose name was also Ferd). My Grandfather, as it turns out, had learned a lot from a man named Michael.

Michael Cullen understood "why" his Business Model was no longer working. Most in his industry didn't – or they didn't want to face it – due to the their unwillingness to put the customer first, which blinded or prevented them from seeing or making the changes the industry needed.

My Grandfather had opened his first corner grocery store in 1917 in Quincy, Illinois. He and his brother soon expanded the operations to multiple corner grocery stores in Quincy and neighboring towns.

Depending on your age, most of us are familiar with the corner grocery store, either through personal experience or through examples on TV or other media. I grew up with Sam Drucker's general store on the popular 1960s television shows, *Petticoat Junction* and *Green Acres*, which is a good illustration.

The Corner Grocery Store Business Model

Typically, the corner grocery store was about 600 square feet in size and carried a variety of food products and basic household goods, generally in small quantities (Value Proposition). They were normally located on the main street in residential areas, to achieve the best visibility, and typically operated with relatively short store hours, closing down at 5:00 PM or so (Customer Channel). They catered to families in a relatively small neighborhood geographic area (Customer Segments). The corner grocery store was typically very high touch and high service. Customers would come in with their list and a store clerk would do the shopping for them, even typically carrying the groceries home for the customer (Customer Relationship).

To provide this type of service, the corner grocery store needed a relatively large number of store clerks for the 600 square foot stores (Key Resources), who busied themselves stocking shelves, shopping for the customers and delivering groceries (Key Activities). Most of the inventory was provided by a variety of local and regional suppliers (Key Partners).

The revenue earned by the typical corner grocery store was generally one dimensional, from simply the sale of products. The pricing was generally established through a uniform rate of markup for all products, typically, for example, 30%. So, if the store bought a product for 10 cents, it sold it for 13 cents. If it bought a product for $1.00, it sold it for $1.30 (Revenue Streams). And, in order to provide this highly visible, full service type of operation, the store needed to pay for relatively high, main street, real estate costs, high low volume inventory costs and high, lots of clerks, labor costs (Cost Structure).

Michael Cullen had begun his grocery business career in 1902 at the age of 18, working for a Company known as the Great Atlantic and Pacific Tea Company (later known as A&P). Over the years he found himself working for a variety of grocery businesses until, in 1930, he was working for one of these corner grocery stores in Herrin, Illinois, known as Kroger.

While the corner grocery store itself was relatively small, the grocery industry was huge. After all, a lot of people needed to eat. While there were a lot of small independent grocers (like my grandfather), there were also a few very big grocery chain store operations. In 1930 A&P had over 15,000, and Kroger had over 5,000, of these corner grocery stores, scattered throughout the country. Kroger was headquartered in Cincinnati, Ohio.

Now, Michael was not the manager of the little Kroger corner grocery store in Herrin, Illinois. He was the assistant store manager. In other words, he wasn't a big shot in the grocery industry. He'd never worked at the Kroger headquarters, had not held a high corporate position and was relatively unknown at the time in the grocery industry.

Yet, from his day-to-day vantage point, Michael perhaps had the most important position of all.

Why The Corner Grocery Store Model No Longer Worked

What was happening in 1930? The country, of course, was in the midst of the Great Depression. Times were tough and people were having a hard time even paying for groceries. This created a lot of resentment towards the big grocery chain stores. But what could the corner grocery store do? All corner grocery stores, including the big chain stores, were operating under a high Cost Structure. Small stores. Low per store volume. Full service. A highly visible costly location. Michael had certainly heard his share of enough complaints from his customers. They loved the service but were simply having a hard time footing the bill.

Besides the Great Depression, what else was happening in 1930. Families generally had at least one car, so they were not confined on a daily basis to simply the neighborhood. Food could be bought and generally stored. Many products were available for sale as canned foods. Often, more than one spouse worked, making it difficult to shop during business hours. Perhaps, Michael thought, people would be willing to give up some of the frills for lower prices, especially if they could get more of their necessary shopping done in one stop.

Pioneer Mindset

☑ *Nine Block It. Know precisely how your Business Model works and test the viability of every decision, business or venture through the lens of the Business Model Canvas.*

The Creation Of The Supermarket Business Model

So, Michael had an idea. Actually, he had a big idea. In fact, he thought his idea was so big, that if he could just write a letter to the Kroger president in Cincinnati, surely Kroger headquarters would see the merit of his idea and immediately start to change the grocery industry.

Michael's idea was this. Instead of a lot of small stores (generally 600 square feet) with a lot of clerks, why not expand the size of the store geometrically to 6,000 square feet with very few clerks (Key Resources). A larger store would provide the opportunity to stock a wider variety of products (which had presently required customers to shop at a number of separate stores) (Value Proposition). Instead of relying on word of mouth and store visibility in the high rent districts, get off of Main Street, where you could also afford to add free customer parking. Use high intensity advertising in the local newspapers (Customer Channels) so he could reach a wider geographic range of customers (Customer Segments). This would produce a higher volume of business with a lower Cost Structure, which would enable prices to be reduced. This effect could be enhanced by using variable price mark ups (instead of the uniform price mark-up), so that certain products could become advertised specials at lower or no mark-up (Revenue Streams).

The customers would not be receiving the same high touch service (they'd shop for themselves and drive their own groceries home), but the presence of one-stop shopping at lower prices would develop the strong following needed to create repeat customers (Customer Relationships). The principal activities of those store clerks who were still needed would revolve around stocking inventory and checking customers through the checkout lane (Key Activities). No longer would the store offer store credit, but instead would be limited to cash and carry only (Revenue Stream and Cost Structure). The larger variety of products would require a broader array of local, regional and national suppliers (Key Partners).

Michael was sure he had a winning proposition. Perhaps predictably, however, his letter to Kroger headquarters went unanswered.

Not to be discouraged, Michael decided to get into his car and drive to Cincinnati. He fully believed if he could just get in front of the Kroger president and tell his story, the corporate office would fall in line. "Mr. Albers is too busy to see you," said the receptionist.

The car ride back to Illinois might have discouraged some, but not Michael. He did what probably few family men would do during the midst of the Great Depression. He went home and quit his job at Kroger. He then sent his letter to the A&P headquarters. After all, he used to work for them and surely they would see the light. Again ... no response.

Now without a job, but still equally determined, Michael got back in his car and drove to New York City. Surely he could find at least one backer for his idea to give it a try.

And he found it. A Vice President for a Company called Sweet Life Foods decided to take a chance.

And on August 4, 1930, Michael Cullen opened the first supermarket in the United States. He aptly named it King Kullen (a reflection of the attitude he needed his culture to exhibit if he was to be successful). Michael had found a vacant old building in New York City which met his specs, and he did what he said he wanted to do.

And it was a huge hit. Police were needed at the grand opening to control the bargain hunters. The first week store volume was "phenomenal". In two years, seven more stores were opened. By 1932, his eight King Kullen stores had annual sales of $750,000 per store (The average annual sales at a corner grocery store were about $17,000). By 1936, he had 15 King Kullen stores. He had profitably increased the size of the store by a factor of 10 and increased the sales by a factor of 40.

Perhaps we will never know for sure all that Michael Cullen might have accomplished had he not died unexpectedly in 1936. However, he had clearly spawned a new industry. His King Kullen is recognized by the Smithsonian Institution as the first supermarket, of which there are now over 25,000 supermarkets throughout the United States. And the conversion of the grocery industry to the Supermarket Business Model in the 1930s has been cited by Harvard Business Review as the model that Walmart and Kmart followed starting in the 1960s.

Michael Cullen had clearly demonstrated how to lead an industry into a new direction. While he had not been the first to attempt innovations within the corner grocery store, he was the first to develop an entirely new Business Model which touched and fully integrated all of the vitally necessary nine building blocks to be successful.

Pioneer Mindset

☑ *The Means of Persuasion. To be a persuasive leader, communicate with credibility (ethos), logic (logos) and emotion (pathos). Understand the principles of take away and reciprocity, the impact of your heartfelt attitude and the power of the analogy.*

Recognizing The "Why"

But what is the most important for our purposes at the moment is to understand that he understood "why" the corner grocery store Business Model could not continue to work (and "why" his would). One of the leading fundamental causes of business failures is that the leaders continue to believe in certain key facts which were true in the past but which are simply no longer true today. Those companies which have the right early detection systems in place to continually challenge the assumptions on which their Business Model is based are those who will detect the need to change early enough to be responsive and effective.

As Jim Collins points out in *How The Mighty Fall*, the "best corporate leaders we've researched remain students of their work, relentlessly asking questions – why, why, why?"

Do we really understand "why" our Business Model still works, or are we relying on assumptions that are no longer true? Perhaps the founder of the Company understood it. Or perhaps the previous owner understood it.

Yet, how often does the following occur:

• The Company leadership keeps behaving as if the fundamental assumptions which have driven the prior success have not changed (when they have).

• New management makes changes which undermine the real (still existing) reasons why the Business Model actually works.

One of the approaches we take in our Business Model Profit programs is to look at whether the customer's job that needs to be done, or the customer's pains or potential gains, has changed such that the assumptions for "why" some part (or all) of the Business Model worked in the past simply no longer does or will work now or in the near future.

Pioneer Mindset

☑ *Avoid Being OBE. Make sure your Business Model is not constrained by "how we've always done it", or you will quickly be Overcome By Events (OBE).*

Overcome By Events (OBE)

Overcome By Events (OBE) is a term of military origin. It is used when a situation changes so rapidly that previously proposed courses of action are no longer relevant. This occurs, for Business Model purposes, when the reason or reasons why our Business Model has profitably worked in the past just no longer holds true.

Little did I know at the time that the reason I was in a supermarket that day, rather than in a corner grocery store, was because a man named Michael realized "why" his (and the grocery industry's) Business Model was no longer working, and he had dared to challenge the thinking of an entire industry from his vantage point as one of the lowest ranking employees within one of the largest food companies then existing in the United States.

Do you have one or more Michaels in your organization? Does the culture in your organization stifle or foster the development of Michaels? Are you and your team constantly asking "Why?" Has your Business Model been OBE?

Misunderstanding How Our Business Model Works

My Dad also owned and operated a small general merchandise and toy store called Shoppers Village, so I wasn't surprised when in the fall of 1964 he brought home a set of building blocks and a model car kit. As someone who was always teaching me about business, he said "Here, see how you can use these to figure things out."

I never fully understood this until 40 years later when I read Dr. Alexander Osterwalder's 2004 dissertation "The Business Model Ontology – A Proposition In A Design Science Approach" (PhD thesis, University of Lausanne).

We can read a lot today about Business Models. However, until Dr. Osterwalder created a language and a structure around this, the study of Business Models had been replete with confusion, misunderstanding and a lack of the tools necessary to design, critique, analyze, innovate and develop Business Models.

To be sure, men and women have been designing and successfully operating businesses for eons. Men and women have also been watching their businesses crash and burn for eons. Many simply didn't understand how their Business Model worked, i.e. how it created, delivered and captured unique value. Perhaps they were just content to follow or fearful of the risk of not following.

Many men and women in business, both today and in the past, have simply patterned their business after that of some other successful example, without necessarily caring to understand exactly how (or why) the business worked. For example, once the supermarket Business Model proved its case, copycats jumped on board and this new Business Model proliferated within a decade. Other examples abound. Once Groupon built a successful (or seemingly successful) Business Model, other imitators (called groupies, copycats or clones) flooded the market (e.g. LivingSocial, GroupPrice, PetSimply, Jdeal).

Definition Of A Business Model

However, to truly build any business which has unique long lasting capabilities, it's necessary to understand the fundamental building blocks as to how any business is put together. Only by understanding the "how" of how a business actually works, can truly unique Value Propositions be developed as part of a truly unique Business Model which is fully capable of successfully creating, delivering and capturing full value.

Dr. Alexander Osterwalder set out in 2004 to define exactly what these building blocks were. His research lead to the following conclusions.

First, every business centers around four key epicenters:

- Offer - What is my offer?

- Customer - Who is my customer?

- Resources - What is needed to produce the offer?

- Finance - How is profit achieved?

However, this is not sufficient detail to produce a workable, useful framework. Instead, based on his research, Dr. Osterwalder found that these four epicenters need to be broken down into the following nine building blocks. (The related question is my summary of what each "building block" means and I've re-named his "Channels" to be "Customer Channels"):

Offer

1. Value Proposition – What do I sell?

Customer

2. Customer Segment – Who buys from me?

3. Customer Channels – How do I reach and deliver to my customers?

4. Customer Relationships – How do I keep my customers?

Resources

5. Key Resources – What do I use to make it?

6. Key Activities – How do I make it?

7. Key Partners – Who outside of my organization helps me do it?

Finance

8. Revenue Streams – How do my customers pay me?

9. Cost Structure – How do I control my costs?

He described these nine components as the building blocks of a Business Model. Apparently my Dad with his set of building blocks was onto something.

The Business Model Canvas

Had Dr. Osterwalder stopped here, his dissertation likely would have ended up in the heap of other doctoral dissertations. However, Dr. Osterwalder took a significant step forward by turning this list of components of a Business Model into a useful tool which business leaders can easily learn to use. He dubbed this the "Business Model Canvas" which looks like the following (with my nine descriptive questions inserted):

The Business Model Canvas

Key Partners	Key Activities	Value Proposition	Customer Relationships	Customer Segments
Who Outside Of My Company Helps Me Do It?	How Do I Make It?	What Do I Sell?	How Do I Keep My Customers?	Who Buys From Me?
	Key Resources		Customer Channels	
	What Do I Use To Make It?		How Do I Reach and Deliver to My Customers?	

Cost Structure	Revenue Streams
How Do I Control My Costs?	How Do My Customers Pay Me?

Source: www.BusinessModelGeneration.com.

Using this Canvas, any type of business, of any size, age, business sector, time and place, can be described, in its essence. This enables any business to be more easily understood by every member within the organization. And it enables every idea to be better evaluated.

> ## *Pioneer Mindset*
>
> ☑ ***Passion.*** *Passion is important. But a bad idea you are passionate about is still a bad idea.*

This is critical to a successful business. If those within the organization do not truly understand how their business works – and what is necessary in order for it to work - the odds are that those working within an organization are pulling or pushing in opposite or competing directions, even though they seemingly believe they are actually helping the cause.

The Business Model Canvas can also be used by an organization's leaders to meet their three principal obligations – to profitably preserve those parts of the business which should continue to be operated, to eliminate those parts of the business which no longer represent the organization's sweet spot, and to create new parts of the business or additional businesses for the organization.

> ### *Pioneer Mindset*
>
> ☑ *Leave No Grudge. The persons you did the job for will be satisfied if you have been diligently pressing their cause with a heartfelt sense of urgency.*

Business Model Thinking

Through the eyes of an eight year old back in 1964 living and working on our farm, I also experienced typical farm life which has served to help me to further understand and explain this whole concept of Business Models based on building blocks.

Besides being in the pony business, my parents also operated an egg production business, so we had a stable full of chickens. We also had, like every other farm in the area, our share of dogs and cats. And, besides the ponies, we had about a half dozen horses of various breeds.

So, how does this help us to understand Business Models? During my Boot Camps and Executive Briefings with business leaders, I pose the question to them that if they had to try to explain the concept of Business Models using different animals to do so, how would they do it. Many explain that each of these animals have a different value proposition or competitive advantage or key capability.

All are correct answers. However, the answer I'm looking for is that they all have the same "building blocks". They all have bones, muscles, eyes, legs, stomach, heart, etc. These are the building blocks which are common to all of these animals. Yet, even though they are all based on the same set of building blocks, they do in fact all have unique capabilities and competitive advantages. They have been designed by God to accomplish or to serve uniquely different purposes within the overall ecosystem (but in each case using the same types of building blocks).

Likewise, whether you have a business which grows vegetables, packages meat products, provides consulting services, delivers packages, repairs automobiles or makes iPhones, each of your businesses is built on the same nine building blocks described by Dr. Osterwalder above.

Let's take a look at how the easily understood grocery business can be described, using the Business Model Canvas.

First, let's compare the corner grocery store operated by Kroger and A&P throughout the country in 1930 to the King Kullen supermarket designed by Michael Cullen. These nine building blocks can be compared as follows, using the Business Model Canvas:

Kroger and A&P (1930)
Business Model Canvas

Key Partners	Key Activities	Value Proposition	Customer Relationships	Customer Segments
A Few Local & Regional Suppliers	Home Delivery	Small Selection Grocery & Household Products	Personal Service	Neighbor-hood Only
	Key Resources Lots of Clerks		**Customer Channels** Rely on Word of Mouth Short Store Hours	
Cost Structure High Rent High Inventory Costs High Labor Costs			**Revenue Streams** High Prices Store Credit Uniform Mark Ups	

King Kullen (1930)
Business Model Canvas

Key Partners	Key Activities	Value Proposition	Customer Relationships	Customer Segments
Many Local & Regional Supplicrs	Self Service	Large Selection Grocery & Household Products	One Stop Shop at Low Prices	Region
	Key Resources Big Stores Free Parking		**Customer Channels** High Power Advertising Long Store Hours	
Cost Structure Low Rent Areas Quantity Buying Power Low Labor Costs			**Revenue Streams** Low Prices Cash Only Variable Mark Ups	

We can look at one of the supermarket Business Model grandchildren by looking at the current Cub Foods Supermarket:

CUB Foods (2017)

Business Model Canvas

Key Partners	*Key Activities*	*Value Proposition*	*Customer Relationships*	*Customer Segments*
Franchisor Distributors Wholesalers In Store Service Partners	Quick Self Service	Wide Selection Of Food, Drug, HBA & Household Products at Low Pricing	One Stop Brand Value Card	Vicinity
	Key Resources Well-Equipped Big Stores Strong IT Free Parking Associates	Essence = Big Name Brands At Low Prices	*Customer Channels* Extensive Media Advertising Retail Stores 24 / 7 Hours	

Cost Structure	*Revenue Streams*
Quantity Purchase Discounts Efficient Inventory Control Efficient Check-Out	Very Competitive Discount Pricing Credit and Debit Cards Variable Mark Up

As Dr. Osterwalder began to speak to various groups around Europe about his Business Model Canvas concept, his audiences invariably asked "Where is your book?" They clearly did not want to read his technical dissertation.

The Business Model Generation Movement

Naturally, having become an expert on Business Model thinking, Dr. Osterwalder would be the last person to follow the normal route for authoring a book. Instead, he decided to enlist the help of other like minded practitioners from around the world. He opened a Business Model collaboration website and invited those of us interested to participate with him in developing what would become the first of its kind Business Model Handbook.

With his Business Model concept in mind, he offered a simple Value Proposition to those who wanted to participate. They would become named co-contributors in the handbook. His Customer Channel for reaching us was through the internet and email. Those who signed up also would become not just his Key Partners, but also his initial Customer

Segments. By having us as a co-contributor team for the handbook, he developed a particularly sticky Customer Relationship. His simple (initial) Revenue Stream was a one-time entry fee which we paid to help fund the project. All of the co-contributors, as well as a group of closely-related professionals who had worked with Dr. Osterwalder, along with the Internet Hub, constituted the Key Resources. Dr. Osterwalder would propose and initially author certain "chunks" for the book, along with posing questions for consideration, which members of the Hub could respond and discuss online, thus constituting the Business Model's Key Activities. Other Key Partners enlisted by Dr. Osterwalder included a select number of firms who could help to design and illustrate a unique new handbook. His Cost Structure was kept to a minimum through the efficient use of the website hub.

Pioneer Mindset

☑ *Determination.* *You wanna be successful? Show up. And keep showing up. On time. No matter what!*

The project took us well over a year to complete. In the end there were 470 of us from 45 countries who participated as co-contributors to develop the handbook, which has been named *Business Model Generation – A Handbook for Visionaries, Game Changers, and Challengers.* Seventy-eight pages of the book can be viewed at www.BusinessModelGeneration.com. The handbook has become an international success, selling over 1,000,000 copies throughout the world. It has been translated now into 35 different languages.

The original group has grown into a community of over 22,000 members on the Business Model Hub. An App is available for your iPad and additional videos and tools are available for those who want to join the Business Model Strategyzer (www.Strategyzer.com).

The Business Model Canvas has been used by over 5,000,000 Business Model innovators (business pioneers, strategies, advisors, etc.). It is also now being used to teach business strategy at major universities. It can be used to describe the overall Business Model for the organization, as well as to describe various divisions, product lines and individual products or services.

Since its essence is to describe how something creates, delivers and captures value, it can also be used at an individual level to describe how any one individual creates, delivers and captures value, e.g. as an employee within a larger organization.

Recognizing this reality, a spin off handbook, led by Timothy Clark, in collaboration with Dr. Osterwalder, and using a similar co-creation Business Model approach, has been developed called *Business Model You: A One-Page Method For Reinventing Your Career.* This was co-created by 328 of us from 43 countries. It has become a very useful tool I use in business leadership development and succession planning (www.BusinessModelYou.com).

The latest spin off handbook is *Value Proposition Design.* This helps entrepreneurs to tackle a main challenge of every business – creating compelling products and services which customers want to buy.

Does everyone in your organization really understand your Business Model? Do they understand the Business Model of your competition? Is everyone on your team pulling in the same direction? Are you in command of your Business Model, which itself is the command center for the profitability and growth of your business?

Pioneer Mindset

☑ *Leadership Unlimited. You can't lead an organization unless you precisely understand how and why its Business Model works.*

Chapter

16

Root Force Culture Deployed

Incredible Result: "Loyalty to our Company is so strong that our Customers and our Team don't even think of switching."

Avoidable Train Wreck: Poor Company culture deflates your team performance and customer loyalty.

Main Play: The "Root Force Culture" Initiative

What This Is: This program, taught to your Profit Strategy Team, puts into practice a profitable, innovation–minded culture driven by the seven Root Forces necessary today for companies to attract and retain great talent and customers and to profitably and quickly grow in the marketplace.

Since my Dad seemed determined that my brother and I would understand business, he often had us tag along when he made his rounds through the Food Center supermarkets.

Each store, to an eight year old, looked like an organized beehive of hard work and activity. And they all seemed to know my Dad – and he knew all of them.

There was something about the atmosphere at the Niemann Food Centers. There was great respect and compassion for others. There was a great trust amongst the people who worked there. There was a generosity of spirit and a dedication to hard work in making the business successful for everyone concerned.

Little did I know or understand everything that it took to keep this business successful and growing. At that time in 1964, there were over seventy grocery stores in my home town of Quincy, Illinois. Of those that existed then, only two of them are still in business today, ours and one other. As I learned over the years, the supermarket business is a tough business. With strong competition and net margins of approximately one percent, this is a business sector which clearly requires a lot of tenacity and courage to be and to stay successful.

> ### *Pioneer Mindset*
>
> ☑ *The Great Culture.* *Create a culture driven by the seven energizing root forces which are fueling tremendous, profitable, lasting growth today: Tenacity, Respect, Trust, Enthusiasm, Compassion, Generosity and Courage.*

So how did my Grandfather, my Dad and my Uncle not only survive, but continue to successfully grow their supermarket business throughout the region, while so many others fell by the wayside?

Niemann Food Center clearly had a great culture.

Much has been written about various aspects of the importance of culture. Over the years of working with business owners, leaders and family, I have also seen that time and again the great successes can be traced directly back to the great culture which permeated the organization. While at the same time, I have seen that the many failures which business owners have described when they have come in to meet with me can be directly traced to the seen and unseen negative forces which have existed within their culture.

The "Root Force Culture" Initiative

"Culture is my main focus as CEO", says Roman Stanek, founder and CEO of GoodData. Yet, HubSpot CEO Brian Halligan contends "that 99% of companies are kind of stuck in the '90s when it comes to their culture." He believes "Companies need to change the way they manage and lead to match the way that modern humans actually work and live." How can we do this?

Zappos is a great example. Its "fun and weird culture" has landed it on Fortune's 100 Best Companies To Work For® list for seven years in a row. They recognize how a "strong company culture can improve employee engagement, increase productivity, promote brand loyalty and enhance financial performance." As Zappos points out, this all begins with a "deep discussion" of the company's core values, the "heart of a company culture".

Culture - The 7 Root Forces

As I have studied this, both with regard to the organizations which I work with, as well as my research into the reasons for success and failure of other lasting organizations, I have found that I can trace all of the successes back to seven root causes within an organization. The truly successful organizations have all seven of these positive root causes (what I call "root forces"), while one or two of these may be predominant.

The seven destructive root forces of behavior and attitude discussed earlier are the mirror image, or exact opposite, of the seven positive root forces which energize the organization. These are as follows:

The 7 Destructive Root Forces	The 7 Energizing Root Forces
1. Hubris	1. Tenacity
2. Contempt	2. Respect
3. Mistrust	3. Trust
4. Contentment	4. Enthusiasm
5. Indifference	5. Compassion
6. Greed	6. Generosity
7. Fear	7. Courage

Each Destructive Root Force is overcome by the owners, leaders and family within an organization when they think, act and lead in accord with these seven Energizing Root Forces.

These extremely strong negative and positive elements of culture permeate both the organization's Dynamic Leadership Core (emanating from owners, family and leaders) as well as its Business Model Command (being reflected in how all personnel treat each other as well as how they treat the organization's customers and key partners).

For example, if the organization's owners, leaders and family are greedy, this will negatively affect pricing considerations for customers and key suppliers and compensation for personnel, and it may jeopardize business cash flow retention needs. If they demonstrate an atmosphere of mistrust, this will permeate the interactions of everyone throughout the entire organization.

The seven Destructive Root Forces and the seven Energizing Root Forces which I have discovered in my research are essentially the business version of the same seven fundamental traits or behaviors which have long been reflected in the culture of our societies.

For example, Christianity has long referred to the personal equivalent of these as the seven Deadly Sins, which are the opposite of the seven Lively Virtues, the roots from which all bad behavior and attitudes and good behavior and attitudes emanate.

Some version of these seven root faults and countervailing root virtues have also been at the center of societal woes and triumphs for thousands of years, as reflected in various literature. For example, Homer's *Odyssey*, Dante's *Divine Comedia*, Chaucer's *The Parson's Tale*, Milton's *Paradise Lost* and C.S. Lewis' *Chronicles of Narnia* all devote serious attention to them.

These seven behaviors are the origin of all other behaviors and attitudes. They underlie other behaviors and attitudes. They are the root cause or root force behind all other behaviors and attitudes.

It readily follows that these seven root behaviors and attitudes of human activity exist in the behavior behind business activity. To deny the impact is at the heart of companies which fail.

Pioneer Mindset

☑ *The Culture Destroyers.* *Avoid the destructive root forces which are destroying once great or potentially great organizations: Hubris, Contempt, Mistrust, Contentment, Indifference, Greed and Fear.*

Visualizing The Impact Of A Company's Culture

We can turn to nature in many ways to see the 3 ingredients necessary for life. Let's choose the tree as our illustration for the life and success of your Company.

The tree's life is dependent on 3 main ingredients – its roots (which fuel it), its trunk (which supports and guides it) and its branches (which reflect its life and which feeds it).

We can easily visualize The Pioneer Success Formula through the visual of a tree:

Impact Of
The 7 Energizing Root Forces

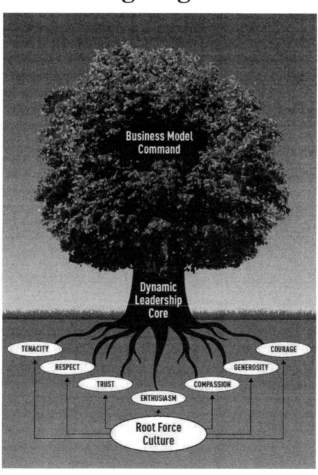

These 7 Energizing Root Forces are critical to the successful life of your business.

The destructive impact of the seven Destructive Root Forces on your Business Model and on your Leadership Core can be visualized as shown below:

Impact Of
The 7 Destructive Root Forces

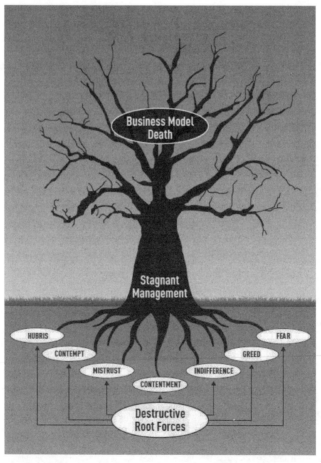

The 7 Destructive Root Forces kill your business.

The 7 Energizing Root Forces Illustrated

We are interested in how to grow your business. Let's look at the seven Energizing Root Forces.

1.   Tenacity: Persistent commitment and determination without unfairly glorifying one's own self.

The Root Force of tenacity can begin with Jeff Bezos, the founder and CEO of Amazon. The story of Amazon is well known and doesn't need to be repeated here. Brad Stone, author of the book *The Everything Store: Jeff Bezos and the Age of Amazon* (2013) describes Amazon's culture as "notoriously confrontational, and it begins with Bezos, who believes that truth shakes out when ideas and perspectives are banged against each other."

Amazon lives by 14 leadership principles, which are the Company's highly prized values, which are often discussed internally and drilled into new hires. One of these reads as follows:

"Have Backbone; Disagree and Commit. Leaders are obligated to respectfully challenge decisions when they disagree, even when doing so is uncomfortable or exhausting. Leaders have conviction and are tenacious. They do not compromise for the sake of social cohesion. Once a decision is determined, they commit wholly."

Tenacity is clearly one of the principal Root Forces which permeates the culture at Amazon. As Stone points out, "Some employees love this confrontational culture and find they can't work effectively anywhere else." Tenacity doesn't need to be too confrontational. When it is, the Destructive Root Forces are starting to creep in.

Seth Godin points out that "tenacity is not the same as persistence. Telemarketers are persistent. Nike is tenacious". (SethGodin.typepad.com)

Tenacity was evident in the approach taken by Michael Cullen when he launched the supermarket Business Model. An excerpt from a 1930 King Kullen newspaper advertisement read: "It's you folks I want to please. The service grocery chain stores oppress the poor and are a menace to the nation. Are you with me?"

2.   Respect: Deep admiration and patience towards someone or something.

"At the core of that call is respect," accordingly to Headsets.com Founder and CEO Mike Faith, as reported in *Small Business Trends* - "Building a Company Culture of Respect" (January 13, 2011). "The customer deserves our respect. Sometimes they could be wrong. But they always deserve our respect." According to Faith, Headsets.com is "Dedicated to customer love. And respect for customers is at the core of that love."

As *Small Business Trends* points out, to ensure that disrespect is a rarity, Headsets.com is extremely rigorous in how they screen and hire candidates. Before they are hired, candidates go through what Faith calls "a day of customer service tryouts" to determine if they are a "fit" for the Headsets.com culture and customer commitment. Only 1 in 30 applicants who have gone through their customer service tryouts makes it into the Company as a headsets.com rep. Is this effective? Headsets.com, which focuses on selling headsets through the internet and their inbound telecom service, is on the 2016 Forbes List of Best Small Companies. It has grown from a $40,000 investment in 1998 to $26 million in revenue in recent years. (www.smallbiztrends.com).

On August 16, 1912, Glen L. Martin formed the Glen L. Martin Company in Los Angeles, California. He had just finished building his first plane in a rented church and decided to take a leap of faith on his risky but innovative new aircraft design – at the urging of Orville Wright.

Four months later and 400 miles away, on December 19, 1912, Allan and Malcolm Lockheed established the Alco Hydro-Aeroplane Company (which they later renamed Lockheed Aircraft Company). They had set up a shop in a garage, constructing sea planes.

As aircraft manufacturing giant Lockheed Martin International states on its website: "A church and a garage. These were humble beginnings. But these were also men of unrelenting vision and unwavering purpose."

Today, Lockheed Martin says it operates its Company on the basis of three core values: "Do What's Right", "Perform With Excellence", and "Respect Others". As the Company describes, we "believe that respect – for our colleagues, customers, partners, and all those with whom we interact – is an essential element of all positive and productive business relationships."

"If you want people to act like adults you need to treat them like adults." This is according to Ricardo Semler, CEO of Semco, a Brazilian conglomerate which specializes in various complex technologies and services such as marine pumps, commercial dishwashers, digitals scanners, filters, mixing equipment, manufacturing liquids, powders and pastes for a variety of industries, logistics and information processing systems, inventory and asset management, biofuels and about another 2,000 different products.

In 1982, at the age of 24, Ricardo Semler took control of Semler & Company, a business which had been founded by his father. Up until then, the Company's organizational structure was a paternalistic, pyramidal hierarchy which had been led by a very autocratic leader. When the younger Semler took office, he instituted a dramatic organizational restructuring. He immediately fired two-thirds of the top management and, in the years which followed, dismantled the rigid management structure which his father had imposed, replacing it with a very flexible organization based on three core values – employee participation, profit sharing and the free flow of information.

Semler felt that all people desire to achieve excellence. He believed that autocracy stifled motivation and creativity. Semco became a self-managed company. Workers chose what they do as well as where and when they will do it. Subordinates review their supervisors. The Company operates like a democracy, with the workers electing the Company's leadership.

When Semler first proposed his ideas, it was rebuffed by his managers. But Semler was clear: "Don't you think they know how to manage their own work?" This is the Root Force of respect. With several hundred million dollars of revenue per year, it appears to work very well.

3.   **Trust: A positive and kind faith in the reliability, integrity, and strength of someone or something.**

Starting as a small shoe retailer in 1901, the American upscale fashion retailer known as Nordstrom grew to over 250 stores operating in over 30 States in the United States and Canada.

This $14 billion annual revenue company is described this way by Harry Mullikin, Chairman Emeritus of Westin Hotels: "Nordstrom has the faith and trust in its front line people to push decision-making responsibilities down to the sales floor.   The Nordstrom shopping experience is "as close to working with the owner of a small business as a customer can get." (*The Nordstrom Way: The Insiders Story Of America's #1 Customer Service Company*).

For years, this trust as a Root Force of Nordstrom's success has been reflected in its very simple Employee Handbook (printed on a single five – by – eight – inch grey card), which was given to all new employees and which contained Nordstrom's one and only rule:

"Nordstrom Rules: Rule #1: Use best judgment in all situations. There will be no additional rules."

In explaining its culture, Nordstom's website explains "We trust each other's integrity and ability. Our only rule: Use good judgment in all situations."

How is trust built within an organization. One critical step is to simply share. As social media expert Dave Kerpen, Chairman of Likeable Media, points out, "Sharing breeds trust, and trust breeds business."

4.   Enthusiasm: Great excitement for diligently achieving a purpose or cause.

Bain & Company, the well known consulting firm, dealt with enthusiasm in a company publication called "The Chemistry Of Enthusiasm – How Engaged Employees Create Loyal Customers" (2012). As Bain explains: "Organizations had been trying for years to cultivate employee engagement ...   Engaged employees go the extra mile to deliver.   Their enthusiasm rubs off on other employees and on customers."

Bain has developed a way to measure this, using a metric which it calls the "Net Promoter Score (NPS). It consists of a single question asked of customers: "How likely are you to recommend [this company or product] to a friend or colleague?" On a scale of 1 to 10, respondents giving a grade of 9 or 10 are considered "promoters" – the company's most devoted customers. Those scoring their experience at 7 or 8 are considered "passives", and those scoring it from 0 to 6 are "detractors".

The NPS is the percentage of promoters minus the percentage of detractors.

As Bain explains, "promoters" are "enthusiastically loyal to the brand, the company and the product. They sing the Company's praises to others and they buy more and stay longer." By contrast, detractors "actively tell others about their terrible experiences." Bain finds that organizations with highly engaged employees "often seem to be powered by an inner force, a mantra that crystalizes the Company's processes and employee behaviors into a compelling summation of 'what we're all about.'"

5.   **Compassion: A proper balance between one's self and the rights and needs of others.**

While some managers may shy away from compassion (as if this might appear weak), a new field of research is showing that organizations which promote a culture of compassion, rather than a culture of stress, create a happier workplace and a better bottom line.

Mark C. Crowley, the author of *Lead From The Heart: Transformational Leadership For the 21st Century* makes this abundantly clear. He explains that companies "are focusing on innovation and unique differentiation – and almost exclusively are looking at people, not machines, to provide it." He goes on to explain that "as workers have become increasingly more critical to the overall success of their organizations, what they need and expect in exchange for their work also has profoundly changed ... They want to feel valued and appreciated by their leaders, and to know their work has significance." Crowley concludes that "future leaders in all workplaces will be required not just to have strong minds, but also generous and caring hearts." (Mark C. Crowley, *Why Workplace Leadership Is About To Get Its First Major Makeover in 100 Years*).

Quoting Dr. Jim Harter, Gallup's Director of Research, Crowley points out that "people will continue to be unhappy in their jobs (and therefore greatly underperforming) just as long as their leaders fail to be their advocates." Citing a worldwide study by Towers Watson, the "single high ascriber of engagement today is whether or not workers feel their managers are genuinely interested in their well-being. Less than 40% of workers now feel that support."

Crowley concludes that where "once the idea of appealing to the hearts of workers was seen as heresy, we've come to understand that it's always been essential."

In other words, an essential element and one of the critical Root Forces which company cultures need to embrace is that of compassion.

6.   Generosity: The habit of giving more value than you expect to receive in return.

Normally when generosity is discussed we think of gifts of money or charity. However, in the context of culture and leadership which builds and executes great Business Models, our focus is not limited to gifts having a monetary value.

As Bruna Martinuzzi, the author of *The Dealer As A Mensch: Become The Kind Of Person Others Want To Follow* says, generosity is "giving someone a chance; giving someone the benefit of the doubt; and giving others a reason to want to work for you." She goes on to state that it "entails giving others latitude, permission to make mistakes, and all of the information that they need to do the job." She suggests that "in a nutshell, all of this translates to generosity of spirit, a quality we admire in leaders."

Bruna explains "a leader with a generous spirit" understands that most people want to feel that they are a part of something bigger and something better and "connects the dots for people – the dots that help them see how the work they perform, no matter how small it may be in the scheme of things, has a bearing on the ultimate vision of the Company."

The Gallup employee engagement tool, the Q12 Instrument, is, I believe, largely a measure of whether this generosity of spirit is present in a company's culture. The Q12 statements look at such factors as whether someone encourages an employee's development, whether an employee's opinions count, whether an employee has received recognition or praise for good work and whether the Company's mission makes the employee feel his or her job is important. These factors are rooted in generosity.

7.   **Courage:** **Embracing purity of thought and action by confronting and overcoming perceived fear, popular opposition, inappropriate emotion, uncertainty and intimidation.**

In his article *CEOs Need Courage*, Harvard Business Review contributor Jeffrey Pfeffer (September 27, 2011), after describing some notable examples of CEOs with courage, concluded: "What separates these CEOs from the pack is not just a more sophisticated and empirically accurate understanding of individual behavior and the sources of organizational success but also the courage to implement these insights even when, or particularly when, they seem to defy conventional wisdom."

A.G. Lafley, former Chairman and CEO of Proctor & Gamble nailed the importance of the Root Force of courage within an organization in his book *The Game – Changer: How You Can Drive Revenue And Profit Growth With Innovation*. He stated "I have tried to promote a more courageous, more connected and collaborative culture – one in which people want to take risks to identify game-changing, life-enhancing innovations. It takes a certain kind of nerve to deal with the unknown, to work on the frontier … . Innovating can mean sticking your neck out; a courageous connected culture means it won't get chopped off, and that you are not alone with taking risks."

The Journal of Business Psychology has even published a study that attempts to quantify the degree of courage within an organization's culture. It created what it calls the "Organizational Courage Assessment" (OCA) which defines four types of organizations: "Bureaucratic organizations (little fear with few acts of courage), fearful organizations (much fear with few acts of courage), courageous organizations (many courageous acts despite much fear), and quantum organizations (many courageous acts with little fear)." *Developing and Validating a Quantitative Measure of Organizational Courage* (2009).

As Seth Godin points out, our "choice is to spend our time avoiding that fear or embracing it." That takes courage.

Pioneer Mindset

☑ *Early and Often.* *Reward your team with benefits that fit your culture and your specific objectives.*

The Prevailing Force

In most organizations that I studied, there occurred a Prevailing Force which had grown or developed on account of one or more of these Root Forces. In essence this Prevailing Force became recognizable as the personality of the organization. This Prevailing Force, when negative, has been the primary cause behind the underperformance, stall or failure. When positive, it has been the primary force behind the growth and ongoing success. This is illustrated in the examples discussed above.

This personality, when positive and intentional, often is reflected in the Company's motto, tagline or advertising and permeates the entire design of the Company's Business Model Command. RAM Trucks are "Guts, Glory" (Courage). Walmart is "Low Prices" (as a result of its Tenacity in controlling costs). Zappos is "Powered by Service" (Respect for its customers). The hugely successful Vala's Pumpkin Patch in Omaha is "Your Fall Family Tradition" (Enthusiasm for the thousands of Nebraska families it serves). Toms Shoes is "Giving" (Generosity towards those without shoes). Salesforce.com is "Customer Success" (Trust by its customers in the service provided).

Often a positive or negative Prevailing Force existing at one stage of an organization's life disappeared or was replaced by a negative or positive Prevailing Force later on during the organization's life. Whether this was intentional or accidental depended on the strength of, and direction coming from, the organization's Dynamic Leadership Core.

Pioneer Mindset

☑ **Brand.** *Let the personality of your brand shine through in every action and decision.*

The 7 Energizing Root Forces in Action

While many focus on just one and sometimes two of these cultural ingredients as keys to organization success, longevity and growth, all seven Energizing Root Forces need to be key elements in an organization's culture if the organization is going to successfully design and re-design (and execute) a great Business Model Command, enabling the organization to truly prosper and endure long term today.

Michael Cullen understood this – and he built his Company around this. In taking on the establishment in the grocery industry, he demonstrated the impact of putting the seven Energizing Root Forces into practice, both by sparking a massive change in that business sector, and by creating a Root Force Culture within his own King Kullen Company which has enabled it to continue to thrive to this day.

This Root Force Culture will permeate your Dynamic Leadership Core to enable it to design, innovate and drive the Business Model Command on which your Company depends.

Pioneer Mindset

☑ *Family.* *Know who your real extended family is.   Protect them.*

The "One Thing" Game Changer

It was 9:00 on the night before the first day of school and my Dad was late getting home after a long business day. Bedtime for my brother Ferd and me, but we wouldn't sleep without a nightly story from our Dad. As a military vet and former professional baseball player, his stories always took us back to some lesson learned in the Korean War or on the baseball field. He always spoke of the members of his platoon and teams as his family. They had a special bond with each other that my Dad spoke about throughout his life. To my Dad, "family" was a very broad, welcome reality.

In the popular 1991 movie City Slickers, the trail boss Curly (played by Jack Palance) kept insisting that Mitch (played by Billy Crystal) needed to find the "one thing" which would change his life (in our case, our organizations) to set it on the right course to lasting success. The movie never revealed what that one thing was. It was up to Mitch to figure it out.

I'll tell you what it is.

There is one thing which will best enable every organization to create a Root Force Culture, meaning a culture which lives by every one of the seven Energizing Root Forces and achieves outrageous, lasting success. An organization where the seven Destructive Root Forces wither away or simply won't take root.

This "One Thing" very simply is to realize, accept and act on the fact that we are all actually family. Family members should (and normally do) think and act towards one another according to the seven Energizing Root Forces. They are generous, compassionate, respectful, trusting and enthusiastic towards each other and will tenaciously and courageously help and defend each other. Members of great Family Business Pioneer families create a culture which helps them achieve amazing outcomes.

This isn't really a new concept at all. Many organizations seek to achieve "family" status. In addition to the military and sports, we see this in fraternities and sororities, alumni, political parties, executive peer groups, social media groups, membership organizations, clubs, customer loyalty programs, national, state and local communities, and many other organizations.

Of course, unless your organization is already built on an "all one family" perspective, a change to this will involve some initiatives. I suggest that a simple mindset exercise is a great start.

If we actually believed that everyone both inside and outside our organization is part of our family, then our attitude and behavior towards each other will automatically reflect the seven Energizing Root Forces critical to outrageous success.

Is it difficult to believe we are actually one family? Society, culture and biases can make this more difficult than it needs to be. However, both religious faith and overwhelming recent scientific discoveries confirm our common ancestry.

An honest, heartfelt mindshift which actually sees everyone we encounter (team members, colleagues, customers, suppliers, partners, etc.) as part of our family puts us in a state of mind where the Energizing Root Forces fuel incredible results.

Pioneer Mindset

☑ **Dignity.** *No matter what, never, ever, take away a person's dignity.*

Chapter

17

Business Model Growth Deployed

Incredible Result: "Our Leadership Team is never satisfied with just doing a great job of managing what we've got. They are constantly eliminating old opportunities we shouldn't be doing anymore and creating new opportunities we should start doing."

Avoidable Train Wreck: External forces (competitors, insurgents, economy, technology, government) start to beat you.

Main Play: The "We Refuse To Be Netflixed" Initiative

What This Is: This program, taught to your Profit Strategy Team, shows how to set up your Business Model Tool Room with the leading tools for designing rapid-response pivots and shifts to your Business Model. This is deployed to keep your Company in a distinct, leading, highly profitable Business Model, with a recognized competitive advantage, a unique value proposition, and a growing, long term, profitable outlook.

"The ponies kicked out part of the fence in the north pasture last night", said my Dad. "Go get Ferd, will you Nick, and get it fixed. Everything you need is in the Tool Room."

Ahh. The "Tool Room". To an eight year old farm boy, the Tool Room was a dream come true. While companies like Amazon, Apple, Disney, Lockheed, Google, Hewlett-Packard and Mattel famously were started in garages, the Tool Room was my second home growing up. It was where I learned how to create, where I learned how to visualize possibilities, and where I learned how to put things together to come up with something completely new.

Working on your Business Model, just like working to build, fix and develop critical components on a farm, is a heck of a lot more productive if you have the right tools and you have been taught how to use them.

Leadership Balance

So, how do we take command of our Business Model rather than let it take command of us? In order for organizations to endure over time, leaders need to balance three critical activities with regard to their Business Models. These are:

- **Preserve**   - **Eliminate**   - **Create**

Every organization, through its leaders, needs to manage (or preserve) its existing Business Model, thoughtfully shut down or outsource (eliminate) certain parts of its Business Model which are no longer its sweet spot, and build (create) new aspects of its Business Model (or entirely new Business Models), if the organization wants to endure over time. (See *The CEO's Role In Business Model Reinvention*, Harvard Business Review, Jan. 2011).

In other words, the organization's Dynamic Leadership Core needs to take command, and be in command, of its Business Model – which itself will be in command of the present and future success of your organization in the business ecosystem.

And, to do so, we, as leaders in our organizations, need the right tools to be able to do this.

The reality is that every Business Model has a limited life. Organizations which are high, long term performers are already working on the creation of their new or revised Business Model before the time that their existing Business Model starts to stall.

Pioneer Mindset

☑ *Strike Zone. Anyone can hit the pitches in the strike zone. Take some chances on some tough ones outside the zone.*

Being willing to embark on a process of preservation, elimination and creation takes a willingness to explore new ideas and entertain creative activity and innovative thought. "The best way to have a good idea is to have lots of them," according to Mihaly Csikszentmihalyi, the author of *Creativity: Flow and the Psychology of Discovery and Invention*. According the Csikszentmihalyi, the requirements for creativity are self-confidence and persistence.

> ## *Pioneer Mindset*
> ☑ *Be Childlike (But Not Childish).* *Recapture that childlike creativity which society and the education system have conditioned out of you.*

Yet, many organizations get stuck into old, tired systems and old, tired thinking which prevent the development of new ideas.

For example, why didn't Microsoft create Google. Why didn't Blockbuster Video create Netflix? Why didn't AT&T create Skype? Why did Xerox essentially give the "mouse" and "windows" to Apple?

It's important that the leaders within any organization understand that new ideas might not necessarily have the proof which they would like to see. A demand for too much proof that a new idea will work can have the effect of inadvertently stifling innovation.

A good example of the willingness to make a logical leap is that made by Mike Lazaridis, the founder of Blackberry. The question he faced was how tiny could keyboards get. He had to make a leap of logic that people would be willing to type with only their thumbs.

Chad Hurley, one of the co-founders of YouTube had this to say about the process of creativity: "It's not about being smarter. It's not about being necessarily more talented. I think anyone that is going to be successful, it's about continuing to try being creative, and having unique insights. It's really just the small subtle things that I think make the biggest difference. And not being afraid to try." (Fast Company Magazine, August 8, 2013).

Many don't make the changes or adjustments. Many do. In a survey of 1,500 CEOs by IBM's Institute for Business Value in 2010, IBM found that "CEOs are breaking with traditional strategy-planning cycles in favor of continuous, rapid-fire shifts and adjustments to their Business Models." (Bloomberg Businessweek, May 18, 2010).

> ### *Pioneer Mindset*
>
> ☑ *SMART. Customers decide based on 5 factors: Skill, Money, Access, Results and Time. Make sure your Business Model uniquely addresses each.*

The "We Refuse To Be Netflixed" Initiative

But how are Family Business Pioneers making these "rapid-fire shifts" and are they being effective?

Fortunately there are "tools" which we can use to be productive in preserving, eliminating and creating Business Models. These tools, when discussing creativity and innovation, are in the form of the right key questions. These are the principal key questions we are using in our Profit Strategy programs, in each case using these through the lens of the Business Model Canvas (in combination with the deployment of OKRs to maximize execution, alignment and engagement):

Preserve

What – What business are we really in?

Why – Why does (or will) our Business Model (still) work (if it does)?

How – How does our Business Model profitably create, deliver and capture unique value?

Grade – How well does our Business Model work?

Challenge – How can we use the Business Model Canvas to challenge our ideas?

SMART – How can we overcome the five main barriers to consumer purchasing: Skill, Money, Access, Result and Time?

Intelligence – What strategies or tactics of my competitors should be used or improved to change my Business Model?

LockIn – How can we lock in our customers, partners and employees?

Advantage – What is or could be our competitive advantage?

TROT – What is the predictable Threat, Result & Opportunity of a specific Trend?

Eliminate

BlueOcean – Which factors could or should be added (that the industry has never offered), increased (well above industry standard), reduced (well below industry standard) or eliminated (that the industry takes for granted)?

SWOT – What are my Strengths, Weaknesses, Opportunities and Threats?

Unbundle – Should we unbundle one or more business functions or features from our Company?

Create

Transference – What feature existing in another field or industry could be profitably transferred to our business?

Fusion – How can we fuse together two or more product features, services or partners?

ValueProp – How can our existing or new value proposition better relieve a customer's pains, create gains or accomplish specific jobs?

BlankSlate – What would be the ideal situation if we were starting from scratch on a blank slate?

Ideation – What if … ?

Freemium – How can we profit more with free products or services?

PESTLE – How will recent or upcoming Political, Economic, Social, Technological, Legal and Environmental trends or issues result in new opportunities or threats?

CherryPick – What profitable segment from a diverse organization can we pick off for our Company?

Collaboration – How can we create and capture more value by systematically collaborating with outside partners?

TRIZ – How can we change the quality, dimensions, content, purpose, user, location, price, experience, volume, or timing of our product, service, processes or organization?

Pioneer Mindset

☑ *The Power of Questions.* *The quality of the questions is more important than the answers you think you already have. The right questions are the power tools of innovation and solution.*

The Impact of Business Model Strategy On Your M & A Program

Every business we work with has some system for achieving organic growth from within. Many also have a well-designed system for seeking and evaluating businesses to acquire and for deciding what part of their Company they may want to sell off – in each case to better achieve their growth objectives.

The "*New M&A Playbook*" (Clayton M. Christensen, etal) points out how companies are closely looking at their own business model and the target's business model in deciding what to buy or sell. Our firm has worked with business leaders on the purchase and sale of hundreds of businesses throughout the world. This business model analysis is something we see is being carefully deployed with the Business Pioneers we work with in making these types of M&A decisions.

"Find Your Tool Room"

The Corona Beer advertising campaign famously urges us to "Find Your Beach". To protect and advance our companies we each need to "Find Your Tool Room".

As an eight year old, my tool room was literally the tool room on our family farm. Today it is wherever my mind can be the clearest to be the most creative. This may be while playing games with my grandchildren, hiking through Superior National Forest near our cabin, riding horses on our family farm, just driving my Ford Explorer along the highway, or walking along "my beach" in Siesta Key in Florida.

The point is that for all of us and for everyone in our Dynamic Leadership Cores, our creative abilities usually flow better outside of the regular office – provided we are willing to commit to the excitement of always trying to come up with that improvement or breakthrough which will enhance our organization and the lives of those who depend on us.

Pioneer Mindset

☑ *The Key To Profitable Growth?* *Your Business Model must be designed to address margin, scalability and OKR execution.*

Whether you call it your garage or lab or tool room, one of the keys to lasting success is to dedicate a team and a space to Business Model Research, Development and Testing. The willingness and guts to decide to commit to this process of reinvention (at the Business Model Command level) may seem to be difficult. Perhaps it will feel uncomfortable. But it doesn't need to be, and it is necessary if your organization is going to achieve lasting success.

As the Harvard Business Review has found, "High performers are well on their way to new business success by the time their existing businesses start to stall. The high performers in our study had typically started the reinvention process well before their current businesses had begun to slow." (*Reinvent Your Business Before It's Too Late*, Harvard Business Review, Jan. 2011).

We are using these Business Model tools described above to work with companies and organizations to show them how to do exactly this.

Pioneer Mindset

☑ *Balance.* *Don't just sit there managing the business you've got. Go eliminate something you shouldn't be doing anymore. And create something new you should start doing.*

Chapter

18

Business Expansion Policy Deployed

Incredible Result: "We are finding and capturing each acquisition and expansion opportunity which is out there to help us grow."

Avoidable Train Wreck: Business expansion opportunities start to be lost or ignored.

Main Play: The "Find It" Expansion Protocol

What This Is: This program, taught to your Profit Strategy Team, shows how to purchase businesses which fit, expand at existing or new sites and develop or acquire new technology rights, all aimed at driving your profitable growth.

A healthy, growing Company will seek expansion opportunities throughout its life. The often repeated line that says if you aren't growing, you're dying, is true. Many business owners who enter or are in their Fourth Quarter often take their foot off the gas pedal. This can have disastrous effects, as it can precipitate a slide down a slippery slope, turn off the interest of possible successors and business buyers, and result in the loss of your customer base, which begins to see your Company as no longer responsive to their growing needs.

Over the past several years companies have become much more analytical in making their decisions on their Expansion Policies. In addition to a focus on strong internal (so-called organic) growth, a strong overall Expansion Policy will focus on consistently looking for opportunities to purchase other businesses, to expand at existing or new sites, and to develop or acquire new technology. The motivation behind this is pretty simple, which is this. One of the principal keys to business success and profitability is to operate from the right locations, for the optimal business market, under the right economic, demographic and technology conditions.

This increasing focus has been due to a number of factors. These include changing demographics, competitive pressures, new strategic sourcing techniques, more sophisticated distribution methodologies, increased shareholder scrutiny, business expansion, merger/acquisition activity, changing technologies, and cost containment efforts.

Adding to this effort to find the right location under the right economic conditions is the fact that businesses today can be much more mobile than they were in the past. Vast improvements in the transportation industries and the voice and data communication industries have enabled many companies to operate from any of several different locations. Therefore, these companies have tended to more aggressively seek locations that have the most favorable business climates.

Business Acquisition

The biggest mistakes we've seen with business acquisition policies is a failure to consider how the 3 ingredients of the Pioneer Success Formula will line up between your existing company and the business you are acquiring. If the 3 ingredients of Business Model Command, Dynamic Leadership Core and Root Force Culture are not thoroughly thought through during the acquisition process, the likelihood of a happy merger is remote.

Site Expansion

The biggest mistake we've seen with moving to or adding new sites is the failure to fully investigate the State and local business climate for the new or expanding sites. This includes the impact on the 3 ingredients of the Pioneer Success Formula. For example, how does the new or expanding site impact the Cost Structure or Customer Channel parts of your Business Model.

State taxes now total about $1.4 trillion annually, which become a significant cost to companies. So, a key component of site expansion policy is the state tax climate and the value of State and local business and tax incentives and inducements.   (This is a planning topic touched on below, which we cover in more detail in our State Tax Anatomy Series).

Competing State Business Climates

As consumers of numerous products and services provided by the business community throughout the country, we are all taught to believe and understand that competition is a good thing. The result of competition is better products and better services at more competitive prices. In order for the business community to be able to accomplish this, business enterprises have needed to become more and more productive and efficient.

The business factors affecting business profitability and success which a State can positively or negatively control or directly impact are the factors which make up that State's business climate. These factors impact the competitiveness of that State amongst other States.

Utilizing State Business Incentives

Every year, State and Local governments award billions of dollars in State Business Incentives to those businesses throughout the country who actively seek these benefits as part of their site location and expansion decisions. These incentives are used by State and Local officials as a way to help incent the addition or retention of jobs and investment in their community.

The availability of most incentives is normally dependent on the Company actually identifying, seeking and applying for the incentives before undertaking a project expansion or relocation. Often these incentives need to be negotiated with the State or Local communities as part of an overall site selection and incentive package. A typical incentive package will be based on the level of projected new jobs and/or new investment the Company will add to the community. Some incentives are being awarded for company restructurings or retoolings that do not require net job increases.

Pioneer Mindset

☑ *Quickness.* *Always find the quickest way to the cash.*

Nebraska's Approach to Tax Incentives

My home State of Nebraska provides a good example of the potential tax incentives available to growing companies in many States.

Nebraska provides many of the State Business Incentives in use today. Nebraska's incentive programs create a package that is substantial enough to impact a Company's location decision. At the same time, its incentives are performance-based, generally requiring the Company to meet and maintain certain designated new job and investment thresholds in order to earn the tax benefits.

Nebraska's program is of particular interest to me because I have been the principal designer and drafter of Nebraska's main economic development incentive programs, beginning with the 1987 Employment and Investment Growth Act (known as LB775) through its successor in 2005, the Nebraska Advantage Act (known as LB312), including several additional incentive programs enacted in between. These programs have incented the creation of over 850 expansion projects, with over $30 billion of capital investment and over 100,000 new jobs in Nebraska.

For over 30 years, the Employment and Investment Growth Act and the Nebraska Advantage Act have been Nebraska's principal incentive package. These substantially reduce a Company's income, sales, withholding and personal property taxes for the life of the project if certain new job and investment thresholds are met by qualifying types of businesses.

The "Find It" Expansion Protocol

Growing companies need to develop an express policy towards business acquisition, site expansion and technology development which lines up with their Pioneer Success Formula.

This provides you with the opportunity to further enhance your Company's growth and value throughout your First, Second, Third and Fourth Quarters.

Pioneer Mindset

☑ *Galaxy Quest. Never give up. Never surrender. Get back on the horse. Adapt as appropriate, but don't wimp out or concede to mere pushback.*

Your Protection Playbook

Wealth Protection For What You're Building

Your Protection Playbook

Wealth Protection For What You're Building

Eric's Game Plan: "Ticking Time Bombs"

Eric* and his partner Joe had a very profitable 25 year run with their industrial supply company, although the past couple years had been difficult.   They had just adopted some well-considered strategic innovations to the "Customer Channel" and "Revenue Stream" components of their Business Model which they felt were keys to sustaining their competitive advantages.   Both were hoping to sell the Company in 10 years or so and enjoy a comfortable retirement.

So the news that Joe's colon cancer had come back and spread to his liver was devastating. The letter from Joe's attorney shortly after Joe's death demanding $5 million cash for Joe's 50% share of the Company was even more unexpected. It seems that Eric and Joe were overly optimistic when they set the formula price in the mandatory death buy-out section of their Buy-Sell Agreement when they signed it 12 years earlier. Eric and Joe hadn't looked at their Buy-Sell Agreement since they put it in the drawer 12 years ago. They had also failed to implement the life insurance funding for their Buy-Sell. And the Company's creditors were getting nervous and talking about "piercing the corporate veil."

These three ticking time bombs had just exploded. There was no way Eric or the Company could cash flow the price, which Eric estimated now overstated the realistic, value significantly in today's marketplace. And any buy-out would hit the company balance sheet and jeopardize future banking and also prompt a creditor push for personal liability to Eric.

What happens when you have an outdated Buy-Sell Agreement that misprices the Company or which doesn't include the funding to implement it?   What could Eric and Joe have done to keep the priorities they had made to each other, their families and their colleagues?

This section of the book addresses the Main Plays which Family Business Pioneers are taking now "with their Fourth Quarter in mind" to achieve "Wealth Protection For What You're Building."

---

*   While this example is real, we've changed the actual names, type of business and other details so that no specific person or business can be identified.

Chapter
19

Business Assets Protected

Incredible Result: "No one can take what our Company has built."

Avoidable Train Wreck: Business disputes and litigation losses deplete your business resources.

Main Play: The Business Asset Protection Protocol

What This Is: You have designed your business entity structure, and you have taken the specific actions needed, to help protect your Company's proprietary rights, intellectual property, key personnel and key assets from existing and future competitors, litigation and potential claimants.

Every time we buckle up or check our smoke alarms, we are protecting the assets and the persons we care about.   This same motivation drives those Family Business Pioneers in their businesses.

One of the first keys to protecting your business is to operate under the best corporate structure.   The second key is to initiate the protection of your key intangible assets.

Structuring Business Entities For Asset Protection

Businesses operate under a variety of corporate and affiliate legal structures.   Often the entire business operation, along with all of its assets, is simply held in one entity, which is typically a corporation or a limited liability company.

There are a number of reasons for operating the business within a legal entity, rather than simply in the name of the business owner as a sole proprietor. These include the ability to limit an owner's personal liability from the debts or liabilities of the business and to provide an entity which is the legal owner of the basket of assets and revenues of the business operation as well as continuity of the venture upon the death or disability of the owner.

Depending on the size, scope and nature of the business operations, more than one legal entity is often used. For example, it is common to have a parent-subsidiary corporate structure or to have a parent corporation which owns more than one subsidiary in a parent-brother-sister operation.

Reasons for this structure may include a desire to shield potential liabilities of one business operation from the assets and revenues of another business operation. This structure may also provide a means to more easily have separate accounting and separate lines of responsibility for each business division or location.

When Business Pioneers begin with their "Fourth Quarter" First, they are considering whether their corporate structure (entity, asset and debt structure) is in line with the protection of their business for the whole game.

Fourth Quarter thinking includes a review of the Business Pioneer's objectives in light of the present business operating structure to determine whether any revisions to that structure are needed.

Identify Valuable, Transferable Intangible Assets

Tangible assets are easy enough to identify. These are typically reflected on the asset side of a Company's financial statements. Under generally accepted accounting principles, the value of such assets is typically identified (with certain exceptions) at historical cost. These assets include cash, inventories, equipment and buildings, to name a few. Generally speaking, a company's financial statement does not reflect the true market value of these tangible assets, nor does it reflect the degree to which you are efficiently using all of the tangible parts of your business to produce profit or to produce a predictable, sustainable, growing cash flow.

Less apparent from reading any company's financial statements is the presence or type of intangible assets which the company has assembled and put into operation to produce that profit and cash flow. While certain intangible assets may have a cost allocated to them when they have been purchased, a balance sheet very likely does not include a recorded list of intangible assets.

Instead, the presence of intangible assets within a company is typically identified by a potential purchaser in the due diligence process when a potential acquisition candidate is being evaluated for purchase. Even when identified, the value of these intangible assets is often determinable only indirectly, for example, by considering the extent to which a company's profit exceeds a reasonable rate of return on the value of its tangible assets.

To realize better value during the life of their business, as well as upon the sale of their business, Family Business Pioneers are identifying the valuable, transferable intangible assets they've built as part of their business.

Various types of intangible assets exist in a successful company. Examples include brands, reputation, tradenames, trademarks, patents, business systems, leadership team, workforce in place, intellectual property, know how, Business Model design, key personnel, leadership development programs and Business Model innovation systems.

By identifying those intangible assets which are truly creating your company's earning capacity, and by carefully protecting them so they remain intact during all Four Quarters, including when you are negotiating your transition or exit, you can improve your Fourth Quarter results.

The Business Asset Protection Protocol

Once identified, the Fourth Quarter Planning process can address whether you've taken the steps to protect the intangible assets you've developed.

You cannot successfully transition from your business under the financial terms you might wish if you have not sufficiently protected your business along the way. Too many businesses – both large and small – fail to survive due to reasons that are often self-inflicted and avoidable.

Ideally, you and your advisors will focus on those areas which often cause companies financial distress or destruction and which may need some "shaping up" for your Company. This will help protect your business while you own it and will also provide a much more saleable business to a buyer.

The Fourth Quarter Planning review can help uncover those areas of your business in which you have not adequately protected your intangible assets. Some of the tools in this area include trademark/service mark and trade name registrations, patents for unique products and processes, trade secret confidentiality agreements, defensible covenants not-to-compete agreements, non-solicitation agreements and employment agreements.

Pioneer Mindset

☑ *Plug The Dike.* *Find and plug your profit leaks before they break you.*

Chapter
20

Ownership Protected

Incredible Result: "We will have only the right Owners at all times."

Avoidable Train Wreck: Company ownership is not correctly controlled or funded with the right buy-sell-hold options.

Main Play: The Company Buy-Sell Agreement

What This Is: Your Owners have agreed to help protect ownership with transfer restrictions and specific, realistic pricing, proper life insurance funding and payment terms for share purchase upon each Owner's death, disability, divorce, departure or dispute, with bring-along rights if the majority Owner decides to sell the Company.

Every owner in an American enterprise is free to transfer his or her shares to whoever he or she would like. And none of your fellow owners are required to ever purchase your shares. That is the American way. Yet that can produce many undesired results. You could find yourself with partners you don't want and you could find yourself without the ability to sell your shares. So, how are Family Business Pioneers fixing this?

The Company Buy-Sell Agreement

A Buy-Sell Agreement is a critical Fourth Quarter Planning tool. This is an agreement amongst the co-owners of a business which addresses the times and the terms for the future purchase or sale of stock of a company.   In a sense, this type of agreement is your own private stock market.

Unlike a public stock exchange, under this private stock market, you and other co-owners are not necessarily free to buy and sell stock to whomever you may please. However, this type of private stock market does create the ability to have some circumstances in which your stock can be purchased or in which you can cause the purchase of another co-owner's stock.

In addition, this type of agreement provides the ability to restrict co-owners from selling their shares to an outside party which the core owners do not want to share company ownership with. In this sense, it also acts as a very solid protective measure for the business operations.

Pioneer Mindset

☑ *On/Off The Ride.* *Create early control of design and terms for future exits because not every owner wants to, can or should ride the train forever.*

Buy-Sell Agreements are prepared based on the needs and objectives of the co-owners. Included below are the various types of provisions which, along with proper price and payment terms, should generally be included, or considered for inclusion, in a Buy-Sell Agreement.

• **Transfer Restrictions.** Owners of a closely held company should not be without limitation on their ability to transfer their shares to outsiders. Co-owners have some right to expect that they can choose their fellow co-owners in a closely held company.   However, American law typically does not permit an absolute restriction on the right of an owner to transfer his or her shares. Therefore, the most common type of transfer restriction used in a Buy-Sell Agreement is the right of first refusal. Under this provision, if an owner wishes to transfer his or her shares to a third party, that owner must first offer the shares either to the Company and/or to the other owners for sale on the same terms and conditions that would be offered to the outside third party. This provides the Company and the other owners with the option to purchase the shares, thereby retaining ownership of the Company within the closely held group of owners. Typically some exceptions would be made to this right of first refusal to enable owners to transfer shares to their spouse and family members, as well as a living trust for estate planning purposes.

- **Purchase Upon Death.** This type of provision operates in one of two ways. First, this can provide the Company (and the other owners) with an option to purchase the shares of an owner who has died. Alternatively, this provision can give the estate of the deceased owner the option to sell (i.e. to "put") the estate's shares to the Company (or the other owners). This gives the Company and the other closely held owner group the option to control share ownership without letting it become disbursed throughout a fellow owner's family, in particular when that owner is no longer around to provide some control over potential disputes within the family. The alternative approach also provides some liquidity to that owner's estate by providing a limited market for the shares in exchange for cash at some pre-agreed value method.

It's critical that your Life Insurance Portfolio be carefully designed with your professional Insurance Advisor so the death options under your Buy-Sell Agreement are properly funded.

- **Purchase Upon Total Disability.** This provision can also be established in one of two principal ways. The Company (and other owners) can have an option to purchase the shares of an owner who has become totally disabled. Alternatively, the disabled owner can have an option to sell the shares to the Company (and/or other owners). This again provides the Company and the closely held owner group with the ability to pull in shares from an owner who is no longer active, whereas the alternative provision provides an ability for a disabled owner to have a limited market for the sale of his or her shares in exchange for cash.

- **Purchase Upon Termination of Employment.** A termination of employment provision in a Buy-Sell Agreement will give the Company (and/or the other owners) the option to purchase an owner's shares upon termination of employment. Alternatively, the provision may give the terminated owner an option to sell his or her shares to the Company (and/or the other owners). This provides the Company with the option to call in the shares, depending on the circumstances of the termination, whereas the alternative provision gives a terminated owner a limited market for his or her shares upon termination. When the owner receives the shares as a share bonus, then it is possible that the share pricing upon termination of employment might be less than fair market value. In addition, it is possible that the owner/employee would not yet be fully vested in all of the shares he or she owns. These terms could be set forth in the Buy-Sell Agreement, or in a separate agreement relating to the share bonus program.

- **Purchase Upon Bankruptcy.** It is common to include a provision that enables the Company to call in the shares if an owner was to declare bankruptcy. This helps to provide the Company with the option to disentangle itself from the individual financial problems of an owner.

- **Purchase Upon Divorce.** Typically, if an owner is involved in a divorce from his or her spouse, and as a result of the divorce proceedings is not awarded the shares in the Company, then, to prevent disputes and business disruptions which might be caused by the marital separation, the owner member of the couple who was initially issued the shares would typically have an option to purchase these shares from his or her spouse, with a secondary option to the Company (and/or the other owners) if the first option is not exercised.

- **"Texas Shootout".** In a "Texas Shootout", the owners are given the ability to each go their separate ways. This type of provision would more frequently be included in an agreement where you have roughly equal owners. If an owner wishes to separate, then he or she can make an offer to sell all of his or her shares to the other owner upon stated pricing, terms and conditions. The other owner either must accept the offer, or refuse the offer, in which case, the initial offering owner must purchase the shares of the declining owner at the same price, terms and conditions initially offered.

- **Drag-Along Option.** This type of provision typically exists when a majority owner or group of owners wish to sell the shares of the Company to an outside third party. Since an outside third-party would most likely want to be able to purchase 100% of the shares, this provision gives the majority owners the right to require the minority owners to sell their shares on the same price, terms and conditions which the majority owner is receiving.

- **Tag-Along Option.**   Under this provision, a minority owner would have the option to require that a majority owner include the minority in a transaction for the sale of the share of the Company. This would occur, for example, when the majority owner did not exercise a drag-along option, but the minority owner, nevertheless wanted to be included in the sale.

Pioneer Mindset

☑ *Perspective Reset.*   *Know when (and how) you need to reset the other person's perspective.*

Chapter
21

Owner Unity Protected

Incredible Result: "Our Owners will always get along. Period."

Avoidable Train Wreck: Avoidable co-owner disputes crush you.

Main Play: The Business Continuity Agreement

What This Is: Your Owners have agreed in advance to protect the critical unity between existing and future Owners with a dividend protocol, retirement guidelines, dispute resolution process, conflict of interest policy, Board of Director decision policy, tax decision process, and key person insurance.

Businesses, regardless of age and size, are often damaged or torn apart due to lack of a well-conceived system for avoiding and resolving disputes. These disputes can arise between co-owners, the spouses of co-owners and co-owner families.

The potential for disputes can become even more acute upon the death or disability of a key owner. The role of a spouse or other family member may take on a new significance when the other co-owners attempt to work out issues with the spouse or family member who may not be familiar with some of the innerworkings and understandings of long-term business partners. This issue can be just as problematic for a one-owner business which now finds itself being owned by a surviving spouse or surviving children.

In addition to issues regarding regular company operations, disputes can arise as to how family salaries are to be set, how dividend distributions are to be determined and paid and who is to run the business as your successor. The risk involves not only adverse financial impact to the Company, but also can pose a threat to keeping peace within a family. Various matters which functioned well when you were around as the "traffic cop" to avoid or resolve disputes might no longer function nearly as well. This can occur despite the best intentions and simply be caused by a difference of opinions.

> ## *Pioneer Mindset*
>
> ☑ *In Shoes.* *Put yourself in the shoes of the person you are serving. If you were that person, would you do what you are recommending. If not, don't recommend it.*

The Business Continuity Agreement

In order to help minimize, avoid and resolve possible disputes amongst co-owners, spouses and family members, the Business Continuity Agreement is being deployed by Family Business Pioneers. This type of agreement operates in addition to a well-conceived Buy-Sell Agreement (discussed previously). The Business Continuity Agreement addresses issues other than buy-sell obligations. The following are some of the features which we recommend be included.

- **Board Approval Actions.** The agreement should spell out those actions which require Board of Director approval. The typical Articles of Incorporation and Bylaws for corporations do not specify this type of detail. Bylaws will typically provide that the Board of Directors is to elect the officers and will specify general duties of the officers. In some instances, the applicable state business corporation or limited liability company act will contain further types of actions which require Board approval. Beyond that, the boundaries of the officers and directors authority may be largely blurred and subject to dispute. This portion of the agreement can set forth the approval requirements for a sale of company assets, capital expenditures, loan transactions, change in accounting principles, acquisition of other businesses, issuance of additional shares, redemption of existing shares and the payment of bonus compensation.

- **Right to Engage In Competing Businesses.** Depending on the circumstances, the parties may agree that co-owners should not be restricted from investing in other types of business which may compete with the Company. On the other hand, you may have reasons for restricting the ability of your co-owners to invest in competing businesses. This is best resolved by a clear understanding of this between co-owners ahead of time.

- **Confidentiality Provisions.** As a business owner, you typically receive and are entitled to receive detailed confidential information regarding your business operations. Typically, the disclosure of that type of information to outsiders or competitors would be detrimental to your business. The agreement should specify a requirement to maintain proprietary information in confidence.

- **Required Resignation.** The agreement can specify that if a co-owner sells his or her shares in the Company, this results in an automatic resignation of status as an officer and director of the Company, unless the parties later agree otherwise.

- **Financial Statement Requirements.** The agreement can specify the nature of the financial statements which the co-owners expect. This may include audited, reviewed or compiled financial statements by an outside CPA on an annual basis along with the details for monthly and quarterly interim statements.

- **Subchapter "S" Protection.** Whether or not your Company is a subchapter "S" corporation today, the agreement can include provisions that require the protection of that status as it exists today and as it may exist upon election in the future. When the owners intend to have "S" status maintained, this agreement can help avoid a costly inadvertent termination of the election.

- **Tax Payment Dividends.** If the Company is a flow-through business, such as an "S" corporation or a limited liability company, then its income is taxed to the owners rather than to the Company. Since the owners are taxed on this, there should be an agreement in place under which the Company and the co-owners have agreed that sufficient dividends will be paid quarterly to the owners to enable them to make the tax payments on the Company income.

- **Share Redemption Provisions.** The owners may wish to have the opportunity to have some or all of their shares redeemed periodically. While this might result in full ordinary income taxation for "C" corporation owners, this type of periodic redemption can be tax efficient for an "S" corporation or limited liability company. Under programs that we have established, the Company's board of directors can determine a redemption pool each year and allow owners to opt in periodically for a pro rata redemption from the funds available in the pool.

- **Annual Dividend Payments.** This provision can establish a policy which the Company will follow for determining annual dividend payouts. This is intended to help reflect a balance between those owners who are full time employees of the Company (receiving compensation) and those owners who are not employed by the Company (and who would expect to see some return through dividend payments).

- **Non-Solicitation of Customers.** These provisions can detail the limitations which the co-owners expect to have in place to prevent other owners from soliciting the Company's customers for other businesses owned by a co-owner.

- **Non-Solicitation of Employees.** These provisions can specify that co-owners are prohibited from soliciting employees of the Company to work in another business operation of the co-owner without meeting agreed approval procedures.

- **Board of Director Composition.** These provisions can specify that each principal co-owner (and his or her family) is permitted to elect a certain number of the members of the Board of Directors.

- **Retirement Guidelines.** These provisions can specify when and under what conditions it is expected that a co-owner would agree to retirement.

- **Profit Strategy Team.** A Profit Strategy Team (also often called an Advisory Board) is being utilized more and more by companies of all sizes as a means to help provide company management with additional perspectives and experience which they might otherwise not encounter. This board can include lower level management members as well as outside business persons or advisors. The terms for this can be specified in the Business Continuity Agreement. This also provides an ongoing means of expertise and guidance upon the loss of a key-owner.

- **Profit Plan Program.** The agreement can specify the company will adopt a Profit Plan Program built on a continuous improvement and innovation process for your Business Model.

- **Company Formalities.** The agreement can also specify that the company will maintain standard corporate or LLC formalities and recordkeeping requirements. This would include holding regular owner and Board of Director meetings and documenting them with regular corporate or LLC minutes.

- **Conflict of Interest Policy.** In order to enable and require directors and officers to avoid conflicts of interest, the agreement can also contain the details of a conflict of interest policy.

The Business Continuity Agreement is not intended to diminish the control of the controlling owners. Therefore, it would typically be amendable or could be terminated upon the determination of a controlling interest of the Company, rather than all parties to the agreement. In addition, the agreement can provide that its provisions can be waived upon the determination of a controlling interest of the Company.

The objective of the agreement is to establish company guidelines, especially as they relate to business continuity issues. This agreement, in effect, lets all of the players know what the rules are, but it retains the ability of the controlling owner to change those rules as determined from time to time.

Pioneer Mindset

☑ **Deal.** *Everyone wants to know they got a good deal. So, show it.*

Chapter
22

Leadership Team Protected

Incredible Result: "Our Leadership Team sees our Company as the best place to achieve their personal and career aspirations."

Avoidable Train Wreck: Leadership team members leave to find better opportunities elsewhere.

Main Play: The Leadership Recognition and Reward Program

What This Is: You have deployed a recognition and reward program with your Leadership Team which earns their loyal performance, addresses their personal and career (leadership and ownership) aspirations, incents them to stay with you and helps to protect them and their families.

One of the top issues that Family Business CEOs report to us is the difficulty in finding and keeping the leadership talent they need.

This step in the Fourth Quarter Planning process is intended to help you and your advisors focus on building and retaining a successful key employee leadership team.

The Leadership Recognition and Reward Program

Having the right team in place builds company value and enhances a sale to a third party. An inside key employee or key employee group could also become a purchaser of your business in a sale to insiders.

Strong key employees will either make your Company more profitable and valuable (or they will make your competitor's company more profitable and valuable if that is the better opportunity for them).

Key Employee Incentives Now

Family Business Pioneers find it is generally in their best interest to provide their key employees with an incentive package that motivates them to continue to excel and to remain on board. The immediate task is to identify these key employees, determine the right incentive package and implement it. A key employee ownership incentive agreement should be designed to maintain your Fourth Quarter flexibility.

This may take the form of a supplemental executive retirement plan or a nonqualified deferred compensation plan for your leadership team. When funded with a life insurance solution, developed as part of your Life Insurance Portfolio with the right Insurance Advisor, this provides an effective means to protect both the employee's retirement and family, as well as the Company.

Such a program will address the employee's desired and expected development, as well as provide the type of cash and equity (real ownership or "synthetic" ownership in the form of a Stock Appreciation Right or Phantom Stock Plan) which will best achieve these objectives.

This step needs to carefully take into account the reality that the key persons you are seeking to retain and develop – most likely Generation Xers – do not have the same objectives as the Baby Boomers. The psychographic, demographic and sociographic trends which influence them present critical factors in designing the right overall retention program.

Pioneer Mindset

☑ *Loyalty. Earn and reward loyalty, and make loyalty so incredibly easy that your customers and team don't even think of switching.*

Key Employee Incentives At Time Of Sale – A Stay Bonus Plan

While it's important to address key employee retention incentives years ahead of your exit, it is also often necessary to address this at the time of your actual transition or exit.

One typical example is the "stay bonus", which can be used to help retain key personnel after your planned sale. This can help provide comfort to a buyer of a successful ownership transition by helping to keep your team on the new owner's "bus".

Key Employee Incentive If You Die or Are Disabled – A Stay Bonus Plan

If you are viewed by your Company personnel as the one person who's presence is necessary in order to keep the Company afloat, how many of your key personnel would jump ship promptly upon your death or disability?   They each need to think about their own continuing financial conditions and need to be in a position to look for the best employment opportunity which arises.

What does this do to the value of your business? If you don't have someone on your depth chart who can immediately step in and assume your position and do so with the confidence of your employment staff, you may find that the value of your Company will dissipate quickly. Not only will key personnel depart, but your key customers, bankers or bonding company may also likely move on if they feel your business is jeopardized.

What does this do to the value that you have spent your life or many years of your life developing? Presumably your spouse and children may be dependent on a continuing income from the Company. If not, you might in any case have been hoping that you could leave them with a company that was ongoing and had value.

What if you had a system in place for financially encouraging your key personnel to stay on board until the rough waters have smoothed out? This would provide your family and your advisors with the opportunity to hire a capable successor who could either keep the ship moving forward indefinitely or who could at least step in to oversee a carefully managed completion of pending projects and an orderly sale (rather than a fire sale at fire sale prices).

One of the best tools for accomplishing this is to establish a Stay Bonus Plan. Under this type of plan, you will have put into place an arrangement to promptly inform key personnel that they will receive a compensation bonus for staying on board during the rough waters. This would be a substantial bonus equivalent to 3-18 months of compensation.

Since this type of bonus would kick in only upon your death or disability, it is capable of being financed through the advance investment in a life insurance and lump sum disability insurance contract. The plan should also be documented and approved in advance by the Company's Board of Directors.

Pioneer Mindset

☑ *Key Colleague Retention?* *More than compensation and benefits. An intense understanding of generational distinctions is the key.*

The Business Owner Salary Continuation or Deferred Compensation Agreement

As a business owner, you of course are also part of your key leadership team and you and your family may need or want additional financial protection.

Assuming that you have been one of the principal driving forces for your Company for some time, the odds are that you have taken an approach to your past compensation, not unlike that of many closely held business owners throughout the country - - you have probably drawn a salary less than the full fair market value compensation which you could have earned, because you have chosen instead to keep those funds working within the Company.

This undercompensation can form the basis for an understanding amongst co-owners that upon your death, disability or retirement, the Company will continue to provide a salary to you (if you retire or become disabled) or to your spouse or children (upon your death). This is known as a Salary Continuation or Deferred Compensation Plan or Agreement.

This can be structured for your Company to provide all or some set portion of your most recent salary levels, to be paid on a periodic basis, for either a fixed number of years or until the death of your spouse.

When this is to be paid due to your death or disability, it can be funded with an investment by the Company in a life insurance and disability insurance portfolio designed by a professional Insurance Advisor. Such an agreement should be established in advance of your death or disability and should be approved by the Company's Board of Directors.

Pre-Funding Financial Gaps Due To Loss Of Key Persons

Regardless of the best laid plans, the loss of a key owner or key employee from your business can still cause a financial harm to the Company. The potential for financial loss due to the death or disability of a key employee (both owner and non-owner key employees) can to a significant extent be lessened with the advance investment in key person life insurance and key person disability insurance.

Your advisors can help you to develop an appropriate key person valuation, which will help you estimate the financial loss and the amount of insurable financial recovery which you can establish today.

Pioneer Mindset

☑ *Heads/Tails.* *Find the win in each outcome.*

Chapter

23

Leader Continuity Protected

Incredible Result: "If I go down unexpectedly, our Company won't."

Avoidable Train Wreck: Company hits the skids if CEO/President is lost unexpectedly by illness, accident or death.

Main Play: The Emergency Succession Plan

What This Is: You have groomed and designated a specific successor to step in immediately if you should die or be disabled unexpectedly. You have created pre-written approvals, a stay bonus program, and notifications to impacted persons which very clearly demonstrate the strength of your Company without you.

As the CEO or President you occupy that unique position in your Company during all of your Four Quarters which requires special attention in case an unexpected disaster hits you.

Upon your death or disability, the continuing financial success (or in some cases survival) of your Company may be dependent upon the ongoing comfort level of those with whom you have been doing business.

What's In Your Green Box

Family Business Pioneer John McArthur of New Zealand understood this extremely well. His story is well known in the international Vistage CEO peer group organization. As the head of his company he found it helpful that he also piloted his own plane. In preparing for a business trip several years ago, his son Jim, also a pilot, warned him about an upcoming storm. John assured Jim all would be fine, but told him that if anything happened, he should retrieve the Green Box in his and his wife's bedroom. As fate would have it, the plane went down. Jim found that the Green Box contained many of the actions suggested in this book.

The Emergency Succession Plan

Family Business Pioneers are taking the step of developing specific contingency notifications and instructions to address this.

Notification of these persons, immediately upon your death or disability, that you have an Emergency Succession Plan that addresses this, can go a long ways to establishing this comfort level to help assure business continuity or, alternatively, to provide for a controlled sale or controlled liquidation.

Pioneer Mindset

☑ **Priorities.** *Life is busy. Prioritize. And delegate everything that doesn't need you.*

The continuing financial success of your Company can be greatly improved by leaving your colleagues and family with clear instructions and clear authority.

The following are examples of these to consider:

- **Contingency Notification Letters** – Pre-written letters to be sent upon your death or disability to your colleagues, your customers / clients, your suppliers and your bank that you have an immediate successor in place.

- **Contingency Press Release** – A pre-written press release to be issued upon your death or disability.

- **Contingency Letter to Family** – Written instructions to your spouse and family for handling business matters upon your death or disability.

- **Contingency Owner Resolutions** – Written resolutions by the owners for directing Board of Director actions upon your death or disability.

- **Contingency Board of Director Resolutions** - Written resolutions by your Board of Directors for handling business matters upon your death or disability.

- **Contingency Board of Directors Instructions** - Pre-existing board resolution process for selecting an interim and permanent successor (or confirming your pre-designated successor) and/or taking contingency options to manage the Company.

- **Contingency Reorganization Plan Instructions** - Pre-written directive as to how the Company is to be divided into more than one entity to be owned/managed by one or more key employees/family members.

- **Contingency Sale Plan Instructions** - Pre-written guidelines for assisting your spouse, family and advisors in selling the Company to a third party or insiders.

- **Contingency Advisor Instructions** - Pre-written designation to your spouse, family and board of directors naming principal Fourth Quarter advisors to assist in advising your family and board on the transition of business matters upon your death or disability.

- **Stay Bonus Agreement** - Pre-written agreements to be used upon the unexpected death or disability of the CEO or President to help retain key personnel during a leadership transition. The Stay Bonus funding should be designed as part of your Life Insurance Portfolio in collaboration with your Insurance Advisor.

- **Video** – A brief video you have recorded to your family and colleagues to be used upon your unexpected death or disability which speaks to your comfort in the successor you have named and which covers other directions you wish to provide.

Pioneer Mindset

☑ *Uplift. Always aim to uplift those you interact with.*

Chapter

24

Personal Wealth Protected

Incredible Result: "No one can take what our Family has built."

Avoidable Train Wreck: Personal risk exposures deplete your personal resources.

Main Play: The Personal Limited Liability Company

What This Is: You have helped protect your personal investments from potential future business or personal lawsuits, accidents, creditor claims or divorce claims by carefully observing asset protection protocols and by transferring your personal investments into an asset protection entity.

So, you've spent years earning and saving. The question is whether your personal investments are being protected from the various litigation, finance and life risks which business leaders and their families face.

The Personal Wealth Protection System

In the litigious society in which we live, it is generally prudent to protect your hard-earned assets through certain asset protection power tools. These types of tools can protect your investment and other assets against unwarranted and unexpected, but potential, creditor claims, which may arise, for example, from business operations, personal accidents, personal injury, or other casualties and contingencies.

The following are some examples of the Fourth Quarter personal asset protection power tools which Family Business Pioneers are deploying:

- **Observance of Corporate Formalities.** It is common knowledge that if you operate your business within a limited liability type of entity (such as a corporation or a limited liability company), then you are generally protected, as an owner, from liabilities incurred by the business operations. However, a significant exception to this rule is the legal principle known as "pierce the corporate veil". Under this principle, if you have not observed the corporate formalities of operating as a separate corporation or limited liability company, then, if challenged, a court has the authority to "pierce the corporate veil" by ignoring the presence of the corporation or limited liability company. Typically this occurs when two principal facts exist. First, when you have not provided reasonable operating funds within the business entity. Second, when you have ignored the usual formalities of treating that corporate entity as a separate legal entity (e.g. because you have not maintained separate bank accounts and corporate business records).

- **Removal of Personal Guarantees.** During the course of the life of your business, you may have been required, in order to obtain bank financing, to sign a personal guarantee on business debts. As your business becomes able to financially stand on its own, the removal of your personal guarantees should be negotiated when your business loans are being refinanced or replaced. This extends not only to your personal liability, but also to your pledge of personal assets as collateral for business obligations.

- **The Personal Limited Liability Company (or Trust).** Occasionally we find that business operations are being conducted by some business owners without the protection of a limited liability entity (i.e. a corporation or limited liability company). For example, if your business is held in your name as a sole proprietorship, or is held in a general partnership or a limited partnership, you run the risk, as the business owner, of being liable for all of the business debts.

- **Bloodline Planning Trust.** When investment assets are transferred out of your name as a gift to a family member, then those assets are not subject to your future personal risks. Gifted assets, however, become subject to the personal liability risk of the individuals who received your gift. By transferring investment and life insurance assets (in collaboration with your professional Insurance Advisor) into a Bloodline Planning Trust for the benefit of your children or grandchildren, you can remove the assets you don't need from your future personal exposures. By placing spendthrift provisions and distribution guidelines in the trust, you can also provide protection for those assets from the personal liability exposures (financial, business, marital, substance abuse, etc.) of your children and grandchildren.

- **Multiple Business Entities.** If you operate certain businesses which are more risky than others, then you can consider placing the businesses into separate business entities, so that a given business risk does not expose all of your business assets to those liabilities.

- **Asset Balance Between Spouses.** Both spouses have a certain amount of potential liability exposure (e.g. due to personal accidents). However, typically, the spouse who is active in business has a greater level of potential liability claims. By balancing your assets between the two spouses, you can minimize the risk of a more substantial loss of assets than if your net worth is entirely in the name of the spouse who is most subject to liability exposure.

- **The Personal Limited Liability Company (or Trust).** Just as you can place a business operation into a corporate entity to shield yourself from those business risks, you can also place your personal investment assets into certain types of limited partnerships, limited liability companies, and asset protection trusts, in order to shield those assets from your business and personal risks. Though not foolproof, under these types of entities, a litigation judgment against you can typically not be collected against the assets of the asset protection partnership, LLC or trust. Asset protection partnerships, LLCs or trusts established in the United States can provide a certain degree of protection. Due to more favorable laws enacted by some countries, a foreign asset protection trust can provide a higher degree of protection, although it also costs a significant amount more to implement and its effectiveness has been challenged in recent years.

- **Proper Insurance Coverage Mix.** The proper mix of business and personal casualty insurance protection, along with business and personal umbrella insurance and long term care insurance, should be implemented and periodically reviewed, depending on changing business operations and personal situation.

Pioneer Mindset

☑ *Risky Business. Don't "take" risks. Manage and profit from risks. Protect what you're building.*

Your Estate Playbook

Lifestyle Continuity For You and Your Family

Your Estate Playbook

Lifestyle Continuity For You and Your Family

Charlie's Game Plan Legacy: "Let My Spouse Deal With It"

With a Master Brewer qualification from the Institute of Brewing and Distilling in London and an MBA from Notre Dame, Charlie* had no problem working his way quickly up the chain of command at one of the country's leading brewing companies. He was set to become the next CEO at age 45 when the Board unexpectedly passed him over. Unfazed, he set out on his own, combining his brewmaster skills, his business acumen, and his life savings to start his own microbrewery business. In twenty years he had grown Silver Bay Brewing Company to six highly successful locations in major cities throughout the country.

At 65, Charlie figured he was just getting started. Teaming up with a new partner and engineering expert, Frank, they had recently created and patented the "Silver Bay Personal Brewery" – the world's first all-in-one brewing appliance for home use. Now they just needed to design and implement the right Business Model to capture its value.

I had never met Charlie. When Charlie's widow, Carol, came to see me shortly after his unfortunate death, she was distraught. He had a Will and a Living Trust prepared by his regular Estate Planning attorney. But he had failed to address essential Business Owner Estate Planning strategies. She said Charlie figured he had many years left. He had no way of knowing that, ironically, a drunk driver would alter his legacy forever.

What happens when you haven't considered that your personal Fourth Quarter could come unexpectedly?

This section of the book addresses the Main Plays which Family Business Pioneers are taking now "with their Fourth Quarter in mind" to achieve "Lifestyle Continuity For You And Your Family."

---

*   While this example is real, we've changed the actual names, type of business and other details so that no specific person or business can be identified.

Chapter

25

Family Lifestyle Continuity In Place

Incredible Result: "I love my Family. Let's be clear. I am protecting them."

Avoidable Train Wreck: Inadequate Estate Plan controls damage your Company and deplete family wealth.

Main Play: The Business Owner Estate Plan

What This Is: You have directed who receives your estate and who is in charge when you can't be. And you have provided your family with enough cash flow (from your business, investments and insurance), with careful timing, distribution and spendthrift controls, so your family's lifestyle can continue upon your disability or death.

Over the years, we have seen many family business leaders who brilliantly and very successfully operated their businesses during their lifetime, only to leave a mess or a disaster to be sifted through and sorted out by a surviving spouse or children upon their death or disability.

This is the type of final act which they generally did not intend to leave, but it was the direct result of their failure either to establish an Estate Plan or to establish an Estate Plan which was properly tailored to them as a family business owner.

The Business Owner Estate Plan

The Fourth Quarter Planning process is being used by Family Business Pioneers to also address the lifestyle continuity they want for themselves and for their family upon their death or disability. Business owners have unique and more involved details which need to be addressed in a tailored Business Owner Estate Plan suitable for business owners.

When Family Business Pioneers have stopped to consider the likely outcome of their present course, they are seeing the need to detect those items which were missing, the presence of which will provide a substantially better outcome for the legacy they wish to leave for their families.

This action addresses the financial security plan you want to leave – to prevent a mess that needs to be cleaned up by others and to have an Estate Plan which fits with your Fourth Quarter Game Plan.

Establishing Your Business Owner Estate Plan

As an initial starting point in the review of the health of your Estate Plan, the elements of a good fundamental Estate Plan are essential. These initial elements consist of the following carefully considered tools, each with the following objectives:

- **Financial Power of Attorney.** If you were to become disabled to the point at which you are unable to handle your financial affairs, the laws in almost all states provide you and your family with two main alternatives for addressing your ongoing financial matters during the course of your disability. First, your family could file an application for the appointment of a conservator with the local probate court. Under this alternative, the family would typically need to hire an attorney to represent the family in court, during which time the family could recommend the appointment of a specific person by the judge to handle your financial affairs. This person has the legal title of a "conservator".   Once appointed, the conservator is obligated to periodically report back to the court to summarize the financial matters which he or she handled on your behalf.

  The other alternative is for you to execute a durable financial power of attorney before you are disabled. This is the preferred option, since it provides a step which you can take in advance to designate a person (and successors) to handle your financial affairs for you. Then, upon your disability, no court process is needed. Instead, the person you appointed is able to immediately step in to privately deal with financial matters as needed.

- **Health Care Power of Attorney.**   The law provides you with two similar alternatives for dealing with your health care matters if you are disabled and unable to do so.   First, your family can make an application to the local probate court to have someone appointed as your "guardian" to handle your medical affairs during your incapacity.

  The second alternative is for you to execute a durable health care power of attorney before you are disabled.   Under this type of tool, you can designate in advance the person (and successors) whom you would like to privately handle your medical affairs should you be unable to do so.

- **Health Care Directive (Living Will).**   Most people understand this tool as the "pull-the-plug" document.   State law allows you to execute this type of advance directive which provides the legal authority to your physician and to the hospital to withhold or withdraw medical treatments which are considered to be ethically extraordinary, i.e. those which present a disproportionate burden compared to the potential benefits.   If this instrument is not executed in advance, then your family and health care providers are left to attempt to determine your wishes and may be in a position to be unable to legally implement them.

- **Pour-Over Will.**   This is the type of Will which is typically used today for persons who wish to avoid the probate court process.   As will be discussed next, this probate court process can best be avoided through the use of a Living Trust.   The Pour-Over Will is used in conjunction with a Living Trust in order to transfer property into the trust upon your death, to the extent of property which you did not transfer into your Living Trust during your lifetime.   The Pour-Over Will is also used by parents who have minor or disabled children, as a means to appoint a guardian and conservator for those children.   The Pour-Over Will is also used to appoint your personal representative (executor) for your estate.

- **Estate Plan Letter.**   This document is a detailed, practical tool which enables you to specify certain wishes, and to detail certain information prior to your death, so that this information is available for your family.   This specifically contains directions relating to your funeral and burial wishes, special gift of personal effects and mementos to your family and friends, a record of your key advisors and close friends, details specifying the location of your key financial and business records and instructions for raising your minor children.

The Living Trust

The Living Trust (also known as a Revocable Trust) has become the tool of choice for parents across the country who want to maximize the Estate Planning opportunities and protections available for their families.

In essence, a Living Trust can be viewed as a bucket which you have created into which you have placed the instructions for how you would like your assets to be handled upon your death.

This set of instructions can include the provisions for distributing your estate to your spouse, provisions for holding your estate in trust for your children, and/or grandchildren for distribution upon certain terms or upon certain ages, and can include provisions detailing your charitable bequests. These instructions are completely revocable and completely amendable by you up until the date of your death.

Typically a separate Living Trust will be executed by the husband and by the wife (although depending on your financial net worth, a joint Living Trust can be utilized). The Living Trust will also typically contain the provisions which can be utilized to help attain the full lifetime federal estate tax exemption for both the husband and the wife.

You may have heard that Living Trusts can be referred to as a funded Living Trust or an unfunded Living Trust. Typically, in both situations, the Living Trust is the same. The difference is whether you have re-titled your assets into the name of your Living Trust.

This is essentially equivalent to an empty bucket (containing only your set of instructions) or a full bucket into which you have placed your assets along with your set of instructions. If you placed ownership of your assets into your bucket during your lifetime, then upon your death, there is no need for the probate court process, because you have already handled the re-titling which the probate court would otherwise accomplish.

In essence, you have filled your bucket and, by naming appropriate persons (known as successor trustees) as part of your set of instructions, your bucket is automatically handed off by you to your successor trustee upon your death. Your Living Trust can also contain provisions which state that if you are disabled, then your Living Trust bucket is also handed off to your successor trustee during that period during which you are disabled.

Comparing The Difference A Living Trust Can Make

During your life your Living Trust can:

- Allow you to manage and have total control over the assets of the Trust during your life.

- Allow you to amend or revoke your Trust any time for any reason.

- Allow you to add property to, or take property out of, your Trust at any time.

- Protect against conservatorship proceedings (or living probate) if you become legally incompetent or disabled.

After your death your Living Trust can:

- Distribute your assets to your spouse, children or other heirs as you've directed or continue to hold your assets in trust for certain beneficiaries (such as minors, young adults, grandchildren and spendthrifts) until an age or ages when they are financially responsible.

- Include special protection provisions to safeguard children or grandchildren who have substance abuse, dependency or other special issues.

- Name a Trust Protector to oversee the Trustee and make certain critical decisions.

- Include supplemental needs trust provisions to help preserve government benefits for disabled children or grandchildren.

- Avoid or substantially reduce estate taxes, depending on the size of your estate, by obtaining the $11,200,000 (as of 2018 under the Tax Cuts and Jobs Act of 2017) lifetime estate tax exemption for both spouses for married couples (total $22,400,000 exemption).

- Avoid probate for all assets and property transferred to the Trust during your life.

- Receive all assets probated after your death from your Will that were not transferred to the Trust during your life.

- Receive all life insurance and retirement plan proceeds where you've named the Trust as the beneficiary.

- Reduce the risk of a Will contest and court challenges to your Estate Plan.

Pre-Funding Personal Financial Gap Needs

Upon your (or your spouse's) death or disability you and your family will obviously face a different financial landscape than that which you would be facing without this adversity. The scope and extent of this is best addressed through a detailed Financial Needs Analysis performed by a Financial Advisor.

For example, if you and your family rely on your salary to cover living expenses and personal debts, the failure to have sufficient life insurance or disability insurance payable on your death or disability will either result in a financial shortfall to your family or could put a bind on your business if the business needs to both replace you and continue to pay your salary.

In addition to covering living expenses, your death could result in estate taxes, which may also put a bind on your family or your business if your ownership needs to quickly be turned into cash.

The Fourth Quarter Planning process can estimate your present ability to meet these needs and recommend changes to improve your shortfalls.

Business Owner Estate Plan

Business Owner Estate Plans generally should address several other matters beyond those detailed above, such as:

- Allocation of business ownership and control.
- Family business retention or sale
- Successor Leadership
- Income and Estate Taxes
- Debt financing or pay off.
- Personal guarantees.
- Family personal and financial dynamics

Some of this is addressed in the Living Trust or in the other Main Plays discussed in the Estate Playbook.

Pioneer Mindset

☑ *Wisdom Always.* *Proactively deploy great judgment and wisdom. Always.*

Chapter
26

Bloodline Wealth Opportunities In Place

Incredible Result: "I don't want to just protect my Family. I have created long term business and personal opportunities for them."

Avoidable Train Wreck: Bloodline wealth opportunities wasted.

Main Play: The Family Bloodline Opportunities Trust

What This Is: Your Company, investments, life insurance and vacation home will be owned, used, invested, preserved and grown to promote family harmony, entrepreneurship, education, and responsibility and protected against potential lawsuit, creditor, spendthrift, bankruptcy, divorce or substance dependency issues.

Those Family Business Pioneers who have worked hard to build a family, to build a Company and to build other wealth are usually highly motivated and are very careful to preserve and protect what they've built.

Often, however, not all of their children have the same capabilities or exhibit the same drive to preserve, protect and build. Their grandchildren may be even less likely to preserve, protect and build.

Sudden Wealth Syndrome

While the popular story is rags to riches, the frequent full story is rags to riches to rags in two or three generations. Psychologists, in discussing "Sudden Wealth Syndrome", explain that heirs, like lottery winners, have a tendency to lose their inheritance. The statistics show that 65% of family wealth is lost by the second generation and 90% is gone by the third generation.

This is not a new phenomenon. The Biblical story of the Prodigal Son shows us this problem has existed for at least 2000 years. This is something known today as "affluenza", where the offspring of the wealthy pursue instant gratification and lack purpose or self-esteem. (Often overlooked is the related impact, known as "Elder Son Syndrome").

The founders of a family business may or may not be successful in instilling in their offspring the same capabilities which created their wealth in the first place.

And even if your children and grandchildren are extremely responsible, life happens. Bad things happen to good people. The unexpected happens to good people.

Ok, so let's win, for the good of our family. The Bloodline Planning Trust helps the business owner win – for the benefit of his or her family.

The Bloodline Opportunities Trust is enabling Family Business Pioneers across the country to help preserve, protect and grow their wealth for the benefit of successive generations.

Pioneer Mindset

☑ *Meet It Head On. The unexpected will happen to you – you just don't know when. Ensure that your team and family have access to enough contingency cash to overcome your unexpecteds.*

The Family Bloodline Opportunities Trust

The Family Bloodline Opportunities Trust (which can operate as a "Family Bank") has "family bank" features, which is providing an incredible opportunity for Family Business Pioneers to preserve, protect and grow their family's wealth.

The biggest reason family fortunes are lost is because those who built the wealth haven't provided clear guidelines, protections and controls for handling the wealth they leave to their loved ones. This can lead to family fights and disagreements, uncontrolled use, bad investment strategies, bad business decisions and the resulting loss of family wealth or the family business.

Even if your children and grandchildren are mature and careful, life's events still pose risks to the wealth they are given during your life and to the wealth they inherit upon your death. This may arise from business ventures that impose personal liabilities, divorce, lawsuits, substance abuse or dependency problems and misjudgments.

The Bloodline Opportunities Trust is a remarkable power tool being used to overcome these issues. By placing family wealth into a Bloodline Planning Trust (either during your life or at your death) this can be set up to last for as long as you would like. Under the careful direction of a professional trustee, family wealth can be carefully grown and used for both the short term and the long term benefit of your family.

What Does The Family Bloodline Opportunities Trust Own?

The Family Bloodline Opportunities Trust can be set up to own some or all of the following assets:

- **The Family Business.** By placing future Company ownership into the Bloodline Opportunities Trust, you can enable the Company decision-making to be made by the family representatives you appoint or by a professional trustee. Other features:

    - The Trust can own all or part of your Company or affiliates or the real estate to be leased to the Company.

    - Family members active in the Company could hold controlling shares or minority shares in your Company.

    - The Trust can be authorized to loan funds to your Company to work in sync with the Company's bank financing and bonding.

- **Your Life Insurance.** The Trust can be set up to own and receive your life insurance to be used for your family or your business (in collaboration with your professional Insurance Advisor).

- **Family Investments.** By holding some of your family investments in the Trust, you have the opportunity to specify how you want your family wealth to be preserved, managed and used to help achieve your family's life long hopes and dreams. Features include:

- The Trustee can be authorized to pay for specific family needs, such as health or education or a downpayment for a home.

- Just because your children don't want to own or work in your business doesn't mean they don't want to go into business. The Trust can provide equity or loans to a business started by your heirs to work together with other bank or equity funding.

- **The Family Vacation Home.** This can help parents and grandparents to ensure that the special home (vacation home, cabin, ranch, beach house, condo, etc.) which you want to continue making memories for the family can successfully be passed on and maintained within the family by succeeding generations. This typically includes the following features:

  - Guidelines to address the decision-making, scheduling and expenses of the vacation home and divorce and liability protection, as well as guidelines for future purchase and sale of ownership interests by one or more family members and for future trust termination options.

  - The Trust can hold the home itself or the home can be held in an LLC owned by the Trust.   The family (children, grandchildren, great grandchildren, etc.) would be named as beneficiaries of the Trust. They would be entitled to use the vacation home but would not have any direct ownership of the vacation home (or the LLC).

  - A funding mechanism, such as a Vacation Home Endowment Fund, funded by either a share of the parents' estate, a life insurance policy, or a dedicated investment fund established by the parents.

  - Investment management and banking guidelines for managing the Vacation Home Endowment Fund.

The Family Retreat

As parents, we all seek "teaching moments" for our children. The business owners I work with often ask if I will meet with them together with their children at a Family Retreat. This is a program where we teach their adult and young children about the "Sudden Wealth Syndrome" pressures they face and where we discuss their parent's or grandparent's game plan for helping to overcome this. Most recognize this is being done with love to provide long term care and protection.

Pioneer Mindset

☑ *Heart and Soul.* *Listen and learn from the passion which fuels the heart and soul of the great business pioneers you should be working with.*

Chapter
27

Family Ownership Allocation In Place

Incredible Result: "We'll be fair to all children, which includes the freedom to own, control and operate the Company for those with the passion to do so."

Avoidable Train Wreck: Wrong family members become Company owners or receive control.

Main Play: The Family Ownership Matrix

What This Is: You carefully cover how you will transfer your Company ownership to your family during your life and after your death. This includes who will receive controlling shares, and whether a "sweat equity" share of your Company will be allocated to an adult child or children active in the business and whether and how an equalizing share of (and vote in) Company ownership, personal investments or life insurance will be allocated for children not active in the business.

While the Estate Planning needs of a business owner include the same issues as non-business owners, Family Business Pioneers are seeing how their business ownership brings into play a series of additional Estate Planning issues and options to be addressed.

Meeting Business Owner Estate Needs

As the owner of a business, you will often have Estate Planning needs which extend beyond the typical Estate Plan. This may be due to certain financial or business needs of the business or because of particular family desires which are already present or may arise upon your death or disability.

> ## *Pioneer Mindset*
>
> ***Onsite.*** *Get out of the office and out of town. Go onsite to see the reality of what is actually happening in the real world and learn the impact on the position you are taking or on the business you are building.*

The Family Ownership Matrix

Foremost amongst these needs is to decide how you will transfer ownership of your Company to your family during your life or upon your death.

Do you have children who are active in the business? Do they want to become owners, and if so, when and on what terms? Are they ready to become owners? Have they earned the right to become an owner?

Do they show the Pioneer Mindset illustrated throughout this book. If not, are they coachable so they can learn to think and act with the Pioneer Mindset.

In order to help address these types of specific Estate Planning issues, we advise Family Business Pioneers to deploy a Family Ownership Matrix in their Fourth Quarter Game Plan, which can include the following:.

- **"Sweat" Equity Allocation.** You may decide that your Company ownership or your estate is not to be divided exactly equally between your children due to a difference between the role which your children have played (or are expected to play) in the success or operation of your business. Your Estate Plan can include an allocation with regard to your business assets which recognizes the "sweat equity" contribution of those children who have been active in the business but who have been (or will otherwise be) under-compensated based on their contribution to the success of the business.

- **Specific Transfer or Bequest to Business-Active Children.** If you have one or more children who are active in the Company and one or more children who are not, you may want to consider making a specific transfer (sale, gift, or stock bonus) or bequest of your Company ownership interest to the active children, so that they have ownership control as well as the valuation benefit of additional ownership on account of their decision to be active in your business.

- **Non-Active Children Equalization.** When the Company ownership has been specifically allocated in your Estate Plan to one or more children active in the business, an equalizing share can be allocated to non-active children through a specific bequest of other financial assets. If your estate does not have sufficient other financial assets to fully equalize the shares, then at least two other options exist. This can include a split off of certain business assets (such as building facilities or intellectual property) into a separate leasing or licensing entity which can be allocated to the non-active children. This would still leave the Company operating assets intact in the business entity to be owned by the active children. As an alternative, your Life Insurance Portfolio can be carefully designed (in collaboration with a professional Insurance Advisor) which would help fund the equalization to the non-active children.

- **Ownership Voting.** You may also choose to divide your estate or Company ownership equally, but to give voting control to your child or children active in the business. This can be done by converting your stock into voting and nonvoting shares or by using a voting agreement or voting trust.

Pioneer Mindset

☑ *Other Person's Perspective.* *Perceive everything from the perspective of the other person. Listen. Ask. Listen. Repeat.*

Chapter
28

Family Business Continuity In Place

Incredible Result: "If my Family wants to be involved with our Company, I won't allow our great Company to come between them."

Avoidable Train Wreck: Business and estate disputes within your family.

Main Play: The Family Peacekeeper Protocol

What This Is: You require the agreement by present and future family members to certain business continuity terms. You have a family employment policy and a market-driven compensation and dividend process. You have appointed a Family Council to work with your Board and CEO/President. You have created a financial reserve from your estate (or from your life insurance) to help support your Company's bank credit or bonding needs.

While Dad and Mom are still around and in control of the Company, and can serve as "traffic cop" as needed, many issues are more easily resolved. But what happens when that's no longer the case. What power tool are Family Business Pioneers putting into place to take care of this?

The Family Peacekeeper Protocol

While the Business Continuity Agreement (discussed earlier) is being used to help prevent disputes among both unrelated and family co-owners during your lifetime, the same concept is also being implemented to help avoid ongoing or new disputes specifically amongst family members (during your life and after your death). This agreement is signed by each family member before shares of ownership are transferred to him or her during your life (as a condition to receiving a gift or the right to purchase) or after your death (as a condition to inheritance).

Pioneer Mindset

☑ **Responsibility.**   *Empower your team.   Hold everyone highly accountable.   Blame yourself first and credit others first.*

A Family Peacekeeper Protocol normally includes provisions such as, a dividend payout policy, a stock redemption policy and voting agreement provisions (as in the Business Continuity Agreement with non-family discussed previously).

Pioneer Mindset

☑ **Peace and Expectations.**   *Never believe or act as if family position itself entitles someone to something they didn't earn.*

The Family Peacekeeper Protocol also typically includes:

- **Family Business Representative.**   An Estate Plan normally appoints a personal representative (executor) and a successor trustee to handle financial and business decisions for your estate.   In those situations where that representative or trustee is not well-equipped to make business decisions impacting your ongoing business, a family business representative can be appointed in your Family Peacekeeper Protocol or your Living Trust to make business decisions relating to management of the business.   You have at least two ways this can be done.   First, this representative can be given authority in your Family Peacekeeper Policy to override your regular trustee's authority.   Second, the representative can be viewed as essentially an advisor, whose decisions are subject to the overriding decision-making authority of your regular successor trustee.

- **Family Employment Policy.** Some closely held family companies have a restriction on hiring any family members while others have no restrictions at all. In order to maintain company harmony and to provide some performance motivation for a family member, we have found it helpful to include a family employment policy which specifies the pre-requisites before a family member can be hired.

- **Family Compensation Policy.** Compensation of family members is best set up based on what would be paid to non-family members for each job position. While you may set the compensation of family members while you run the Company, we find those who use an outside compensation specialist have greater success in keeping family peace.

- **Business Sale Instructions.** As part of your Family Peacekeeper Protocol , if you have not completed your exit from your business at the time of your death or disability, but believe that the best alternative for the family is that the business be sold, then your Family Peacekeeper Protocol can contain sufficient details to provide instructions on how and to whom your business can best be sold or transferred should you die or become disabled before you complete your exit.

- **Dispute Resolution.** If you have more than one child, or the potential of differences between your spouse and one or more children, it is possible your estate or business will encounter a dispute once you are no longer present. Your Family Peacekeeper Protocol can include a dispute resolution provision which prevents a dissatisfied child from disrupting business operations. A dispute resolution provision can range from the appointment of a mediator to help resolve disputes, to instead including a provision which disinherits a child who challenges your Estate Plan.

- **Financial Resource Reserve.** If your Company needs your ongoing financial support in order to thrive (e.g. due to business finance and bonding needs), then your Family Peacekeeper Protocolor Living Trust can designate that a reserve portion of your estate be held as a financial resource to help support the business, its balance sheet and its credit and bonding needs.

- **Family Council.** Your Family Peacekeeper Protocol can designate a Family Council to be established to enable your spouse and adult children to be apprised of ongoing business operations and to discuss resolution of business matters impacting the family. Depending on the make up of your family and your use of a board of directors, in lieu of a Family Council, you can consider having your children serve on your Board of Directors as either voting or non-voting board members, as an additional way to keep the family members involved in or apprised of the ongoing challenges associated with the business.

Pioneer Mindset

☑ *Great Enough.* *Don't let a fruitless quest for perfection delay getting the great done now.*

Chapter
29

Family Business Retention In Place

Incredible Result: "With Family ownership comes responsibility to act in the best interests of all. So, we have pre-set the rules for who gets to remain Owners."

Avoidable Train Wreck: Wrong family members remain Company owners or remain in control.

Main Play: The Family Buy-Sell Agreement

What This Is: To be given or to inherit Company shares, your family must sign the Family Buy-Sell Agreement. This has proper insurance funding and has been designed to thoughtfully control buy back or retention of next generation ownership in case of a family member's death, disability, dispute, divorce, desire to sell or bankruptcy.

We discussed the Company Buy-Sell Agreement elsewhere in the Protection Plan section of this book. A Buy-Sell Agreement is almost always used when the Company is owned by unrelated or extended family (e.g. siblings) co-owners.

The Family Buy-Sell Agreement

Family Business Pioneers are also using a Family Buy-Sell Agreement, whether the Company is owned by multiple family members already or by just one family member now, but where it will become owned by children (adult children or minors in a Trust) through gifts or inheritance. A Family Buy-Sell Agreement enables the family members (at the parents' direction) to have a pre-agreed understanding amongst themselves (and their children/heirs), as to how, when and under what terms business ownership will be kept and passed on to family heirs or purchased and sold upon future events and conditions (including after the parents are gone).

Establishing A Family Buy-Sell Agreement

An agreement which governs the ownership of shares in a Company is a must when the Company has more than one owner. Such an agreement is not limited to just companies which presently have more than one owner.   Upon the death of the sole owner, that owner's Company shares would typically be distributed according to the terms of the owner's Estate Plan. The executor or trustee charged with handling the estate or living trust of the owner does not necessarily have the authority to add stock restriction or buy-sell provisions before distributing the shares to family members pursuant to an Estate Plan – if those ownership terms and restrictions were not already in place at the owner's death.

In the absence of such an agreement, after the owner's death, the shares could be owned by multiple children, some of whom might find themselves in disagreement as to the Company operations or share ownership going forward.

Therefore, it's prudent for even the sole business owner to enter into an agreement before death. Since it takes two parties in order to have a binding agreement, this agreement would be between the sole owner and the Company and would be binding on successors to the share ownership pursuant to an Estate Plan distribution.

Family Buy-Sell Agreements are prepared based on the needs and objectives of the family. The various types of provisions included in a Buy-Sell Agreement discussed in the Protection Plan should generally be included, or considered for inclusion, in the Family Buy-Sell Agreement.

These may include, for example, provisions relating to:

• Transfer Restrictions	• Purchase Upon Bankruptcy
• Purchase Upon Death	• Purchase Upon Divorce
• Purchase Upon Total Disability	• "Texas Shootout"

- Purchase Upon Termination of
  Employment

- Drag-Along Option

- Tag-Along Option

Just as with the Company Buy-Sell Agreement, it's critical that your Life Insurance Portfolio be carefully designed in collaboration with your professional Insurance Advisor so that the death options under your Family Buy-Sell Agreement are properly funded.

In addition, a Family Buy-Sell Agreement will include provisions for when and how shares in the Company can be gifted or transferred to descendants. This becomes critical in family businesses where owners are often expected to be employed at the Company and where Companies often don't grow fast enough to support multiple families.

The specific trigger events, must/may buy-sell options and payment terms may be different in the Family Buy-Sell Agreement between parent-child or child-child family members as compared to the Company Buy-Sell Agreement between unrelated or extended family co-owners.

Pioneer Mindset

☑ *Know Who Is To Complain.* *Check the reality and scope of your proposed course of action based on who could complain about, be harmed by or challenge the decision, transaction, outcome or solution.*

Chapter

30

Family Estate Tax Reduction In Place

Incredible Result: "We haven't built all of this for Uncle Sam to take away or to deplete."

Avoidable Train Wreck: Estate tax hit.

Main Play: The Estate Tax Reduction Strategy

What This Is: You have achieved control over potential government impact by reducing your projected estate taxes (or by pre-funding with life insurance) and assuring your Company does not need to be sold, liquidated or compromised in order to help your family pay your estate taxes.

The role of Federal Estate Tax in family businesses has changed significantly over the past few decades. With the "permanent" increase in the Estate Tax lifetime exemption effective in 2012, and the "temporary" doubling in the exemption effective in 2018, the number of small family businesses impacted by the Estate Tax has been reduced. However, this tax remains in play for many family businesses under present law (all of which is dependent on future tax law developments).

The Estate Tax Reduction Strategy

Under the Federal Estate Tax law as it presently exists as of 2018, you are subject to this tax if you die with an estate worth more than the sum of your marital deduction (if applicable) and your lifetime exemption.

Under the Tax Cuts and Jobs Act of 2017, the Estate Tax lifetime exemption is presently $11,200,000 (and is indexed to increase with inflation). This reverts back to $5,490,000 in 2026 (adjusted for inflation).

You have a taxable estate if the value of your Estate (less your marital deduction) exceeds your lifetime exemption amount.

Depending on the State in which you live or have assets, either or both a State Estate Tax and Inheritance Tax can also apply.

Pioneer Mindset

☑ **Simplify.** *Take the simplest route possible. Add complexity only to the extent necessary.*

The following are some of the tools which Family Business Pioneers are using to reduce or eliminate their Federal Estate Taxes. These are based on specific provisions which have been established in the law to enable taxpayers to plan their affairs in a legal manner for reducing the estate taxes which would otherwise be due from their families.

- **Annual exemption gifts.** The present Estate Tax laws permit you to make gifts of up to $15,000 to as many persons as you would like free of federal gift tax. This is an annual exemption which is available to both spouses. It is typically used for annual exemption gifting to children, grandchildren, and/or children's spouses. These gifts can include shares in your business or other investment assets. A gifting program should never be started until you've determined the coverage of your and your spouse's lifetime needs.

- **Gifting Vehicle.** Often, a parent or grandparent would prefer not to make their gifts directly to their children or grandchildren in the form of cash. A common technique to address this objective is to create a family limited partnership or a family limited liability company. These types of techniques can also be viewed as creating a bucket, into which you place a certain amount of cash or other investment assets. Then, just like giving shares of your Company, you can gift shares of ownership interest in the bucket to your children, grandchildren, and/or children's spouses. Under this arrangement, you or certain family members might or might not retain some portion of the ownership.

Other Estate Tax reduction vehicles to be considered may include the grantor retained interest trust (known as a GRAT, GRUT or QPRT), the grantor trust (sometimes technically referred to as the "intentionally defective" grantor trust or IDGT), or a generation skipping trust. Details of these techniques are beyond the scope of this book and can be addressed further in the Fourth Quarter Planning process.

- **Lifetime Exemption Gifting.** You can during your lifetime deploy up to $11,200,000 of your lifetime exemption to avoid payment of the gift tax, should you wish to gift more than the $15,000 annual exemption amounts. This can be done, for example, if you wish to have a means to move future growth out of your taxable estate. For example, if you owned an asset which today is worth $1 million, but which on the date of your death had grown to $2 million, then you would need $2 million of your lifetime exemption to avoid paying estate taxes on that portion of your estate. If instead, you gifted that asset today, using $1 million of your $11,200,000 lifetime amount, then the asset (and the future growth) has been removed from your estate using only $1 million of your lifetime exemption amount. The family limited partnership or the family limited liability company can be utilized for this type of lifetime exemption gifting as well. Note, however, that the tax basis of a gifted asset would not be "stepped up" to fair market value on your death, so this Estate Tax savings could be offset somewhat by an income tax cost.

- **Life Insurance Trust.** If your combined estates (husband and wife) are presently valued at over your lifetime Estate Tax exemptions (including the value of your life insurance), then a commonly used Estate Tax reduction technique is the life insurance trust. This is a powerful Estate Tax planning technique for the following reason. Let's assume, for example, that you and your spouse have estates consisting of at least $22.4 million in investment and business assets, along with $1.5 million in life insurance. This life insurance would be valued (and subjected to the 40% Estate Tax) at the full face amount of $1.5 million upon your death. However, during your lifetime, it's valuation is relatively small (basically equal to the unearned portion of your last premium payment and any cash value).

Except where this has been designed to provide yourself with retirement benefits, this life insurance (designed in collaboration with a professional Insurance Advisor) is in place in order to provide funds for a spouse and for surviving minor or young adult children or for certain business purposes. Therefore, for that reason, it can be an ideal asset to gift to your children, since they will be the ultimate recipients of the proceeds anyway. It is particularly ideal because its present gift tax value is, as previously stated, extremely low in comparison to its future Estate Tax value, because the Estate Tax value literally blossoms into existence upon your death. Therefore, it is an asset which you can easily gift, typically using your annual exemptions (and/or part of your lifetime exemption).

Since, however, you may not wish to have the life insurance proceeds immediately available to your children upon your death, a trust can be used to hold the proceeds until that point in their lives at which you would like the proceeds to be distributed. A trustee can be appointed to make distributions as needed for their living, education, and health-related expenses. In addition, provisions can be included which provide that the funds can be used for your surviving spouse as needed for your surviving spouse's support (without pulling the life insurance proceeds into your surviving spouse's taxable estate). Since this technique constitutes a gift of an asset out of your taxable estate, the estate rules for "completed gifts" need to be met. For this reason, your gifting of life insurance into a trust typically needs to be an "irrevocable trust" which provides that you cannot revoke the gift at a later date.

- **Discount Planning.** When you own less than a controlling percentage of a Company, the Estate Tax value is based on a discounted value method. In other words, if you own 49%, the value isn't 49% of the whole. It is less, because the Estate Tax law recognizes that the market for a minority share should be discounted. This enables us to align family ownership between spouses, children and trusts to reduce Estate Taxes even if the family as a whole owns 100%.

- **Disability Gifting**. If you have established the above type of gifting program, then you would typically not want this to be disrupted if you became disabled. The law allows you to establish a Gift Power of Attorney in which you have appointed someone to continue your gifting program should you become disabled.

- **Payment of Estate Taxes**. If you anticipate an Estate Tax liability despite the above gifting tools, and you anticipate that your estate will not have enough readily available liquid assets to pay the Estate Taxes, then the Estate Taxes can be pre-funded with discounted dollars through your investment in life insurance as part of your Life Insurance Portfolio designed in collaboration with your professional

Insurance Advisor. Since Estate Taxes become due only upon the death of the second spouse, a second-to-die life insurance policy can provide a more economical way to fund life insurance for married couples, since the life insurance risk is based on two lives rather than simply one, resulting typically in a lower annual premium investment.

Pioneer Mindset

☑ **Focus.** *Only begin everything that should be started now.*

Your Succession Playbook

Personal Freedom On Your Terms

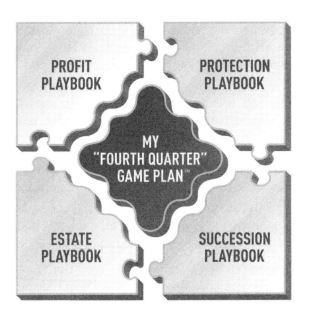

Your Succession Playbook

Personal Freedom On Your Terms

Art's Dilemma: Leaders With Conflicting Objectives

I wasn't surprised by our meeting with Art.* We had seen it many times before. Art had founded and built a very successful retail business. He had operations across the region which were consistently producing significant year-to-year profitable net cash flow. Pete, his second-in-command, had been working with him for the past twenty years. Art had decided recently that he was ready to transition from the Company, and he wanted to get this done soon.

However, as we began to visit, it became obvious Art and Pete clearly had very different views about the future.

Art had assumed Pete would purchase the business from him at a full fair price. Pete thought much of the ownership should be bonused to him based on his two decades of dedicated services. However, they had never really discussed this in any detail.

Pete also believed the Company's Business Model had become the victim of Art's recent short-term thinking. If he was to be Art's successor, Pete wanted to know the Company would be primed to endure for a long time. In addition, Pete had recently been approached by a competitor to take a key position and ownership with his Company, which Pete was giving strong consideration to. Art had also been talking to possible outside buyers but so far no one was interested.

What happens when you and your possible successor haven't dealt with each others vision soon enough? And when the great business you thought you had built just isn't of interest to potential buyers?

This section of the book addresses the Main Plays which Family Business Pioneers are taking now "with their Fourth Quarter in mind" to achieve "Personal Freedom On Your Terms."

---

*   While this example is real, we've changed the actual names, type of business and other details so that no specific person or business can be identified.

Chapter

31

Cash Target Ready

Incredible Result: "I know the score and whether I am ahead or behind."

Avoidable Train Wreck: Insufficient cash-in-pocket to meet your business and personal needs or objectives.

Main Play: The "Rubber Meets The Road" Report

What This Is: You have a realistic view of the true, "transferable", fair market value of your Company, based on normalized, forecastable EBITDA and reliable market-based pricing multiples, and this (after tax) value (when combined with your other wealth and insurance) will provide the cash resources you and your family need or want for the long term.

As Family Business Pioneers begin to consider their Fourth Quarter, with possible retirement (or cut back) from active duty and possible transfer of ownership, one of the initial questions they are answering is whether they have the cash (or cash access) to meet their needs and wants.

You can more effectively start to think about and discuss in detail your Fourth Quarter and your eventual exit or retirement if you know what we call your Cash-In-Pocket Target. The question is what is your number.

Knowing Your Cash-In-Pocket Target

The Cash-In-Pocket Target is the sum total of the following:

- Cash needed or wanted to support you and your spouse for the rest of your lives if you completely moved on to your next adventure today.

- Cash needed or wanted to support your dependent children until adulthood if you completely moved on to your next adventure today.

- Cash needed or wanted for children and grandchildren education.

- Cash you'd like to leave your children and grandchildren upon your death.

- Cash you'd like to have or leave for special causes (such as your next personal or business adventure or favorite charities).

- Cash needed to cover taxes and debts.

This target takes into account not just the capital you need to maintain your standard of living, but also the excess capital above your needs to address the additional family, business, charitable and community objectives you wish to achieve. Depending on the precision you want, this step may also entail having your Financial Advisor, Insurance Advisor or CPA perform a Financial Needs Analysis for you, as well as preparing a Wealth Plan to best utilize and project the growth of your investable capital.

Cash Needed Or Wanted From Sale Of Business

Once you've determined your "Cash-In-Pocket Target" you can determine the net cash needed from the future sale or transfer of your business. This looks at not only the liquid assets you presently have on hand, but also the amount you (and your spouse) need from your business after you exit to achieve financial independence. This is key to starting to determine how you can meet your prime objectives.

Normalizing Your Financial Results

Business owners of privately-held companies typically receive income from their companies other than through simply dividends or the eventual capital gain on the sale of their stock. Specifically, most active owners receive a salary and other compensation for their services. In addition, those who own real estate, equipment or intangible assets utilized by the Company will also receive rental and royalty income from the lease or license of this property to the Company.

Often, the true fair value of such services or the use of such property is a range, rather than one fixed number. This is because the value of these services or property is not necessarily precisely determinable. Often, the width of this range can be several tens of thousands of dollars between the low end and the high end.

Depending on the tax structure of the Company, business owners may find it more tax advantageous to pay this compensation, rent and royalties from the Company to the individual owners at the high end, rather than the low end. This is particularly true if the Company is organized as a "C" corporation.

While this may present tax planning opportunities during the normal life cycle of business ownership, it can present a detriment to the selling price during the Fourth Quarter Planning process. This is because when compensation, rent and royalties are paid by the Company at the high end, this results in less net income and less net operating cash flow being reflected as earned by the Company.

Since a buyer will typically determine a purchase price in reference to some multiple of net income and/or net operating cash flow, the above practice can have a detrimental, downward impact on the selling price opportunity available (which greatly exceeds the tax benefits the owner felt he or she was receiving).

Business owners often attempt to overcome this during the selling process by contending that these company expensed amounts should be "normalized" to reflect a more realistic value as to what an unrelated company would have negotiated with an owner-employee, lessor or licensor for the actual market compensation, rent and royalty. During the selling process, this puts the business owner in the awkward position of contending that he or she has been overpaid. This can also put the business owner in a compromised position should tax authorities seek to contend that the overpaid amounts represented nondeductible "constructive dividends" paid by the Company, resulting in a retroactive tax liability.

Another issue which can arise if these amounts are at the high end of the market range is that minority shareholders of the Company, if any, could complain that the payment of these amounts is a breach of a fiduciary duty owed to them. Since a business owner's Fourth Quarter Game Plan will often involve the beginning of selling part of the Company (or awarding stock bonuses for shares in the Company) to key employees, this raises the potential of a shareholder dispute going forward through this process (in particular if this has not been agreed to ahead of time).

Proper tax and corporate planning during the Fourth Quarter Planning process, done in conjunction with your CPA, can help to optimize and resolve these competing objectives.

By beginning to move the Company's payments to the owners for compensation, rent and royalties more to the mid-level range of fair value, the opportunity arises to better reflect a realistic Company valuation and better selling price.

The Fourth Quarter Planning process can guide a business owner through this normalization process step-by-step.

Why Do You Need To Know Business Value?

A universal ownership objective is to secure the income stream you will need to support the lifestyle you and your family plan to enjoy. Knowing the value of your business – and how to value your particular business in your particular market – can be critical if you are to successfully complete the Fourth Quarter Planning process. Knowing this value - and knowing how this value is determined – becomes important for the following reasons:

- Your business is generally your most valuable asset. Financial freedom depends on maximizing its value and converting that asset to cash (with minimum tax consequences).

- If you plan to transfer your business to an "insider," you need to know the relationship between business value, tax consequences of transfer, and cash flow requirements of the buyer.

- To find out whether your business is actually marketable to a third party buyer (and at what price).

- To find out which type of third party buyer will likely be interested in your business — and what specific features incent that type of buyer to buy at the best price.

- To provide guidance as to what areas of improvement in your business could best impact price.

- The type of buyer you sell to determines whether the "sale price" (at least for your "ownership" interest) should be high or low and whether other (more tax effective) ways to realize value from your business should be utilized.

Why Does Your Fourth Quarter Advisor Team Need To Know Business Value?

Your Fourth Quarter advisors need to have a solid understanding of your Company's valuation for a number of reasons:

- It impacts whether your objectives can be met.

- It impacts determining whether you are operating under the optimal tax and legal business entity format.

- It impacts if your business growth, stability and eventual exit can benefit from beginning to transfer some ownership to key employees.

- It impacts an understanding of a realistic selling price (and terms) to a third party.

- It impacts development of the cash flow model and type of sale techniques to help make a sale to insiders feasible and most attractive as to tax impact for both the seller and buyer.

- It impacts how to define and determine value upon contingencies (upon death, disability, divorce, disputes and casualty loss), as well as how to fund a purchase upon these trigger events.

- It impacts expected estate consequences (relating to tax matters and family equalization).

Various Types Of Valuations

During the Fourth Quarter Planning process, a number of different types of business valuations are often discussed. These different types of valuations all tend to have the same objective, which is to establish a value for your ownership interest in the business which you (or your family in your absence) expect to receive, or would be satisfied to receive, in full exchange for your ownership interest. These differing types of valuations can come into play at or during various parts of the exit process.

Your business valuation initially provides some idea as to what your Company is worth, as a means not only to provide you with an estimate of the value which your efforts have achieved, but also to provide your advisors with a valuation estimate for their planning purposes in helping you to achieve your objectives. Differing types of valuations can also be used in determining the price to be established for a transfer to insiders, the price to be established for a transfer to outsiders, and the price to be used in a Buy-Sell Agreement in the event something happens to you prior to your planned exit.

Some of the different types of valuation approaches include the following:

- **Preliminary Value.** This is a rough estimate of the value of your business, which can be determined relatively quickly, but which lacks much of the due diligence and analysis which would be part of a full business appraisal. This type of preliminary valuation can be performed by a Financial Advisor, a CPA, or some attorneys, with the proviso, however, that it represents only a guide, but should not be viewed as a full, documented valuation of your business.

- **Walk-Away Value.** This is simply the value which you have determined you need at this point in time as a price to walk away from your business. This valuation may be significantly higher or lower than the true value of your business, and it simply represents the number you would be happy with.

- **Lowest Defensible Value.** It may seem odd that a seller should be looking to establish the lowest defensible value. However, this counterintuitive valuation approach is extremely useful when planning for an exit in which you are looking to minimize the total tax impact on both the seller and the buyer. To the extent that the total tax impact is minimized, this provides additional dollars on the table, which can either be provided as part of the compensation paid to the seller, or as a reduction in the total cash flow needs that the buyer must come up with in order to be able to accomplish the purchase. In essence, the objective of the lowest defensible value is to provide the ability to transfer actual ownership at a lesser price (defensible for tax purposes), while at the same time providing the seller with other exit compensation (e.g., deferred compensation for past services that have not yet been fully compensated) or to defend a lower price to a family member. Because of the interplay of tax rates imposed on a seller to exit, as compared to the tax rates imposed on a buyer who is earning taxable cash with which to pay the seller, a combination of different types of compensation (e.g., sales price, consulting fees, deferred compensation, no-compete payments), can result in a more favorable overall outcome for both parties.

- **Appraised Value.** This represents the valuation of your business, based on a careful analysis of your Company's historical results and the projected future results, with the application of current valuation principles and economic factors to reach an estimated value, documented in a written appraisal by a qualified business appraiser. This valuation typically represents the appraiser's determination of that price which a hypothetical buyer would pay to a hypothetical seller, each being under no compulsion to buy or sell, with each being aware of the relevant facts. This valuation may reflect the value of the Company as a whole, or may reflect the valuation of a majority or minority interest in the Company, which may or may not be a pro-rata portion of the value of the Company as a whole, depending on the application of minority and marketability discounts or control premiums.

- **Negotiated Value.** This reflects the price for the Company arrived at pursuant to negotiations between two unrelated parties; i.e., between a buyer presumably interested in paying the lowest price, and the seller, presumably interested in receiving the highest price. Always recognize that a deal is comprised of price and terms, so a proposed price by itself does not equate to value.

- **Buyer-Specific Valuation.** This is a valuation based on the expected business value in light of the buyer-specific needs. For example, if your business possesses certain synergistic elements which would complement the business of the buyer, then this valuation may reflect a premium as compared to the price which might apply to a purely financial buyer.

- **Market Outlook Valuation.** This is an estimated value typically provided by a transaction intermediary (such as a business broker, a middle market intermediary, or an investment banker) with the objective of providing you an estimate of what your business would bring on its sale today, under current economic conditions based on the industry which you are in and the types and extent of buyers existing today in the marketplace.

- **Adequate Consideration.** The price for the sale of stock to an Employee Stock Ownership Plan ("ESOP") cannot exceed "adequate consideration", meaning the fair market value determined in good faith by the ESOP trustee.

Valuation Methods

There are a number of valuation methods which are used, either by themselves or in combination, in each of the above types of business valuations. In the end, a true valuation for a closely held business is that price and terms which an informed, willing buyer pays to an informed, willing seller. The following valuation methods are essentially simply the means by which buyers and sellers choose to inform themselves to determine their willingness to pay a certain price.

When the stock of a publicly held company is being valued, the process is much more precise. This is because stock in publicly held companies is valued every day by thousands of buyers and sellers who consider hundreds or thousands of relevant facts in reaching a determination as to what they will buy and sell the stock for. This, of course, depends on numerous factors which are internal and external to the Company. Prevailing economic and financial sector conditions, as well as industry outlook, reflect some of the external factors. Internal factors include those various elements which reflect upon the profitability or cash flow of that particular company. The valuation which results is a true, as close to perfect as possible, valuation of that business at a particular moment, taking into account all of these external and internal factors. Even with this arguably near perfection in the public markets, there is room for better judgment, which reflects why some investment advisors will do better than others. In addition, there is room for immediate or rather rapid price changes in any given stock. A company that is worth $10 per share today might easily be "worth" $12 per share a week later, then be down to $8 per share a week after that.

The valuation methods used in valuing closely held companies reflect attempts by Financial Advisors to approximate the conditions of a public market, while reflecting the fact that the stock is not actually being traded on a public market. In the end, from a strictly financial and economic perspective, the value of a company today is the present value of the future stream of net cash flow which that business enterprise will produce. This present value is a discounted future cash flow. In other words, it reflects the fact that a dollar today is worth more than a dollar received tomorrow or next year. A dollar received next year may, after application of the discount rate being reflected by the person doing the valuation, be worth, for example, only 75-95 cents today, in present value terms.

Some of the valuation methods used in valuing a closely held company include the following:

- **Book Value.** This may also be referred to as historical cost, adjusted book value, or depreciated book value. In essence, it represents the original cost (less depreciation where applicable) of all of a company's assets, offset by the total of the company's debts. This results in a net book value of the equity of the business. Depending on the type of business, this method of valuation might be highly relevant or it might be next to completely irrelevant. Rather than simply using straight book value, at times, it may be appropriate to use a multiple of book value. This may be true in particular, if there is evidence, for example, from the public marketplace, of companies trading hands at or within some range of book value multiples.

- **Recent Third Party Sales.** This method can reflect the valuation of a company when shares of stock in the company have been recently bought and sold between unrelated parties.   This provides a reasonable indication of value to the extent that the amount of shares was significant, the two parties engaged in a meaningful negotiation which appropriately reflected valuation factors, and the transaction was relatively recent in time.

- **Price/Earnings Ratio.** This is also known as the PE ratio, which is a ratio of price to earnings. This is commonly used in reference to stocks traded on a public stock market. Often, stocks within a certain industry may trade within a certain PE ratio range at a given time during an economic cycle or under certain economic conditions. Stock traded on a public stock exchange is generally reflective of a minority share of stock in that company (and therefore, reflects a minority discount), but with no "lack of marketability" discount, because of the fact that the stock is generally easily marketable. Therefore, all other factors being considered equal for the sake of discussion, the PE ratio provides a useful reference to determine a company's valuation. In its essence, it reflects the rate of return that a buyer and seller would expect to see for the given risk level and future expectations of that company. For example, if a company was to be valued, if the marketplace for that type of company demanded a 10% rate of return, and the company was earning $8 per year, the price/value of that company should be $80. This is because 10% of $80 results in $8 of income. The PE ratio for the stock would be 10 ($80 divided by $8).

Once the appropriate PE ratio factor is known, it is necessary to determine what earnings will be used to determine the pricing. This will typically be some function of expected future earnings, which may be based on some average or weighted average of previous years as a reflection of expected future earnings.

- **Discounted Future Cash Flow.** Under this method, the present value of future expected dollars is literally discounted to today's net present value to determine the worth of the company. Typically, the expected future cash flow is estimated by management (based on historical results and reasoned future expectations) for the next 4-10 years, and a terminal valuation at the end of that 4-10 year period is also determined (i.e., as a reflection of discounted, net cash flow after that timeframe). The sum of the net present value of these future cash streams reflects the valuation of the business.

- **EBITDA Multiple.** This is similar to a PE ratio; however, it reflects a valuation of the operations without a deduction for depreciation, amortization, or income taxes, and without reflecting the interest inherent in the debt structure of the company. EBITDA is Earnings Before Interest, Taxes, Depreciation and Amortization. The EBITDA to be used might be the most recent year or some simple or weighted average of the past few years, or some reasonable projection, as a basis for estimating future expected years. For example, if the EBITDA for the company is $100,000, and the appropriate multiple is 5, then the business (before debt) is worth $500,000 for purposes of that valuation (assuming a normal working capital level).

Premiums and Discounts

Once the valuation of the Company as a whole is determined, the per-share true value is not necessarily a pro-rata portion of that total.

This is because of the presence of premium and discount factors which influence the valuation of a share of stock.

The most common premiums and discounts fall into two main areas. The first area has to do with control or lack of control. If a share of stock is part of a controlling block of shares of stock in the Company, then the per-share value, according to market influences, should be higher than the per-share value of a minority share of stock, i.e. of a share of stock which is not part of a controlling block of stock.

For example, if a Company is worth $1 million as a whole, and there are 1,000 shares of stock, the implication is that each share of stock is worth $1,000. However, if you are the owner of only 100 of those shares of stock, it is less likely that a buyer would pay you a full pro-rata price, because the buyer would be purchasing a block of stock that does not have control over the business enterprise. In this case, a minority discount might be applied to the transaction.

These minority discounts can range significantly, but would commonly be in the range of a 20%-40% discount. Therefore, instead of your 10% share of the $1 million Company being worth $100,000, it might only be worth $70,000 (assuming a 30% minority discount).

By contrast, the owner of 90% of the company might be entitled to a control premium. In other words, a buyer might be willing to pay more than $900,000 for that owner's 90% share of the Company. In this case, if the control premium matched the minority discount, then the controlling owner might be entitled to a price of $930,000 for 90% of the corporation.

In practice, if the whole Company is being sold, then it is likely that each seller would receive a pro-rata share of the overall price, based on percentage of ownership.

The second most common form of discount is a "lack of marketability" discount. This comes into play because a closely held Company is not freely marketable on a stock exchange. A purchaser would typically be less than willing to pay a full pro-rata price for the Company if the stock cannot be turned around and freely sold in the future. Since there is no public stock market for your stock, a lack of marketability discount could be applied in determining the value of your shares, whether these are minority shares or majority shares. The range of "lack of marketability" discounts is also broad, and depends on the circumstances, but might range from 10%-30%.

Valuation Facts

In order to value your Company, it is necessary for the person doing the valuation to be provided with specific details regarding certain key facts affecting the Company's financial and business outlook. Some of these facts can be gleaned from the following information:

- An analysis of the strength or weakness, and remaining life, of the Company's Business Model.

- Strength of the Company's Business Model Profit Strategy program.

- Credible financial statements (including income statement, balance sheet and cash flow statement) for the past five years.

- Company income tax returns for the past five years.

- Management forecasts of business operations for the next five years.

- Breakout of valuable, protected intangible assets.

- Inspection of company facilities.

- Company status as a leader in its particular market and product sectors.

- Industry and economic outlook.

- Status of litigation and other legal, business and competitive threats to the company.

- The degree to which it has protected (and registered) its trademarks and service marks.

- Depth of key leadership.

- Comparison of the Company's financial results benchmarked with other similar companies in the same industry.

Pioneer Mindset

☑ *Systems. Embrace the value of scalable systems.*

Relevance Of Rules Of Thumb

Certain rules of thumb are often mentioned with regard to valuation of a Company. For example, you might be aware that another company in your industry recently sold for two times sales or 2.5 times book value.

By and large, these types of rules of thumb are not relevant to the value of your Company. The factors that went into determining the price for that Company may have had little to do with the multiple of sales or a multiple of book value, but instead dealt with the other types of facts and valuation methods discussed above. In the end, any price can be reflected as a multiple of sales or a multiple of book value, but that does not necessarily mean that that's a reflection of what your "basket" of tangible and intangible assets are going to be worth.

Other rules of thumb which are more reflective of the net comparable results of a Company may be more relevant. For example, if companies in your industry are trading at four times EBITDA, this may be a reflection of the value of your Company, since EBITDA often represents a true reflection of how well a given company is producing a net cash output.

The "Rubber Meets The Road" Report

The above reflects simply some methods for arriving at some indicated valuations for your Company. They do not represent a substitute for a good business appraisal by a qualified business appraiser.

However, they do provide a way to develop a preliminary valuation, which is very useful in the Fourth Quarter Planning process. This is because the preliminary valuation can be arrived at fairly quickly which can help keep the Fourth Quarter Planning process moving forward without the need for an interim stoppage to obtain a full business appraisal.

Once the Fourth Quarter Game Plan is designed, depending on the alternatives chosen and depending on the need for a more formal valuation, one of the Plan implementation steps can be to proceed with a full business appraisal, with the Plan then adjusted or accommodated to reflect the more certain indicated Company valuation.

This Company value estimate provides the key number needed to determine if your overall cash resource needs will be met.

> ### *Pioneer Mindset*
> ☑ *Measure It.* *Understand the impact of every action on future quality of earnings, cash flow and company value.*

Your Life Insurance Portfolio

A successful Fourth Quarter is dependent on having the right cash at the right time. This is to meet both your Personal Cash Needs and your Business Cash Needs. A critical component to this is the collaboration between your CPA, Insurance Advisor and Business Continuity Attorney to determine how your net Cash Flow and your Life Insurance Portfolio needs to be designed to fit into your Game Plan.

Will Our Present Plan Produce "Enough Cash At The Right Time"?

Personal Cash Needs	If I Retire	If I'm "Hit By The Beer Truck"
• Lifestyle Continuity	$____	$____
• Children Goals	$____	$____
• Grandchildren Goals	$____	$____
• Bloodline Opportunities	$____	$____
• Vacation Home Retention	$____	$____
• Estate & Income Taxes	$____	$____
• Personal Debt Pay Off	$____	$____
• Charities	$____	$____
• Estate Equalization	$____	$____
Total Needed	$____	$____
Existing Cash/Liquidity	$____	$____
Deferred Comp (from Biz)	$____	$____
Cash If Business Sold	$____	$____
Existing Life Insurance	$____	$____
Total Available	$____	$____
Long (Short)	$____	$____

☑
☐ We're looking good so far.
☐ Ok. Short as of now. Let's deal with it.
☐ Not sure. Explore. Find Out.
☐ Check on Life Insurance Fit and Endurance

Business Cash Needs	If I Retire	If I'm "Hit By The Beer Truck"
• Buy-Sell Agreement	$____	$____
• Deferred Compensation	$____	$____
• Business Debt Pay Off	$____	$____
• Credit & Bonding Support	$____	$____
• Business Expansion	$____	$____
• Key Person Loss	$____	$____
• Business Continuity	$____	$____
• Key Person Stay Bonus	$____	$____
Total Needed	$____	$____
Existing Cash/Liquidity	$____	$____
Existing Life Insurance	$____	$____
Total Available	$____	$____
Long (Short)	$____	$____

☑
☐ We're looking good so far.
☐ Ok. Short as of now. Let's deal with it.
☐ Not sure. Explore. Find Out.
☐ Check on Life Insurance Fit and Endurance

Chapter

32

Key Successors Ready

Incredible Result: "Our leadership depth chart is as solid as the best professional sports team."

Avoidable Train Wreck: Wrong successor, no successor, or great successor leaves (to go help your competition).

Main Play: The Leadership Development Program

What This Is: You have developed key members of your Leadership Team who could immediately (or who already) hold your Company's top three executive positions today, who align with your culture, who can operate successfully without you and who have completed the shift to a pioneer leadership mindset.

A company's results in all of your Four Quarters depends on the strength of several aspects of your leadership team. This is becoming even more critical for Family Business Pioneers as they look ahead to their Fourth Quarter.

Most importantly, to be successful in the future we are heading into, business leaders must have a Pioneer Mindset. This mindset is teachable if your leadership team is coachable. If they don't learn this, don't count on them to capably lead your Company into the future.

Active Board of Directors

A Company's leadership team begins with its Board of Directors. Many companies do not take advantage of the strength and guidance provided by an active Board of Directors. We highly encourage this with the Family Business Pioneers we work with.

Most family companies should be utilizing an active Board of Directors which consists of certain key insiders and at least one outsider who can provide insight to your industry and business. This Board also helps provide leadership continuity and immediate oversight in the event of your unexpected death or disability.

Profit Strategy Team (aka Advisory Board)

Depending on the nature of your business, most owners should consider establishing a Profit Strategy Team (aka Advisory Board). The members of the Profit Strategy Team do not need to have management responsibility, which enables you to focus specifically on enlisting the assistance of capable persons outside your Company who do not want the responsibility or potential liability of being on the Board of Directors. A Profit Strategy Team can be tailored to help you address specific business needs such as business model strategy, executive performance, production efficiency, strategic planning, strategic sourcing, business acquisitions, cost containment, distribution network, customer engagement, employee engagement, brand management and product/service development.

Pioneer Mindset

☑ *Kirk Out.* *Discover who on your team can unleash what they do best by remaining a Captain rather than being promoted to Admiral.*

Peer Group

Accomplished Family Business Pioneers throughout the world are achieving great success through the exchange of information and ideas in peer groups. As the authors state in *The Power of Peers – How The Company You Keep Drives Leadership, Growth & Success*, its "just not that easy to find individuals who know precisely what it's like to sit in the CEO's chair."

CEOs, throughout their time in action, as well as their expected successors, are finding the true advantage of having a group of peers to watch your back and to provide valuable insights from a CEO's perspective. Vistage International is a great example. It is the world's leading peer group organization. It is designed to help CEOs and executives drive better decisions and better results. Its member companies grow 2.2 times faster than average U.S. businesses.

Pioneer Mindset

☑ *Linchpin. Don't allow your company to become dependent on the presence or performance of any single person.*

Management Recruiter Firms

Absent your own depth chart for the Company, you will want to be prepared to quickly access the depth chart which exists throughout your industry. If you have strong talent in your Company today, you would be naive to believe that they have not been in contact with, or been contacted by, executive or management recruitment firms to fill the gaps in leadership talent encountered by other companies throughout your industry. Whether your key employees have told you about these calls doesn't mean the calls are not occurring. Many strong management personnel have themselves developed a management recruiter contact to keep them informed of opportunities which come up through the industry to provide them with better opportunities if they aren't available with your Company. This is one of the reasons for developing a great culture and for deploying the key employee retention tools discussed elsewhere in this book.

Business owner's should normally be no less aggressive and strategic in planning for the possible loss of any given key employee. If your inside depth chart is insufficient, we suggest you develop your own ongoing relationship with a management recruiter firm, particularly one which is familiar with your industry. To the extent that you incur an adverse financial impact from the loss of any key employee, this can be lessened by the speed with which you are able to replace that individual. An ongoing relationship with a management recruiting firm which is already familiar with your business will help this to occur.

Pioneer Mindset

☑ *Align. Develop Leaders (and your successor) who align with where your Business Model and Business Culture need to go.*

Leadership Development

An Owner/CEO's transition from a business is generally not immediate, but instead is often accomplished through a transition of both ownership and leadership responsibilities over a period of time, normally during your Fourth Quarter. According to a study by the Raymond Family Business Institute, about half of CEOs over age 60 who plan to retire within five years have chosen a successor. Leadership development becomes critical to transitioning your leadership responsibilities over the period of time you have chosen.

Jack Welch, former CEO of General Electric, speaking about succession planning in 1991 – nine years before his anticipated retirement, had the following to say:

"From now on, choosing my successor is the most important decision I'll make. It occupies a considerable amount of thought almost every day."

How do you select a successor who can keep the train on the tracks in today's environment. Larry Bossidy and Ram Charan in *Confronting Reality – Doing What Matters to Get Things Right* have stressed the fact that businesses which want to last today need to raise the bar with regard to leadership. In addition to the leadership qualities which have always existed, they have pointed out that two leadership qualities that are indispensable today are business acumen and a constant need to know about what is new and different.

Pioneer Mindset

☑ *Own It. Think and act like you are the business owner and CEO, even if you aren't (yet).*

Are You A Family Business With A Nonfamily CEO

If your Company is a family business in which the CEO is a nonfamily member (or where you are a family member CEO who is considering a nonfamily CEO to succeed you), you will typically face unique challenges and the potential for disruptive disputes. To be successful, an effective nonfamily CEO needs to possess strong business skills, while at the same time be adept at navigating the variety of family dynamics and personal relationships that exist in a family business.

The presence of a sound corporate Board of Directors as well as a Family Council can be crucial to a successful nonfamily CEO's efforts to sustain and grow the Company.

Pioneer Mindset

☑ *Two Ears. Empathy first. Then debate and resolve.*

The Leadership Development Program

In his groundbreaking study and the best selling book *"Good To Great: Why Some Companies Make the Leap and Others Don't"*, Jim Collins stressed the importance of getting the right people "on the bus", getting the wrong people "off the bus", and the right people in the right seats on the bus. This is a key to not just profitably operating and growing a successful business, but also key as you address your Fourth Quarter plans and contingencies.

The expected retirement of a key owner or other key employee, or the unexpected loss of a key owner or other key employee due to death or disability, can pose a significant financial hit to any company. Pre-planning to be prepared for this can reduce the adverse impact.

So, what should you do now? The immediate answer is not unlike that encountered every day by professional and college sports teams. They have a depth chart. In an ideal situation, there is always a back up player for whichever specialty position needs refilling due to the loss of a player, whether by death, injury or retirement. In the context of a business operation, the first line of defense is to have a Company depth chart. Those next on the list are ideally always close to ready to step in as needed.

Pioneer Mindset

☑ *Bench Strength. Only God knows when your time is up. Have your successor ready now.*

Chapter
33

Company Ready

Incredible Result: "We are profiting today by always being in prime purchase condition."

Avoidable Train Wreck: Company not always in prime condition to be operated, transferred or sold.

Main Play: The "House-In-Order" Checkup

What This Is: Your business, financial, accounting and legal controls position you to always operate effectively, tested by always being able to meet a potential buyer's rigorous due diligence review. You have minimized necessary contractual consents needed to sell the Company. Your business structure is designed to fit your specific Business Model and is also based on what you want to ultimately transfer or keep.

Family Business Pioneers who are finding the greatest success always have their companies ready to sell – because the same factors which a smart buyer will look for in deciding on whether to purchase your Company are the factors which impact how well your Company performs while you own it.

Business Model Alignment

The first step in having your Company always ready is to be sure during all of your Four Quarters that your Company is always aligned with your Business Model. Your corporate structure, business contracts, legal strategies, state and federal tax strategies, employment policies, research and development, production, fulfillment, marketing, advertising, pricing policies, cost controls, etc. all need to fit precisely with the elements of The Pioneer Success Formula discussed previously.

Creating Accounting System Credibility

Whether you are a startup or next stage company looking to attract investors, or a well established company looking to obtain an attractive line of credit, or you are looking ahead to a Fourth Quarter that may involve the sale of your business, no matter what you think your business may be worth, and no matter what you believe your earnings are or have been, none of this matters unless the investor, banker, business buyer or your successor also believes it. They will believe it only if your accounting system is credible, and only if you utilize methods of accounting which provide a sufficient reflection of the true net income, net cash flow, and net owner's equity of your business.

To put it very clearly, your investment in a good outside CPA is one of the best investments you will ever make.

A credible accounting system and a proper regime of accounting methods is extremely important to most business owners as continuing owners of a business. This is really the only way that an owner can have an accurate idea of exactly how well or how poorly his or her Company may be performing. A frequent reason companies end up in bankruptcy is because they failed, due to bad accounting, to realize the actual financial condition of their Company.

The most effective way to answer the question as to whether your accounting system is credible, and whether your accounting methods accurately reflect the performance of your business, is to take off your owner's hat and put on your investor's, banker's or buyer's hat. Would you invest in, lend to or buy your Company based on the reliability of your accounting system?

Outside Accountant's Report

First of all, knowing what you know about your business, answer the question of whether you would find a high degree of comfort in believing your own financial statements if they were placed in front of you by a third party. There are several reasons for the role of an outside independent CPA during the life of a business. The CPA performs an attest accountability function, based upon an outside look, as to the reliability of a set of financial statements. The CPA lends this accountability, typically in one of three possible levels of comfort in the Compilation, the Review or the Audit.

Pre-Exit Prep

Regardless of how you have chosen to use an outside CPA firm in the past, as you approach the possible sale of your Company, business owners need to focus on obtaining at least a reviewed or audited financial statement, for at least three to five years prior to your exit. Many financial buyers and strategic buyers will require reviewed or audited financial statements for this period of time at a minimum. If your potential buyer is itself a publicly held company, and if the acquisition of your business is material, then the publicly held company will probably not be in a position to even consider buying your business unless you have at least three years of audited financial statements.

Assuring Ongoing Inside Control To Sell Company

In order to have your business in an ongoing position to be sold to a third party, whether based on present plans to sell the business in the near future or based on a decision to always be in a position to sell should the right offer come along unexpectedly (or if you should die or become disabled), certain steps should generally be taken well in advance of a sale.

One of these steps is to assure that you have the necessary control to be able to sell your entire Company – whether this is through a sale of the stock or assets of your Company. You don't want to be in a position where a minority shareholder can unreasonably hold up the sale of the Company.

You can typically authorize the sale of all or substantially all of the assets of your Company, followed by a liquidation distribution (under most state business corporation laws) if you own at least two-thirds of the voting control of your Company.

However, if your sale will be of the Company's stock, buyers will often want to be able to purchase 100% of the stock. By negotiating a must "come along" or "drag along" provision into your Buy-Sell Agreement in advance of your exit, you'll know you have the option to deliver 100% of the stock in your Company in the event of a sale.

Under such a "drag along" provision in a Buy-Sell Agreement, the terms will typically provide that the majority owner can require that the minority owners must also sell their stock to the buyer. This will typically mean that the terms for the minority owner would be the same as that of the majority owner.

Absent such control, and absent the ability to purchase the stock of non-consenting minority shareholders under a Buy-Sell Agreement, it may be necessary to utilize a reverse merger (also known as a squeeze out merger) to cash out the non-consenting shareholders. This can present delays and disruptions if it needs to be done at the time you are trying to sell the Company. Plus, it's just not a pleasant step to have to take.

Ongoing House-In-Order

Every buyer will expect to "kick the tires" before purchasing your business. This is typically referred to as a "due diligence" review and will entail the review by the buyer and its legal counsel of various documents and other information pertinent to your business.

The objective is to learn the details about your business which the buyer wants to know before completing a purchase and to determine the scope and extent of potential liabilities and surprises.

If you are not prepared for this at the time of your exit, or if such a review uncovers significant issues, then your sale can be delayed or indefinitely sidetracked or a particular selling opportunity can be lost. While both parties to a business sale typically hope to be cooperative and constructive in negotiating and implementing a business transfer, never forget that the buyer is still an opponent during this process who is attempting to negotiate price and terms which might not be in your best interests. Be prepared and don't underestimate the scope of the effort the buyer will bring to bear.

You should always have your "house-in-order" and ready to sell. By reviewing and preparing for a "due diligence" review ahead of your exit, you can be prepared to handle a buyer's questions, objectives and negotiating tactics to help achieve a more successful exit when the time comes. This review can also help you avoid issues that could sidetrack or derail you in all Four Quarters.

Minimizing Need For Outside Consents

Various outside third parties with which you regularly transact business may have a strong interest in having some control over who owns your Company as a condition for that person to continue to do business with you. For this reason, various types of agreements and business relationships will have provisions buried within them which prohibit the sale or control of your business - or which prohibit the sale of substantially all of the assets of your business – without first obtaining their written consent.

Therefore, as you look ahead toward your Fourth Quarter, these types of agreements and business relationships need to be reviewed to determine if they present potential roadblocks to proceeding as you may otherwise wish to proceed.

One of the objectives of this book is to suggest to business owners the fact that they should always operate their business with a view towards their future exit. It makes sense, therefore, to negotiate flexible future exit alternatives into agreements and business relationships if and when an outside third party seeks to impose constraints during the course of your business operations.

This is not always possible and, in fact, might be adverse to the business if a certain element of control would provide a favorable comfort level that would enhance a relationship with an important third party. Nevertheless, these types of provisions should not be freely granted when negotiating an agreement, but should instead be looked upon with the continuing view towards your expected or unexpected exit.

Pioneer Mindset

☑ **Build It.** *Be dedicated to building an enduring business, not just working a job so you can one day retire.*

Typical Consents Needed

One of the most frequent contracts in which you will find "change of control" provisions is in a loan agreement with a third party bank or other financial institution. This is especially the case when the bank is lending largely on the basis of the strength of the current owner or owners.

While less common, it's also possible to find "change of control" provisions in certain customer and supplier agreements, as well as within the body of certain government granted licenses or permits.

Franchisor's Consent

Of particular interest to franchisees is the "change of control" provision in a franchisor/franchisee agreement. Here, the franchisor will often want to maintain control, or at least have the option to veto a change in control, so as to have the opportunity to evaluate whether a new business owner will be satisfactory for the franchisor's standards of operation.

Structure Business Entities For Your Fourth Quarter

Depending on the make up of your Company's businesses and assets, and your objective for what components you wish to ultimately sell or keep, it may be necessary to restructure your business entities. For example, you may wish to retain a particular operating division, either due to personal preference or because you don't believe it will be an attractive or feasible part of the business mix that your anticipated buyer will want to acquire.

You might also wish to retain the real estate which your Company uses and lease this to the buyer.

Another type of asset class which can in the right circumstances be retained is specifically identifiable intellectual property that your business utilizes. This may be a particular process, technique, know how, trademark, etc. which you wish to keep and license to the buyer.

Business entity restructuring may also be necessary due to the change in leadership you anticipate upon your exit. For example, if you have two distinct divisions which require different leadership talents that you could handle but your successor doesn't have, it may be necessary to divide the Company into more than one entity to suit the leadership talent you have available to you. A corporate restructuring may also be desirable where you have more than one child who is capable of managing the Company and you wish to place each in the leadership of a particular Company division.

You may also find that due to your tax savings plans it becomes necessary to revise your Company corporate structure. This may, for example, be due to "S" vs. "C" status under your Federal Income Tax Plan or to better address your nexus factors under your State Income Tax Plan. Or you may restructure to meet your Estate Tax Plan.

The "House-In-Order" Checkup

In a separate Chapter I discuss the business sale process. By understanding that process today and by keeping your house in order through an up-to-date "House-In-Order" Checkup, you will be better ready for the ultimate sale of your Company, whether this occurs on your timeframe or pursuant to an unexpected offer.

Pioneer Mindset

☑ *Ready To Sell.* *Nothing will keep your business in better shape than always having it ready to sell.*

Chapter
34

Tax Reduction Strategy Ready

Incredible Result: "We are living up to our patriotic duty to help control the size of government by paying the least taxes legally allowable."

Avoidable Train Wreck: Income tax hit.

Main Play: The Income Tax Reduction Strategy

What This Is: Your personal and your Company federal and state income and capital gain taxes will be minimized during all Four Quarters of your time in action (and upon the future transfer of your Company) because your Business Model, your business contracts which implement it, and your corporate structure, have all been designed with the proper tax strategy actions to help achieve this.

If you were to look closely at each of the 9 building blocks of your Business Model, you would see the various ways where the Federal, State and local governments have imposed their income, sales, use, property, franchise, etc. taxes. However, those Family Business Pioneers who venture to look closer are finding the many ways that, with the proper design and implementation of their Business Model, much of these taxes can be lawfully avoided or reduced.

It's beyond the scope of this book to detail all of the potential transaction designs and tax planning tools which can act to minimize personal and Company taxes during the course of a business owner's

Four Quarters. However, below are some of the tax planning actions which can be addressed relating to the actual transfer of your business.

Tax Reduction Steps Not To Take

During the life of a business, some business owners are tempted to implement tax reduction steps which push the limits of acceptable tax planning beyond the realm of acceptable boundaries. Many are aimed too far at reducing reportable taxable income. I won't detail those here. Opportunities for prudent tax planning should be the focus.

Pioneer Mindset

☑ *Double Check. If you wouldn't be happy seeing your words or action on the front page headline, don't say it or do it.*

The Income Tax Reduction Strategy

A Fourth Quarter Game Plan provides the opportunity to significantly reduce both the seller's taxes and the buyer's taxes upon the sale and purchase of a business.

Most business owners are familiar with the fact that a sale of their business will typically result in federal and state income tax obligations which will be created and due upon the sale of a business. Depending on the (a) business structure, (b) terms of the sale, (c) the location of the seller, and (d) pre-exit tax planning by the seller, these federal and state income taxes will either be maximized or minimized. In addition, depending on the state within which the business operates, there is the potential for sales/use taxes, franchise taxes or other transfer taxes, particularly if the transaction is an asset sale which is not covered by an exemption.

What is less frequently known or understood is the fact that a buyer also needs to pay federal and state income taxes upon the purchase of a business. This is because in order for a buyer to pay the purchase price, the buyer needs cash. In order for a buyer to possess cash, the buyer needs to earn cash. Those earnings, like other earnings, will be subject to federal and state income taxes.

For example, if the buyer needs to pay the purchase price of $1,000,000, the buyer needs to earn pre-tax cash of approximately $1,700,000. Assuming, for illustration, combined federal and state income tax rates of approximately 40%, then $700,000 of this pre-tax cash would be paid in federal and state income taxes, leaving a balance of $1,000,000 to pay the purchase price.

The reason for this is that the buyer can typically not deduct the price paid for the business (although when assets are purchased, some portion of the price may be deducted over time as depreciation). If the million dollar price was fully deductible currently against income taxes, then there in effect would be no tax on the buyer. This is because the buyer would need pre-tax cash earnings of only $1,000,000 to pay for the business, because the deductible purchase price (if that were possible) would offset the million dollar pre-tax cash earnings to result in no income taxes on those earnings.

Below are some of the pre-exit tax reduction election and other tax steps which can be taken to help minimize the potential income taxes to both the seller and the buyer.

"C" vs. "S" Corporation Asset Sale or Stock Sale

Where the Company is a corporation that has elected to be an "S" corporation, then the double seller's tax could be avoided. This is because the "S" corporation would not have a tax obligation on the sale of the assets. In order for this to be fully effective, the "S" election (to convert from a "C" corporation) must be made at least 5 years in advance of the owner's exit.

The "S" election has the added benefit that each year's taxable income (less distributions) will increase the tax basis of the owner's stock, which will decrease future tax on the sale of the company. The difference between annual income tax rates on "C" corporations and "S" corporation pass through income (after the new 20% deduction on qualified business income) needs to be part of this analysis.

The Tax Cuts and Jobs Act of 2017 has added new life into whether to be a "C" or "S" corporation. When the new top "C" corporation tax rate (21%) is combined with the potential capital gain exclusion (IRC Section 1202) for the sale of "qualified small business stock" of a "C" corporation (subject to various requirements and limitations), and the elimination of the corporate alternative minimum tax, compared to the new 20% "S" corporation deduction (IRC Section 199A), the question of "C" vs "S" is less clear. (The possible move to "C" status also brings back into play the possible application of the accumulated earnings tax (and the steps needed to avoid this).

Avoiding State Capital Gain Taxes

Those states which impose an income tax also typically impose the tax on the sale of a business. One of the most frequent pre-exit steps business owners consider taking in advance of selling their businesses, if they are residents of a taxing state, is to first consider changing residency to another state which does not impose an income tax (e.g. Florida, Texas, Washington, Nevada, Wyoming, South Dakota).

To be effective, this needs to be done before entering into any type of a sales agreement. By establishing residency in a no-tax state, the state income tax (or capital gains tax) could be avoided completely on a stock sale. However, moving to another state is not always consistent with business leadership and sale objectives.

The other main way in which to avoid a state income tax upon the sale of a business is to reside in a state with (and to meet the specific requirements for) an exemption to such taxes upon the sale of business.

For example, in Nebraska, one of my partners and I had the opportunity in 1987 to explain to the Nebraska Governor and Legislature that Nebraska's tax on business owners who sell their companies was counterproductive. It was just causing our business owners to move out of Nebraska and so the State wasn't collecting the tax anyway. We convinced the State to enact a statutory exemption for the sale of stock by a business owner. This enabled Nebraskans to stay in Nebraska. The Nebraska exemption provision applies if there are at least five shareholders and at least 10% of the corporation is owned by shareholders who are not related to the other 90% (a provision also designed to encourage employee ownership).

Minimum Defensible Price With Deferred Compensation

If part of the purchase price could be deducted by a buyer, then the overall buyer's tax can be reduced. While it may not be possible to deduct an entire purchase price, it is possible to establish the selling price at a lower amount by establishing a deferred compensation agreement with the business owners.

Provided that the federal income tax requirements for establishing deferred compensation are satisfied, this deferred compensation acts as a liability on the balance sheet payable to the business owners which must be satisfied once the buyer assumes ownership of the Company. Therefore, it's possible to provide the sellers with a combination of consideration for their stock and past (perhaps under compensated) services, this being a combination of the selling price and deferred compensation.

While deferred compensation is taxable to the recipient as ordinary income (rather than capital gain), it is fully deductible by the payor (the buyer), which therefore has the result of decreasing the buyer's tax. Depending on the negotiations between the parties, this decrease in total seller/buyer taxes may be negotiated with some or all of the tax savings to go to the buyer or the seller.

Pioneer Mindset

☑ *Keep More.* *Diligently seek and find the many ways within the nooks and crannies of your Business Model to patriotically cut taxes.*

Chapter
35

Inside Route Exit Option Ready

Incredible Result: "We built our Company together. My Team is ready and able to take it forward."

Avoidable Train Wreck: No effective inside route exit.

Main Play: The Inside Route Exit Plan

What This Is: You have one or more key persons, partners, family members, or an ESOP who could and would purchase the Company now, on the price, terms and feasible financing you've agreed to with them, and they have the ability to successfully own and operate the Company into the future.

Take a deep breath. Get a cup of coffee. We are now going to take a bit of a deep dive into a fair amount of critical information about how to eventually exit from your Company to the benefit of you, your family and your team.

The way you intend to ultimately exit from your Company is one of the most important Fourth Quarter objectives which Family Business Pioneers are considering early on. This can impact many early decisions.

When we talk about transitioning or exiting from your business at the end of your Fourth Quarter, our focus is on two types of exits:

- Active Duty Exit.
- Ownership Exit.

This chapter focuses on these alternatives. Having some idea of your inside route exit alternatives early on helps to direct your actions which impact these options.

Active Duty Exit Routes

As the Company's principal leader, you have a number of ways to leave active duty. These are, for the most part, obvious, but need to still be considered and communicated to your Fourth Quarter advisor team so there is an understanding as to precisely what your objectives are. It is important in the exit process to eliminate as many wrong assumptions between yourself as the owner and your advisors who are seeking to help in your Fourth Quarter planning. In addition, it is helpful to avoid incorrect assumptions between you and the other members of your key management team.

Your "active duty" exits include the following:

- **Complete Retirement.** This is at a designated date or age.

- **Leadership Transition.** For example, if you are presently the Chairman, CEO and President, a leadership transition would include handing off your President duties and later your CEO duties and later yet Chairman duties, to a successor, over a period of time.

- **Active Consultant.** Here you agree to stay on in an active consulting role while handing off all officer and director duties to your successor. This status as an active consultant might be for a pre-agreed period of time, or be set up for a date to be established in the future.

- **Retainer.** This involves being an inactive consultant, but you agree to remain available as an advisor to your successors if and as needed.

- **Disability.** In this case you have decided to work and retain your positions of leadership until you are no longer able to productively continue.

- **Death.** You have decided that you really have no intention of retiring at all and would be content to literally "die at your desk," as they say.

Each of these alternatives involves personal as well as business and financial considerations. If you are ready to move on and hand over the reigns, you are going to pick one of these, or some combination of these alternatives, depending on what is best for you, your family, your business, and the perceptions and objectives of your key leadership team. Good leaders on your team, if in fact they are as good as you believe, will typically want to have the opportunity to take over one of the top positions. Nothing in business is static. If your key leadership do not see this opportunity as a possibility, you may face the prospect of losing a key performer as a tradeoff to your personal desire to remain fully active longer than perhaps you should.

When these active duty exits are viewed in the context of your ownership exit options, you may or may not have the freedom of choice. Your buyer of your business may well insist on one or the other of these options. This, of course, varies from business to business, and from situation to situation. A strategic buyer may well be purchasing your business without a need for you to continue for any period of time, or perhaps, to continue only in a retainer capacity. On the other hand, a financial buyer might insist that you stay for a period of time to help transition management duties, in particular, depending on the management depth in place behind you.

Ownership Exit Routes

It is important in the Fourth Quarter Planning process to understand where you, as an owner, want to end up. In the context of Fourth Quarter Planning, this revolves largely around six principal objectives, as stated in a previous chapter.

It is the "Who" objective that is considered now. This objective, however, cannot be considered in isolation. Depending on "What" you want to transfer or keep, and depending on "When" you want to transfer ownership, the objective of "to who" may well need to be dependent.

If you were to take a trip from Omaha, Nebraska to northern Minnesota, you could travel via a number of routes to arrive at the same destination. You could take Interstate 80 east to Des Moines, then turn north to Duluth, Minnesota on Interstate 35, then take Hwy. 61 to Lutsen. Or, you could take any of a number of diagonal routes through various small towns in Iowa and Minnesota.

You also could have chosen from a variety of methods of transportation. You could walk any of these routes and eventually arrive. You could ride a bicycle and arrive in about two weeks. You could travel by car and make the trip in less than a day, or you could charter a plane and be there in a couple of hours. You also could have chosen some combination of these and other routes and methods, including travel by train or boat.

With each of these routes and methods of travel, you can achieve your destination. However, each involves a different combination of cost, time, comfort, satisfaction, and personal preference.

Choosing an exit route and exit method to depart from ownership of your business is a similar process. There are seven main exit **routes** for exiting ownership from your business. There are at least 30 exit **methods** for exiting all or part of your business ownership. It is with that understanding that the following discussion of "ownership exit routes" needs to be considered.

Exit Route: Employees

Your employees may be the most natural fit as a buyer of your business. They will typically have a good understanding of how the business works, as well as some motivation to see the business continue after your departure, with the possibility of it continuing under their control. Whether they are financially capable of purchasing your business, and how this might be structured to address financial capabilities, needs to be carefully developed. Some of the methods by which employees could acquire your business would include a purchase by a key employee group (with third-party lender financing or seller financing), a purchase by an employee stock ownership plan (possibly leveraged through bank financing), or a sale to just one key employee (either with bank financing or seller financing).

Exit Route: Family

Your family is a second, natural, potential exit route for your business ownership. Often, for estate planning and other financial reasons, an owner may have already transferred a sizable portion of ownership to a spouse, children and grandchildren.

If your objective is to retain ownership and continue to profit and oversee the business until your death, then your ownership exit may be through the bequest that you leave to your family, via your Estate Plan upon your death. Of course, you may decide to simply own the Company until your final, literal exit. Here, you might have resigned from your active duties years in advance and simply remained as a passive owner as you mentored a key employee or family member to take over your management duties, or you might have continued to retain your management duties until your death.

Assuming instead that you would like to transfer your ownership in exchange for some cash with which to retire on, the exit methods to accomplish this could include a direct, negotiated sale to family for the full price, or a part sale/part gift for less than the full price.

Exit Route: Co-Owner

Another natural, possible purchaser of your business is one or more co-owners. Whether this makes sense depends on the exit objectives and financial capabilities of your co-owners. The method of purchase by a co-owner would typically be either through a negotiated direct sale transaction, or through a previously agreed trigger event under a Buy-Sell Agreement. Depending on the independent means available to the co-owner(s), this type of sale would either be self-financed by the co-owner, bank financed, or seller financed and may or may not include "earn-out" provisions.

Exit Route: Third Party Strategic Or Financial Buyer

A strategic buyer is a person who is interested in your business because of the synergies which it can add to the buyer's business. This may be a competitor or similar business looking to expand into your area, or it may be a person looking to add market share who is already in your area. The strategic buyer might be specifically interested in certain parts of your business, such as your distribution network, your customer base, your intellectual property, or your product or service lines. Besides being a competitor, the strategic buyer may be a supplier or customer, or someone who is looking to actively become involved in managing your specific type of business. The exit methods can include a direct, negotiated purchase or a limited auction.

A financial buyer is a person who is interested in owning and profiting from distributions or from the future sale of your business, but who is typically not interested in having to manage your business. This can include an individual investor, a group of investors or a private equity fund. The exit methods for this type of buyer can include a direct negotiated purchase or a limited auction.

Exit Route: Public Market

Another type of financial buyer would be the public stock market. The exit method for this route would typically be through an initial public offering (based on a number of different pricing options).

Exit Route: Liquidation Buyer

This route would be chosen when the liquidation value of your business exceeds its going concern value. In other words, if you can receive more from liquidating and selling the parts of your business than you can from trying to sell it as a going concern, then this route makes sense. Potential buyers can range from equipment dealers to real estate developers to technology licensors and to competitors or others in the business interested in some or all of the parts of your business. The exit method would either be an auction or a directly-negotiated sale, in either case, with the expectation of this being a cash transaction.

Exit Route: Partial (Or Twice)

Redemption/Refinance.   This route leads you to a partial ownership exit. One exit method is a refinancing of your business to add debt borrowing to your balance sheet from a third-party lender, such as a bank or other financial institution, with the objective of using the loan proceeds to redeem part of your ownership. This, in essence, lets you take some of your chips off the table while keeping control of the Company as you move forward. This route, of course, only works if you have a balance sheet and a net cash flow which is strong enough to support the debt service payments.

Recapitalization.   Another partial exit route is to sell part ownership to a third party and retain either a majority or minority position for sale at a later date. The most common method is a recapitalization leveraged buyout by a private equity firm. Typically a private equity firm will not be interested unless you have annual EBITDA (Earnings Before Interest, Taxes, Depreciation and Amortization) of at least $2 million to $10 million.   A private equity firm will typically want at least 80% ownership, leaving you 20%, and will want you to remain to run the Company for a certain period. The firm will also want to have about 10% ownership available to issue to new or existing key employees, which will either be dilutive to both you and the private equity firm, or not dilutive to you, depending on the terms which can be negotiated.   A sizable portion of the price will be financed with debt. The recapitalization gives you the opportunity to continue to still achieve some later equity upside from the sale of your retained 20% and to "stay in the game" to continue to manage the Company, while you have taken the balance of your chips off the table.

Franchise. If you have developed your business systems so they can be efficiently replicated and if you have a highly profitable niche which many others would like to own, then you can consider franchising the business. This involves a close review of about a dozen key factors.

Joint Venture. Lastly, you may consider forming a joint venture with another Company as a step towards your eventual exit.

Pioneer Mindset

☑ *Confusion.*   *A confused mind won't buy or agree. Be extremely clear about what you are offering and why.*

Impact Of Exit Route Decision

Regardless of which exit route you choose, the remaining steps in the Fourth Quarter Planning process need to be addressed. This is because they either apply to specifically carry out the exit route you have chosen, or because they may apply as a backup for which you want to be prepared, should you choose or need to change exit routes into the future.

Determine Inside Route Outlook

In an ideal world, when you are ready to sell your business, an overabundance of ready, willing and able outside buyers, with cash, would be knocking on your door. However, in today's world, this is often not the case. For this reason, as well as to meet personal preferences, many business owners would like to sell their business to leadership team, to family members or to a partner ("insiders").

There are three principal directions to exit ownership of your business through a transfer to an insider or insiders. These consist of:

- Sale to co-owner (s) (either directly or as a stock redemption).

- Sale to key employee (s) (either directly or through an ESOP).

- Transfer to family (during life or at death).

Some combination of these is often utilized with a transfer to insiders.

One of our objectives is to help determine whether a sale to an insider (family or non-family) is even financially feasible. If so, this step will help manage and overcome the problems associated with a transfer to insiders. This step is intended to apply for either an immediate or possible eventual sale or transfer to insiders.

Many business owners we visit with have already considered various alternatives for transferring ownership to insiders. Many have also already gifted shares to family members, often for estate planning reasons or perhaps because one or more children have been active in the business.

The first decision in this step is to understand your most likely inside transferee and your expected timetable. If you are the sole owner and you are absolutely certain you intend to exit through the lifetime gifting or death inheritance of your stock to your family, it remains important to realize you should consider having a backup plan to be prepared for an outside sale opportunity. Again, all plans are firm … until changed.

However, if you anticipate a sale to a partner, key employee (s), ESOP or family, then the purpose of the step is to assess the desire and ability of such insiders to actually purchase your stock and to develop the best means to do so. With a sale to insiders, owners often face a common problem — the proposed buyer does not have enough cash to meet a fair price and the seller is required to assist in financing the transaction. A number of pre-transfer steps and actual transfer design tools can help address this.

Whether or not your proposed inside buyer has independent cash, every buyer will look to the future cash flow of the business to justify the price being paid to you – either to see whether the business will "cash flow" the debt service to you and/or to determine the potential for future profit on the purchase. To determine this, your Fourth Quarter advisors can perform an estimated future cash flow analysis. The results of this help determine the pricing as well as the terms of payment and security for payment.

Employee Stock Ownership Plan ("ESOP")

If you would like to sell to the Company's employees rather than just to your key employee management team, you should consider establishing and selling to an ESOP. This enables you to reward and incent your employees while enabling them to buy you out with pre-tax dollars (because in certain instances the price paid can be deducted by the Company).

The ESOP was the creation several decades ago of attorney Louis Kelso (1913-1991). I had the opportunity to visit with Mr. Kelso at an ESOP conference before he passed away. He told me that the main reason he designed the ESOP was to expand our nation's economic prosperity by extending the ownership of productive assets to the Company's workforce. Mr. Kelso convinced the then U.S. Senate Finance Committee Chair Russell Long to champion the program through Congress in the 1970's.

The ESOP enacted by Congress aims to achieve its economic objectives by allowing the Company to deduct the purchase price paid to purchase your stock. It also provides you as the seller the ability to defer the tax on your gain if after the sale the ESOP owns at least 30% of the Company and within fifteen months (starting three months before the sale) you invest the proceeds in qualified replacement securities (generally domestic company stocks and bonds).

According to the National Center for Employee Ownership, 32 million Americans own stock in their employer (through a 401(k) plan, ESOP, options, direct stock grant or similar plan). There are about 7,000 ESOPs with a total of about 14 million participants.

The ideal ESOP, from a tax perspective, owns 100% of an "S" corporation, because it is effectively income tax exempt. The ESOP is not suitable for every company, however, and certain technical requirements must be met. Before deciding to pursue this exit route, we will first evaluate whether a company (in light of the business owner's future exit objectives) is a suitable candidate for an ESOP.

Plan For A Tax Efficient, Bankable Sale To Insider

Exiting your Company through a sale to one or more insiders is not easy and, as will be seen below, can involve terms and conditions which at first may appear counterintuitive to a business owner.

As a starting point, the business owner needs to first and foremost understand that the most likely way to be successful in a sale to one or more insiders is to accomplish this in at least two stages. In other words, you will likely be less successful if you believe that a sale to an insider or insiders should occur in one phase at or near the time of your actual ownership exit.

The Problems With A One-Phase Transfer To Insiders

Under the right circumstances, a one-step transfer of your ownership to insiders can work. This requires the simultaneous presence of capable inside purchasers coupled with your intention to exit now. This is because the type of ownership-interested, capable key insiders whom you would like to purchase your Company may very well not be interested in hanging around without some commitment from you if you plan to exit several years in the future. In addition, even if your capable key insiders were interested in hanging around until you exit, a bank is unlikely to finance 100% of a key-employee stock purchase, leaving you in the position of providing seller-financing which could run several years after you have exited management of the Company, resulting in a higher probability of default.

The Two-Phase Ownership Exit

Under a two-phase ownership exit, a portion of your stock would be transferred to your inside buyer or buyers now, while the balance would be transferred at a later date. There are at least eight possible scenarios for how the second phase of the transfer might occur. You don't necessarily need to decide phase two today in order to accomplish phase one. This two-phase approach has the following advantages:

- Providing stock ownership to key employees today can provide an incentive for higher personal achievement in their job performance.

- Providing stock ownership to key employees today can help reduce the risk that they will be attracted to a job offer from a competing Company.

- Providing stock ownership to key employees today improves the likelihood of a bank financing the balance of their purchase in the future upon your final exit.

- Providing stock ownership to key employees today, particularly if they have been required to invest part of their personal funds in the purchase of some or all of that stock, gives them some "skin in the game," which serves as an additional motivation to help the Company be successful.

- Providing some stock ownership to key employees today, while you retain the balance of your ownership, enables you to continue as controlling owner, as well as becoming a mentor to your key employees to further develop their skills and leadership talent under your watchful eye.

What About Minority Shareholder Issues?

Business owners have reason to be concerned about transferring partial ownership to key employees, who would now constitute minority shareholders. If not fully planned, this could raise issues on how such stock is to be voted and whether you can receive the return of such stock if your key employee leaves the Company. These types of issues can be dealt with through Buy-Sell and Business Continuity Agreements, discussed elsewhere in this book. For now in the discussion, let's make the assumption that minority shareholder issues can be dealt with to your satisfaction.

Evaluating Whether Your Key Employees Actually Want To Be Owners

It's important to determine, rather than assume, that your key employees in fact actually want to be owners. A key employee may have discussed a desire in the past to be an owner and may actually tend to think or act like an owner. However, if you don't have a high degree of comfort that you have one or more key employees who can actually become the Company's leader, then you need to face the fact early on that an inside transfer might not be your best exit route, but instead should become a backup route, with a sale to a third party taking the place as your primary exit route.

Equally important with regard to whether a key employee could be a successful owner is whether your key employee or key employee group is of such an age that they may have little interest in spending a number of years acquiring stock ownership, only to then be faced with their own rather immediate need to attempt to sell the Company, in particular before they have had enough time to realize full value. If your key employee group or a member of your key employee group is over the age of 50, then you need to seriously consider their ownership objectives and whether you should instead be providing simply some means of ownership incentive, such as phantom stock or a stock appreciation right plan.

How Much Skin In The Game?

When considering the transfer of stock to a key employee or a key employee group, you need to determine how much risk you want them to bear in the first step of the purchase. Sometimes owners are willing to allow the key employees to pay for their stock solely out of future cash flow which they receive as dividends on the purchased stock. Often, though, owners want their key employee groups to have some skin in the game and to bear some risk of loss by putting in some of their own money, or pledging some of their own assets as security for the purchase of their stock. This becomes a balance between the financial capabilities of the key employees and the departing owner's desire to become less exposed to the risk of the business.

Pioneer Mindset

☑ *Always Three.* *There are always three possible scenarios. Left end of the spectrum. Right end of the spectrum. Or somewhere in between. Anticipate and think accordingly.*

Free Cash Flow

In order for a key employee group to purchase your stock, assuming that some or all of the purchase price is to come from the key employee group's share of dividends on that stock, it's important that the Company have a known and consistent "free cash flow." "Free cash flow" is the cash flow that's available for distribution to the stockholders. This is sometimes called "discretionary cash flow." This represents the cash generated by the business that is not required for either the operations or expansion of the business or for the debt service/capitalization of the business.

In order to properly plan for a sale of stock to insiders, it's necessary to have a solid estimate of the future free cash flow expectations. This can be developed with your CPA. It can be easily illustrated. If the free cash flow of the Company (after distributions to pay income taxes) is projected to be $800,000 each year, and the first step of the stock sale to the key employee group is 10% of the Company, then the key employee group will have approximately $80,000 available to pay for the stock each year. If free cash flow is inadequate, and assuming the key employees do not have substantial cash of their own, then the key employee group is not going to be in a position to pay full value for the stock. If that's the case, then either the pricing needs to be reconsidered (with possibly a portion connected to deferred compensation) or you need to further consider whether your primary exit route should instead be a sale to an outside third party. In addition, you need to consider whether you can meet your exit objectives on the timing for your exit and instead need to work on developing a stronger cash flow for your business.

Subchapter "S" Or LLC Status

The sale of stock to insiders is generally best accommodated if your business entity is a "flow-through" entity for income tax purposes. A flow-through entity is either an "S" corporation or a limited liability company ("LLC"). Under either of these arrangements, the business entity itself does not pay income taxes, but instead the business entity's income is automatically taxed to the business owners. Typically, this type of business entity would distribute sufficient cash to the owners to pay for this tax liability.

The principal advantage of this flow-through entity structure is that dividends can be paid by the Company to the owners without additional tax. In other words, the dividends can be placed into the hands of the owners having incurred only one tax (i.e. a federal and state income tax only once).

By contrast, a regular "C" corporation must pay income tax on its earnings and the shareholders must pay a second tax when those after tax earnings are distributed in the form of dividends. Since dividends are not deductible to a "C" corporation, this results in a true double taxation on the same income.

When an "S" corporation or LLC is utilized, the key employee group can receive its share of Company dividends free of additional taxation and use the dividend proceeds dollar-for-dollar to pay for their stock investment.

This means that as you look ahead to your Fourth Quarter, it is time to consider whether you should make an election to become an "S" corporation if you haven't already. When you're not in exit mode, it may well have worked just fine to be taxed as a "C" corporation, in particular if you were only receiving deductible salary compensation and bonuses from the Company and were not receiving any non-deductible dividends. It's important once you are in exit-mode planning that we review with your CPA the specific considerations which go into switching from a "C" corporation to an "S" corporation.

No Loss Of Control

The transfer of stock to key employees does not mean that a business owner needs to give up control over that stock. Nor does it mean that the owner must give up the ability to recall the stock if the owner determines that future events or conditions warrant this.

What is meant by control and how does this impact the business owner? The following elements of control can typically be relevant:

*   **Annual stockholder meetings.** The principal occasion for a shareholder to exercise his or her ownership rights as a shareholder would be at a shareholder's meeting, whether an annual meeting or a special meeting. Typically a pre-exit transfer of stock ownership to key employees will be less than a majority of the stock, e.g. typically 10%-25%, whether initially or over time. This amount of ownership by the key employees provides a better ability for the key employees to obtain bank financing for the purchase of your remaining stock when you complete your exit. However, this percentage of ownership does not give the key employees control of votes during shareholder meetings. As long as the Company's Articles of Incorporation and Bylaws have been duly structured, the majority owner can maintain control over the voting which occurs at a shareholder meeting. In addition, voting control can be further established through a Business Continuity Agreement.

Another alternative is to issue only non-voting stock to the key employees in the pre-exit phase. If your corporation is not presently set up to issue non-voting stock, this can be easily handled through an amendment to the corporation's Articles of Incorporation (or Operating Agreement for LLCs). This alternative exists even if the corporation is an "S" corporation. While the tax rules limit an "S" corporation to only one class of stock, non-voting stock is not considered a second class of stock for purposes of these rules.

- **Control as to selling the company.** Corporate laws generally require that certain major events, such as liquidating a corporation or selling all or substantially all of the assets of the corporation to a third party, require at least two-thirds approval by the shareholders. As long as you maintain this percentage of ownership, you have retained the ability to control the decision regarding such a sale. In addition, you can provide in a Business Continuity Agreement that your control for this type of decision is maintained.

- **Control over selling 100% of the stock to a third party.** Suppose that the best exit in the future becomes a transfer to an outside third party rather than a transfer of the balance of your stock to inside employees. Suppose further that an outside third party only wishes to buy your stock if it can acquire 100% of the stock (i.e. also acquire the stock held by your key employees). This objective can be accomplished through a Buy-Sell Agreement through such provisions as a "drag along" provision in the agreement which requires the key employees to sell on the same terms and conditions which you are able to negotiate for the sale of all the stock of the Company.

- **Stock recall.** If your key employees turn out to be problematic, you may want to have the ability to recall, or re-acquire, the stock which had been previously transferred to them. This objective can be met through provisions in a Buy-Sell Agreement.

- **Helping assure key employee loyalty.** You may have transferred stock to your key employees for three principal reasons. First, to provide an incentive to the key employees to perform and to remain with the Company. Second, to provide you with the first step for accomplishing your overall exit. Third, to demonstrate your commitment to them, which you expect would be reciprocal. In addition to transferring stock to your key employees, a business owner also typically wants to begin to transfer leadership duties. While this has the advantage of starting to provide you with more free time, it can result in some shift of operating control (e.g. through customer relationships) to your key employees, which provides some risk that a key employee will leave and begin competing against your Company. All business decisions have the potential for upside and the potential for downside. This is simply another occasion for managing, reducing, or eliminating the downside risk.   In this instance, it can be done through the combination of non-compete terms, employee non-solicitation terms, customer non-solicitation terms, and confidentiality terms, all of which provisions can be included in a Business Continuity Agreement.

While the conventional expectation of most business owners is that non-compete terms are not binding, this is generally a risk if the employee is only an employee (and not an owner) and is generally a risk when the terms of the non-compete are too broad and overreaching. These issues can often be substantially dealt with. In addition, an employee non-solicitation provision and a customer non-solicitation provision, as well as a confidentiality provision, are generally more enforceable and often target precisely the human capital, customer relationship capital and intellectual property capital which you are most interested in protecting in any event. To the extent you have protected this, you have also discouraged that key employee from believing that he or she can leave the Company and take this along.

These types of provisions in a Business Continuity Agreement are important not only to you, but also to the other members of the key employee group, who likewise should want to see a high degree of loyalty to the enterprise, which benefits everyone provided they remain loyal to the Company. Its extremely important to prevent a former key employee group member from harming your Company. Therefore, attention needs to be paid to these details.

Tax Consequences Of, And Payment For, Stock Transfer To Key Employees

The transfer of stock to your key employees will typically occur in one of two ways. First, you might want to transfer some of your stock to them. Second, the corporation might want to issue new stock to them. Payment for this stock also will generally occur in one of two principal ways. First, the stock could be bonused to them or, second, the stock could be sold to them. If the stock is sold to them, then payment for the stock typically occurs in one of two ways. Either they will pay cash up front for the stock or they will sign a promissory note in which they pay for the stock over a period of time (with part of the note possibly forgiven each year the employee stays with the Company).

The key employee funding for such payments would also typically occur in one of two ways. First, they would pay for the stock out of their own assets or, alternatively, their payment of the stock would be funded through dividend payments they receive pro-rata on their shares of stock.

Security for their payment of stock would also typically exist in either one of two ways. First, you would receive no security or collateral backing up their obligation or, alternatively, some assets would be pledged to secure the payment obligation against potential future default.

Lastly, the price paid for the stock is usually established in one of two ways. First, it could be a fair market value based on a pro-rata percentage ownership of the Company or it could be a discounted value (e.g. reflecting minority discount, lack of marketability discount, or some bonus compensation element).

Your actual terms with your key employees might also be some combination of these alternatives.

Typically we would see the following choices. The stock sold would consist of shares which you own (rather than newly issued shares by the corporation), the stock would be sold at a price (bonused or some combination), the stock pricing would reflect minority and lack of marketability discounts, the repurchase price (if for some reason you decide to recall the stock) would be based on the same type of pricing as the initial purchase, the stock would be paid for in installments over time (rather than cash up front), the installment payments would be funded through dividends (though this might be partially from employee compensation and savings), the employee would provide collateral as security for the purchase (although this might be limited to simply pledging the stock purchased as collateral rather than pledging other employee assets as collateral).

One other set of alternatives for the transfer of stock to employees would be to transfer them stock with or without requiring the execution of a Business Continuity Agreement and Buy-Sell Agreement or to require this as a condition for the transfer. Typically these agreements should be required.

Rolling Vesting

If part of your combination of stock issuance to employees will be stock which is fully or partly a stock bonus, then you should consider issuing this stock on a rolling vesting approach. Under this approach, the stock bonus represents part of the overall compensation to the employee in the form of performance incentive and employment retention compensation.

Under this approach, the amount of stock to be bonused would be based on a performance incentive which applies either to each individual key employee or to the performance of the key employee group as a whole. The standards of performance can be tied to the business results that you wish to see. This might include, for example, revenue growth, net profits, cost control, or other relevant business or financial ratios.

Simply because stock is then issued under this type of stock bonus formula does not mean the stock can be retained should the key employee terminate his or her employment. Instead, the key employee should always have some risk of leaving some of his or her stock ownership on the table should the employee leave the Company. Under a rolling vesting approach, the employee will vest in a given year's stock issuance over a period of subsequent years that the employee remains with the Company.

For example, if the employee is issued 100 shares of stock in 2017, based on performance in 2016, under a rolling vesting format, the employee could vest in those 100 shares at the rate of 20% per year over five years. If the employee leaves in one year, then the employee would only have earned ownership in 20% of the 2017 100 shares. If the employee leaves after two years, the employee would have ownership in 40% of the 2017 100 shares.

Likewise, if shares are issued in 2018, the employee would have a similar vesting schedule for those shares. This doesn't mean that the employee can retain ownership of those shares upon termination, but instead reflects the number of shares to be considered as owned, and therefore the shares for which the Company would pay a price to recall those shares upon termination of employment.

Securities Law Considerations

Stock issued directly by the Company to key employees is subject to securities law compliance, as is every other stock sale by an owner or issuance by a Company to shareholders or potential shareholders. A full discussion of this is beyond the scope of this book. Briefly, the securities law provides for certain exemptions from its registration requirement for non-public or otherwise limited stock issuances. Even when an exemption exists, it is important that an employee receive financial information regarding the Company. This is particularly true if the employee is purchasing stock from the Company with the employee's funds.

Tax Considerations

When stock is bonused by the Company to an employee (or issued at a price less than its fair market value), the bonus component will typically constitute taxable compensation to the employee (and an offsetting deduction to the corporation). This taxation typically occurs when the stock is either transferable by the employee or no longer subject to what the tax law refers to as a "substantial risk of forfeiture".

Depending on the circumstances, the Company can decide to "gross up" the employee for these tax consequences by paying a cash bonus to the employee as part of the overall stock bonus, so that the tax impact is covered by the Company (which is receiving a tax deduction to offset this payment and stock bonus). Under certain circumstances, a transfer of stock by a controlling shareholder to an employee might be viewed as an indirect stock issuance by the Company which is subject to these compensation rules.

Explaining Your Stock Transfer Proposal To Key Employee Group Members

Obviously the terms and conditions of a stock transfer or stock bonus to your key employees requires a series of discussions, explanations, and feedback. One of the expected primary concerns from the key employee group members will relate to their ability to pay for the stock which they are becoming obligated to purchase. It is important to have a demonstration of the Company's cash flow and dividend payout expectations, which will typically be the primary means of funding their purchase. It is also important to consider designing some flexibility into the promissory note to help alleviate the risk to the key employee group of a default should the Company face a downturn and be unable to pay the full dividends on time as expected.

Why Family Business Pioneers Are Doing This

It is a fair question as to why an owner should be interested in bonusing stock to key employees or selling stock to key employees which will simply be funded by Company dividends to be paid on that stock. Wouldn't the owner be better off to simply retain the stock and therefore retain full ownership of the dividend proceeds.

For some business owners, this might be the better scenario. This really depends on a couple of factors. First, can you attract and retain the type of key employees which you need to profitably continue to grow and maintain the Company without providing stock ownership to those key employees. If they in fact are good, they will want to be owners, and if you can't provide it, you should expect they will look elsewhere. In addition to the objective of having strong leadership to help you grow the Company, if your eventual exit is a sale to a third party, the ability to sell, as well as the ability to sell at a full fair price, will depend on the strength of your leadership team in your absence. While this may vary depending on whether the outside buyer is a strategic buyer or a financial buyer, as a general principle, the value of your Company will be worth more to the extent that it can operate successfully without you.

Second, if you anticipate that the balance of your stock will upon your exit be transferred to your key employees, this will be facilitated if they have already achieved a certain level of minority shareholder status. You might decide to provide seller financing for the sale of the balance of your stock.

However, if one of your objectives is to not retain that risk, by hoping that a bank will provide financing for the balance, then this is more likely to happen if your key employee group already has a significant minority ownership interest and a proven track record as representing key owners.

Addressing The Second Phase Of Your Exit – Keeping Your Options Open

We have discussed so far the concept of transferring a significant minority interest in the stock ownership of your Company to your key employees over a period of time. This type of incremental stock sale approach tends to have less overall risk and tends to help achieve overall objectives better than simply expecting to be able to sell 100% of your stock to a key employee group upon your exit.

However, this phase one sale of a significant minority interest of your stock to your key employee group should not be viewed as limiting your flexibility for your final exit. Overall, the objective is that phase one has enhanced your feasible alternatives for your final exit. In phase one, you will have transferred a non-controlling portion of your stock to your key employee group. Once that phase is completed, you have a choice of at least eight possible approaches for addressing your exit. These include the following:

- **Keep your remaining stock until death.** You might decide to keep the balance of your stock until your death and then pass on the stock to your family. This would enable you to continue to receive distributions on the stock until your death and for your family to continue to receive distributions after your death. Your family could decide down the road the final exit for the family from the Company.

- **Sell the balance of your stock to your key employee group in installments.** Under this alternative, you could sell the balance of your stock to your key employee group over time. This could be at a preset price or it could be at a price which fluctuates with the value as the Company goes forward.

- **Sell to new key employee group members.** You could use some or all of the balance of your stock to provide additional incentive for attracting and retaining additional key employee group members to your Company or to recognize other employees who have risen within the ranks of your Company to this status.

- **You could sell the balance of your stock to an Employee Stock Ownership Plan (ESOP).** This type of sale can have certain company performance benefits as well as tax favored advantages.

- **Sell to key employee group at your retirement for cash.** Under this alternative, the balance of your stock would be sold in one transaction upon your retirement to your key employee group. Anticipating that they would not have the cash to fund this, the expectation would be that your prior implementation of phase one has now put them in a position to secure bank financing which would be used to cash out your stock.

- **Sell to key employee group at your retirement for a package.** Under this alternative, you would sell the balance of your stock at one time upon your retirement in exchange for a promissory note equal to the low end of the range of your stock's value. In order to receive the full financial benefit of your stock ownership and your years of service which may have been under-compensated, this package could also include a deferred compensation or salary continuation agreement.   This approach provides a tax advantage to the key employee group buyers, because the Company can deduct the deferred compensation and salary continuation payments.   That portion of the payments would be subject to ordinary income taxation to you, which can, however, be minimized by a longer compensation payment and if this is spread over time and into potentially lower tax brackets.   This needs close review with your CPA

- **Sell to an outside third party.** You might decide that your best option at the time of your final exit is to sell the Company to an outside third party.   Your Buy-Sell Agreement should include provisions which anticipate this in two aspects. First, the Buy-Sell Agreement should include a "drag along" provision by which you can require your key employee group minority shareholders to sell their stock as part of this overall sale to the third party who likely will expect to be able to purchase 100% of the stock. It is possible that the third party might decide to leave the key employee group members as minority shareholders which can be negotiated at the time. Second, in order to receive the full incentive impact intended initially by your stock transfer to key employee group members, your Buy-Sell Agreement should also include, typically, a provision known as a "bring along" or "tag along" provision. Under this, your key employee shareholders would have the right, should they so elect, to require that you include them in the sale to a third party. The combination of these provisions provide you with the control to cause a 100% sale of the stock to happen while at the same time provide the key employees with the incentive to help grow the Company to reap the benefits of a potential favorable sale to an outside third party.

- **Repurchase the stock from the key employee group.** You might decide upon your exit to move into a different direction than that originally anticipated during phase one. If that is the case, you want to have the ability to re-purchase the stock from the key employee group members or from a selected number of key employee group members. Again, to achieve the incentive elements intended by this stock transfer in the first place, this re-purchase should be based on some formula or method for determining that selling price so that the key employees have been able to share in the potential upside while they were owners.

Is Your Plan Bankable?

It's extremely important to be working today with a bank that understands Fourth Quarter Planning and which will pro-actively work with you to help develop a Fourth Quarter Game Plan that fits you, your Company and your bank. As you develop a Fourth Quarter Game Plan, you want to structure it in a manner where a bank is willing to step in to provide the financing for the buyer's purchase when you exit from your ownership.

Planning For A Tax Efficient Transfer To Family

Whether or not you plan to transfer your Company to an outside buyer, to your key employees, or to your family, you should consider the use of certain tax-advantaged ways to transfer all or part of your Company to family members during your lifetime or upon your death (each closely coordinated with your CPA). These are summarized below.

Company Transfer Alternatives To Family At Your Death

The following alternative should be considered and determined for transferring all or a portion of your Company to family members at your death.

- **Spouse Inheritance**. Transfer of the Company to your spouse on your death through the provisions of your Estate Plan, specifically your Living Trust. The key tax planning action is to be sure you have a Will or Living Trust which provides you with optimal Estate Tax marital deduction.

- **Child Inheritance**. Transfer of the balance of your ownership in the Company to your children upon your death or upon the last to die of you and your spouse. The key tax planning action is to reduce your direct ownership of your Company to less than 50% before your death, so your Estate can claim a minority discount off of the taxable value (to the extent this discount remains feasible under IRS rules).

- **Grandchild Inheritance**. Transfer of the balance of your ownership in the Company to your grandchildren upon your death or upon the last to die of you and your spouse. The key tax planning action again is to reduce your direct ownership of your Company to less than 50% before your death, so your Estate can claim a potential minority discount off of the taxable value. In addition, use of your Generation Skipping tax exemption can help reduce overall family death transfer taxes.

Company Transfer Alternatives To Family During Your Lifetime

The following alternatives can be considered and determined for transferring all or a portion of your Company to family members during your lifetime.

- **Annual Gifting Program.** Transfer of part ownership in your Company to your children, grandchildren, and/or children's spouses up to your annual Federal Gift Tax Exemption amount ($15,000 per recipient as of 2018). This can save about $6,000 per gift in future Estate Taxes as well as saving the tax on future appreciation.

- **Lifetime Exemption Gifting.** Transfer of shares in your Company to your children, grandchildren, and/or children's spouses up to your Total Lifetime Gift Tax Exemption amount of $11,200,000 (as of 2018) for you (and $11,200,000 for your spouse). This enables you to save future Estate Tax on the value appreciation of the gifted assets.

- **Fair Market Value Cash Sale.** Transfer of your Company to designated family members at full fair market value for cash. If your Company value will grow faster than the invested cash, then the excess will escape future Estate Tax. If you don't want to receive the maximum price, you can sell it for the "lowest defensible value", using the low end of the value factors along with reasonably high end potential marketability and minority discounts (depending on ownership structure).

- **Installment Sale.** Transfer of your Company to designated family members at a price equal to full fair market value or lowest defensible value with payments to be made over time pursuant to an installment promissory note. This enables you to help fund the purchase by your family, while moving excess appreciation Estate Tax free to the next generation.

- **Part Sale/Part Gift**. Sell to family members at less than the lowest defensible value and report the sale as part sale and part gift.

- **Stock Redemption**. Redemption of your stock by the Company at full fair market value for cash. This could apply when you intend to completely terminate your stock ownership and to fully retire from all positions with the Company. It would apply when family members already own the balance of the shares of the Company. Care must be taken to achieve capital gain rather than dividend treatment.

- **Grantor Retained Annuity Trust**. Your shares of the Company could be transferred to an Irrevocable Trust which in turn provides you with an annuity for a specified number of years. After the term elapses, the Company ownership would pass to the Trust beneficiaries, typically designated family members. This is similar to a part sale/part gift. The annuity payable would typically be stated in terms of a fixed dollar amount. The excess of Company growth over the GRAT interest rate would pass free of Estate Tax.

- **Grantor Retained Unitrust**. Similar to a GRAT, however, the annuity payments are a fixed percentage of the fair market value of the trust, re-determined annually. This enables the excess of Company growth over the GRUT interest rate to pass free of Estate Tax.

- **The Grantor Trust**. This is a sale of your Company to a Grantor Trust (sometimes technically called an "intentionally defective grantor trust") in return for a promissory note, with the intended result that the Company is not included in your estate, while the sale is disregarded for income tax purposes. Due to a lower required interest rate, this tax planning technique can enable a larger portion of future Company growth to pass to your family free of Estate Tax.

- **Charitable Trust**. This involves the transfer of your Company's shares to a charitable trust which is either a form of charitable remainder trust (in which the charity receives the Company after a period of years) or a charitable lead trust (where the charity receives the Company for a number of years, after which the Company is transferred to family members). These tax planning techniques can generate both Income Tax and Estate Tax savings.

- **Spin-Off Real Estate**. The real estate used in your Company can be spun off to you (e.g. by sale or dividend) and leased back to your Company (and separately retained by you and later sold or gifted to family).

- **Spin-Off Intellectual Property**. Certain intellectual property used in your Company can be spun off to you (e.g. by sale or dividend) and licensed back to your Company.

Various business, financial, family and tax considerations (such as impact on tax basis step up) apply to each of these alternatives which we want to carefully consider with your CPA and other Trusted Advisors before final decisions are made and before any of these techniques are actually implemented.

The Inside Route Exit Plan

The Inside Route Exit Plan should be designed early in your Fourth Quarter Planning to provide you with either a known primary or backup exit plan for your and your family's ownership in the business.

> ## *Pioneer Mindset*
> ☑ *Victory.* *Know when to declare victory and move on.*

Chapter

36

Outside Route Exit Option Ready

Incredible Result: "If the best interests of my Family and our Team are served by bringing in an outside owner for our Company, we know we'll be successful doing this."

Avoidable Train Wreck: No effective outside route exit.

Main Play: The Outside Route Exit Plan

What This Is: Due to your known Business Model's unique design, your Company culture, your leadership team, your proven performance, your realistic future outlook and a professional M&A market test, a financial or strategic outside buyer would pay top dollar for your Company right now on terms you'd agree to.

Just as Family Business Pioneers are looking at their inside route exit options early on, they are also looking into their outside route exit options early on and making decisions accordingly.

This part of the Fourth Quarter Planning process is intended to answer some fundamental questions:

- Is there or will there be a market for the sale of your business to an outside third party?

- How do you plan ahead for and pursue a sale to an outside third party?

- What kind of price and terms can you expect or require?

The answers to these questions early on can help direct your business decisions throughout your time as an owner.

The results of this review will help you decide whether you should plan for a sale of your business to an outside third party as your primary or fallback plan.

Understanding Potential Outside Exit Routes

There are four principal directions to exit ownership of your business through a transfer to an outside third party (which were discussed briefly in the preceding chapter). These consist of:

- Sale to third party financial buyer (financial or strategic).

- Sale to the public market.

- Sale to a business liquidation buyer.

- A partial sale, to a strategic, financial buyer or the public, or through a joint venture or franchise.

We've found that most business owners have some idea about who might be a potential outside purchaser of their business. Rarely, however, does a business owner have a good assessment of the full potential market. That's because unless you are actively studying this market on a frequent basis, you simply don't know its reach. This is why we include in the Fourth Quarter Planning process the option to pursue an Outside Route Assessment with the help of an M&A advisory firm.

One of the primary reasons business owners have reported dissatisfaction with their exit is that they didn't understand their alternatives. Until you know the actual market outlook for your business, it's difficult to select the best exit route for you and your family. You may prefer to transfer the business to a key employee group and you may feel so strongly about this that an outside sale simply isn't an option for you.

However, we've found that business owners normally want to know what they are leaving on the table by excluding one or more options. With an Outside Route Assessment we can look at your value strengths and detractors and be better able to recommend specific value and marketability enhancements. This can detail the best routes to pursue to target the best potential type of outside buyer. And it will detail an expected sales price range based on specific sale transactions for similar companies in your industry.

Private Equity Groups As An Exit Strategy

Due to the existence of several thousand Private Equity Groups ("PEG") which possess several billion dollars of funding for the purpose of purchasing companies, the potential often exists for a sale to a PEG. Not all companies are attractive to the PEG community. Generally, PEGs find the following characteristics to be appealing.

- Predictable, steady revenue stream. This is preferably generally insulated from market cyclicality.

- Profitability in excess of industry norms. This includes profit margin and other financial ratios.

- A significant level of Earnings Before Interest, Taxes, Depreciation and Amortization ("EBITDA"). A minimum EBITDA of $2 to $5 million or higher is generally needed to attract meaningful attention from PEGs, though many will consider a lower level.

- Strong growth potential. This should be evidenced by a track record of profitable growth and/or an ability to grow with an infusion of outside capital.

- Unique products, services, technical skills and customer bases. PEGs prefer companies with defensible niches with high barriers to entry.

- Strong leadership team with a deep bench. PEGs do not want to manage routine operations. They want a seasoned and committed leadership team which can assist them in growing the business.

Being Prepared With The Right Attitude

The eventual exit from active duty and ownership will typically be a major event in the life of a business owner, after which some will transition well and some not so well. Some owners will take a sneak-preview of life after business by taking an extended vacation before reaching the decision to sell, to, in essence, experience a taste of retirement to see how well it suits you.

Once you decide its time to sell and begin the actual sale process, it's best to be both prepared to leave and prepared to not leave – that is, be prepared to stay on if the transaction can't be completed. Unless you maintain the ability to walk away from any deal, you will lose negotiating leverage.

The sale of a business can be a very trying time for a business owner. The transaction intermediaries will tell you that unless a deal has been in the ditch at least a half dozen times, it's not a real deal. Have your S.W.A.T team (Business Continuity Attorney, transaction intermediary or business broker, and M & A attorney) assembled well in advance to help pull the deal out of the ditch and keep it on track. But be prepared to walk away from any deal that you find will not meet your objectives.

The Competition For Quality Buyers

Various organizations have projected a substantial, baby boom driven increase in the number of businesses being offered for sale in the next several years. This increase in competition for quality buyers raises the need to develop a Fourth Quarter Game Plan with an understanding of the business sale process.

Are You Ready To Let Go?

Understanding the business sale process isn't limited to just learning the technical aspects. It's important to first address your planned readiness to sell. Entrepreneur Jimmy Calano and author of "Make Your Move" provides a good insight into the mental steps an owner should walk through when approaching the sale of your Company. He was co-founder and former CEO of CareerTrack, an international training company. This was an organization he helped grow to 700 employees and $82 million in revenue, conducting business in 24 countries. After heading the Company for 13 years, he sold it to a multinational company.

His advice as you contemplate the sale of your Company is to first take some time to decide if you are ready, willing and able to let go. He suggests that you do this by first listing out: your reasons for selling, your fears about selling, what could go wrong, your deal team, how you will mentally prepare yourself, the things that you won't miss, your "Dream List" of what you'll do with your days after you've sold, the positive habits and routines you promise to develop, and the goals you plan to achieve after the sale.

You Can't Win If You Don't Know The Playing Field

Just as it's difficult to be successful in running a business without understanding the playing field, it is difficult to be successful in selling your business if you don't understand the field of play.   One of the objectives of the Fourth Quarter Planning process is to provide the business owner with enough understanding of the business sale process to be able to prepare appropriately and to engage the right expertise at the right time to help accomplish a profitable exit through the sale of your business.

Many business owners fail to build the optimal position for profitably selling their business.   Often this results in leaving large amounts on the table.   This can arise because of any number of reasons, including the failure to properly design or place your business into a position to be ready for sale, as well as a failure to properly approach the buyer's marketplace.

Pioneer Mindset

☑ *Negotiate Everything.*   *Understand the power of framing, the power of anticipation and the power of perspective. And always create and keep the option to walk out.*

Understand The Business Sale Process

The business sale process typically consists of four principal stages, including:

- Pre-Sale Planning.
- Marketing The Business.
- Negotiating The Sale.
- Completing And Closing The Transaction.

Pre-Sale Planning

The Fourth Quarter Game Plan is designed to help accomplish your pre-sale planning (whether for a sale to an outsider or to an insider). It will help in making sure you have properly structured your business organization.   It will also help you focus on growing the value of your business, protecting it through the date of your sale, as well as putting you in a position to be able to sell your Company.   Pre-sale planning will help increase your odds of completing a sale.

In planning the sale of your Company, it's important to keep in mind the factors which determine what a buyer is willing to pay. These include (i) the return on investment the buyer expects on the purchase of your business (vs. other investments), (ii) the buyer's expectation of your business' future performance (e.g. predictable, growing future cash flow, management capabilities, proprietary technology and products), (iii) the buyer's own objectives and needs, and (iv) the then-present economic factors affecting the M&A market (e.g. interest rates, capital availability, industry economic cycle).

Marketing The Business

Fourth Quarter Planning involves a review of your potential Exit Routes. This includes a review of your potential third-party buyers, whether financial or strategic. Depending on the industry within which you operate, you may well possess the best working knowledge of the potential financial and strategic buyers for your type of business. We typically work with our business owner clients to engage an investment banker, a transaction intermediary or business broker (depending on the size and nature of your Company) to assist in marketing the business: a business broker (for smaller companies), or a transaction intermediary or investment banker (for middle-market or larger companies). A business broker, transaction intermediary or investment banker may also be known as an "M&A Advisor", or "M&A Broker" or "Deal Maker".

In each instance, we will work together to first do a Marketability Assessment and then to help develop a buyer profile as well as a company information or offering memorandum, which will describe the salient features of your business. This may be known by other names, such as a business description report.

In addition, the investment banker, transaction intermediary or business broker will work with us to prepare some form of a "teaser sheet", which is a document which contains enough information to test a buyer's interest. Once the banker, intermediary or broker has developed a list of potential buyers, the "teaser sheet" can be distributed to potential buyers to determine an indication of interest. This teaser sheet will typically not contain enough information to identify the specific seller.

Once an indication of interest is received from one or more potential buyers, a Confidentiality Agreement will be executed on behalf of the seller, assuming that the buyer is of interest to the seller. At this point, the business description report can be provided for a detail review of interest by the potential buyers.

Depending on the circumstances (such as the size of the company), some form of "auction" will typically be developed. A transaction intermediary or investment banker will generally engage in what is in effect a limited auction in order to involve multiple potential buyers during the same time process.

A business broker, transaction intermediary or investment banker will typically negotiate a retainer for its fee to engage in this process, coupled with a "success fee" if and when the sale is concluded. Often the success fee will be set at a fixed percentage of a given expected value and a somewhat different percentage as to that portion of the selling price achieved in excess of that. This aligns the interests of transaction intermediary with the seller.

A seller engaging an investment banker, transaction intermediary or business broker to sell his or her business should anticipate giving an exclusive term for a period of time, followed by a cancellation option by either party. Normally you should expect a tail period for a certain period of time after termination of the agreement in the event a sale transaction is actually consummated with a buyer which the banker, intermediary or broker brought to the table.

Strategic Value

It's critical during this process to understand and identify the unique value your business can bring to a buyer beyond just the obvious profitable cash flow to every buyer. What are the potential strategic and synergistic values (yes, there's a difference) your business can bring to the strategic buyer? For those who have deployed the Profit Playbook, you will have already identified and benefited from these aspects of your business.

Negotiating The Sale

The bidding process ends when the seller has selected one of the buyers with whom to complete the transaction. Typically, the parties will then enter into a "Letter of Intent" which will include the key terms of the transaction. This will detail the proposed purchase price, the particular business being sold, the method of payment, a proposed closing date, the expected contingencies to closing (such as completion of financing and the due diligence process), and such other factors as the parties determine. The Letter of Intent can also include provisions which provide for a period of time (known as a standstill) during which the seller cannot market the business to another buyer. The Letter of Intent can also contain further details regarding confidentiality requirements and press release requirements. The Letter of Intent creates the framework for an agreement, but it is not intended to be a legally binding document (other than with respect to certain terms, such as the standstill and confidentiality terms).

Following the execution of a Letter of Intent, the buyer will, with the cooperation of the seller, typically engage in a very comprehensive investigation of the business, known as the due diligence process. The transaction intermediary, investment banker or business broker, as well as M&A legal counsel for both the buyer and the seller, are typically involved in the Letter of Intent preparation as well as management and review of the due diligence process.

Following this, assuming that the parties are both in agreement on proceeding, then a definitive "Purchase and Sale Agreement" will be prepared by M&A legal counsel and further negotiated by legal counsel, the buyer, the seller and the investment banker, transaction intermediary or business broker. The initial draft of the definitive Purchase and Sale Agreement is often prepared by the buyer's legal counsel. It will contain the terms of the deal, along with various representations and warranties to be made by both parties, as well as certain covenants regarding actions to be taken or not taken between the date of the agreement and the closing of the transaction. During this process, the buyer and its advisors will also be negotiating its own financing for the transaction as well.

Completing And Closing The Transaction

Following execution of a definitive Purchase and Sale Agreement, the buyer will typically engage in additional due diligence to confirm that the representations made in the agreement have been complied with. In order to complete and close the transaction, a number of additional documents will be prepared by M&A legal counsel in order to actually carry out and implement the completion of the sale.

The overall timing for this process can vary greatly from transaction to transaction. Overall, the time period involved from first engaging the investment banker, transaction intermediary or business broker to closing of the transaction could be expected to take from six months to over a year, depending on the size and complexity of the transaction and the market conditions.

The process of selling a business can typically be very complex and can also involve a lot of time by the seller and the Company's key employment staff. It's important to involve professionals who have demonstrated experience in the process, both as to the business marketing capabilities of the investment banker, transaction intermediary or business broker as well as the merger and acquisition experience of the M&A legal counsel.

Plan For An Outside Route Exit

Once you've decided that your primary or backup exit route includes the future sale of your business to an outside third party, it's important to start to consider the terms under which you will be willing to sell by developing an Outside Route Exit Plan. Such a plan would address:

- **Who will you sell to?** Do you have specific buyers you do or don't want to consider?

- **What is sold?** What are you selling and what are you keeping?

- **What is received?** What overall financial package are you willing to receive to accommodate your needs and the buyer's objectives?

Tax Efficient Terms

Many third party outside buyers will prefer to purchase the assets of your business rather than to buy your stock. There are a couple reasons for this. First, it helps them to avoid the risk that they are "inheriting" potential, unknown liabilities that were not reflected on your balance sheet. Second, it helps them to obtain a depreciable tax basis in your assets equal to the price they paid (rather than your typically lower depreciated tax basis).

The tax impact of this asset purchase preference on you is as follows. If your corporation is a "C" corporation or an "S" corporation that converted to "S" status within 5 years of the sale, then when it sells its assets, it owes a tax on the gain (or on the "built-in gain" portion of such a converted "S" corporation). Then, when your corporation distributes the sale proceeds to you, you owe a tax on your gain. So, you've effectively been taxed twice on the sale.

This double tax can be reduced to a single tax if your business is held in an "S" corporation or in a limited liability company. To move from being a "C" corporation to a limited liability company typically produces a tax on the conversion. However, you can become an "S" corporation simply by filing an election with the IRS. The decision to become an "S" corporation involves at least a dozen factors, which are reviewed (together with your CPA) in the Fourth Quarter Planning process to help determine if you should make the election.

If you've been a "C" corporation, then to fully realize the "S" election benefit on your sale, you need to make the election at least 5 years before your sale.

Following the enactment of the Tax Cuts and Jobs Act of 2017, the question of whether to be a "C" or "S" corporation has become more difficult. This is due to the interaction of the lower (21% top) "C" income tax rate, the new 20% "S" corporation deduction (IRC Section 199A), and the elimination of the corporate alternative minimum tax, which have given new life to the capital gain exclusion on the sale of "qualified small business stock" (IRC Section 1202), specifically for the sale of stock acquired after September 27, 2010.

Obtaining A Higher Stock Tax Basis

Another benefit of the "S" election is that your tax basis in your stock can increase annually, resulting in a lower taxable gain if you (a) sell your stock instead of your assets or (b) sell your assets and distribute the proceeds to yourself in liquidation of the corporation. This is because your stock basis in an "S" corporation increases annually by the excess of the Company's income over the amount of dividend distributions.

Tax Efficient Sale To Outsider - Exit Structure Alternatives

Business owners and buyers have a number of alternatives for structuring the transfer of a business. The choice of structure depends on a number of factors, including the parties' objectives and relative negotiating leverage, the seller's present corporate structure and tax attributes, and the nature of the buyer. Some alternatives for you as the business owner (shareholder) include the following:

- **Double Taxed Asset Sale**. The buyer purchases the assets of your "C" corporation (which distributes the sale proceeds to you). Both your corporation and you as a shareholder are taxed on the gain.

- **Almost Double Taxed Asset Sale**. The buyer purchases the assets of your "S" corporation which within 5 years of sale was a "C" corporation. Your "S" corporation will be taxed on the "built in gain" that existed at the time of the "S" election and you as the shareholder will be taxed when the (after tax) sale proceeds are distributed.

- **Single Taxed Asset Sale.** The buyer purchases the assets of your "S" corporation which has either been an "S" corporation since its inception or for at least 5 years. You as the shareholder are taxed once on the gain.

- **Single Taxed Stock Sale.** The buyer purchases the stock of your "C" corporation. You are taxed on the gain, but the buyer doesn't receive a tax basis step-up in the Company assets (unless buyer makes what is called a "338 election" to treat the transaction as a taxable asset sale, resulting in taxable gain and basis step-up).

- **Partly Taxed Stock Sale.** The buyer purchases the stock of your "S" corporation. You are taxed on the gain, but the taxable gain may be significantly less depending on how long you've been an "S" corporation, since time builds tax-reducing basis in your stock.

- **Tax Deferred Reorganization.** The buyer purchases the stock or assets of your corporation in exchange for stock of the buyer's corporation in a transaction that qualifies as tax free under the Internal Revenue Code. Tax on your gain is deferred until you sell the buyer's stock.

- **Tax Deferred Installment Sale.** The buyer purchases your stock or the assets of your corporation in exchange for an installment promissory note payable to you over time. This can defer some or all of the tax on the transaction until payments are received.

- **Tax Deferred ESOP Sale.** You sell some or all of your stock to an Employee Stock Ownership Plan. This can defer the tax on that stock sold to the ESOP, if you invest the proceeds in qualified securities.

- **Partial Equity Rollover.** Here you will retain partial equity in your business by receiving a portion of the ownership (e.g. 20%) in the entity which is set up to be the buyer. To avoid capital gain taxation on the retained equity, an LLC "drop-down" or an S corporation "inversion" transaction may be utilized.

Summary

These exit structure alternatives illustrate only some of the options available for structuring a sale to an outsider. Other more detailed alternatives, as well as tax efficient choices within each alternative, also exist, which can be addressed in the Fourth Quarter Planning process.   Each proposed sale of a business provides its own set of business, financial and tax planning opportunities.

Understand The Potential Sale Models

As you consider what you want to achieve, you need to begin to consider the various potential selling models which exist for selling your Company. Several different models exist for selling your Company in an inside sale (e.g. to your key employees, family, partners or ESOP) as well as in an outside sale (e.g. to an investor, private equity group, competitor, supplier, customer or industry roll up). These can best be considered by addressing the principal components of the transaction.

Transaction Structure

The principal choices to overall structure include:

- **Asset Sale**. Sale of the Company assets to a new entity set up by the buyer(s).

- **Stock Sale**. Sale of the stock you own in the Company to the buyer(s).

- **Joint Venture**. Transfer of all or part of the Company assets to a newly formed limited liability company or corporation which you (or your Company) will own along with the buyer(s).

- **Equity Rollover**. This enables you to keep a portion of your ownership equity invested in the buyer's company. This may be some form of full tax deferred merger or a partial equity rollover.

- **Franchise**. Franchise your business and sell franchise's to selected qualified buyers.

Pricing

The principal choices to the pricing for the sale of your Company include:

- **Fixed Price**. The price here is determined and fixed under the terms of your sale agreement.

- **Contingent Or Earn Out**. The price here would be adjusted based on the Company's performance after the sale. This could be dependent, for example, on the Company's future revenue, EBITDA (earnings before interest, taxes, depreciation and amortization), net cash flow, net earnings, or key customer retention. Certain collars could be used to set a floor and ceiling on the price adjustments.

- **Combination**. Some combination of fixed price and contingent price.

Valuation

The valuation of the Company on which the price will be based depends on the parties' negotiations and could include the following factors:

- **Appraisal**. An appraisal can be obtained by one or both parties.

- **EBITDA Multiple**. The parties may determine pricing based on a multiple (e.g. 4 to 10) of past (e.g. 1 to 3 year weighted or simple average) or projected earnings.

- **Earnings Multiple**. The parties may determine pricing based on a multiple of past or projected net earnings.

- **Discounted Future Cash Flow**. The parties may determine pricing based on the present, discounted value of future expected cash flows.

- **Sales Multiple**. The parties may determine pricing as a multiple of past or projected revenue.

- **Book Value**. This is appropriate for certain industries.

Payment

The principal alternatives for payment of the purchase price include the following:

- **Cash**. You may require full cash paid at the time of closing of the sale.

- **Installment Note**. You may be willing to accept an installment note from the buyer for the price (typically secured by the assets of the Company or the purchased stock as collateral).

- **Equity**. You may accept equity in the buyer as payment.

- **Combination**. You may agree to the receipt of a combination of cash, a promissory note and equity.

Other Agreed Payments

You may decide to accept some part of your overall payments in other items of compensation such as:

- **No Compete**. You might decide to be paid to agree not to compete in the future.

- **Consulting**. You might agree to an ongoing fee to consult with the buyer about the business.

- **Employment**. You might agree to continue to be employed after the sale for some period of time for an agreed compensation package.

- **Lease**. If you presently own or decide in the transaction to retain real estate or equipment that has been used in the business, you can agree to lease this to the buyer.

- **Intellectual Property**. If you presently own or decide in the transaction to retain intellectual property that has been used in the business, you can agree to license this to the buyer.

Portion of Stock Transferred

You may choose in a stock transfer from the following as to the amount of stock sold:

- **100% Transfer**. The sale of 100% of your stock now to fully exit ownership.

- **Less than 100%**. The sale of less than 100% of your stock to enable you to remain a part owner with the objective of continuing to achieve equity growth with the possible sale of the balance in the future.

- **Multiple Phase Transfer**. Particularly in the sale of your stock to your key employees, family or ESOP, you may choose to sell or transfer just some of your stock now, with the balance over several steps (and in each case leaving you the option to change course in the future as to the sale of the balance of your stock).

Leadership Retention Incentive

In order to properly compensate your key employees, as well as to incent them to remain with the Company upon a sale, you will want to consider providing one or more of the following (preferably well in advance of the sale):

- **Stock Bonus.** Bonusing key leaders shares of stock in the Company.

- **Stock Purchase.** Allowing key leaders to purchase shares in the Company at a full or bargain element price.

- **Stock Option.** Granting key leaders stock options in the Company.

- **Phantom Stock.** Providing key leaders what is known as "synthetic" equity in the form of phantom stock.

- **Stock Appreciation Right.** Providing key leaders "synthetic" equity in the form of a stock appreciation right (with the proper balance between Retention SARs and Performance SARs).

- **Deferred Compensation.** Providing key leaders with a deferred compensation plan (unfunded or funded, e.g. with one of several insurance products).

- **Stay Bonus.** Providing key leaders with a cash Stay Bonus for agreeing to remain with the Company for a certain period after the sale (paid by the seller or buyer).

- **Employment Commitment.** Providing key leaders with an employment agreement and/or position commitment for a certain period of time.

The Outside Route Exit Plan

The Outside Route Exit Plan enables the business owner to see the reality of achieving, and put into place the stages to achieve, a company sale which can meet your objectives.

Pioneer Mindset

☑ *Careful Out There. Know how to pick your spots. Don't sow harmful discord or start any unnecessary fights.*

Your "Fourth Quarter" Game Plan™

Putting It All Together

Chapter
37

The "Fourth Quarter" Game Plan™

Just as a profitable business bases its success on using an established process, so does the Fourth Quarter Planning approach which I have been deploying with Family Business Pioneers for over 3 decades.

Designing Your "Fourth Quarter" Game Plan™

The Fourth Quarter Game Plan is a roadmap intended to help a Business Pioneer to successfully chart a course to win in all Four Quarters.   This Plan addresses business, personal, financial, legal, contingency and tax matters which typically impact business owners. It is a proactive plan. It also addresses contingencies for early death, disability, divorce or future burnout. The objective is to maximize your net value, minimize taxes, maintain your control of the process and help assure your personal and financial objectives are met.

The Fourth Quarter Game Plan also provides a thoughtful plan that will help you accomplish your mission to eventually successfully exit (and pass on) your privately held Company on your timetable and your terms. The plan needs to address key questions which you (and your advisors) must address before and when you exit your business.

Hitting The Mark

Over the years, we have seen business owners who have implemented perfectly sound advice from their trusted advisors. This may include acting on certain tax advice from his or her CPA one year, executing a Buy-Sell Agreement prepared by his or her corporate attorney in another year, purchasing some type of life insurance policy at yet another time, perhaps having discussions with a business broker or investment banker at some other time, all after the execution of an Estate Plan several years prior to all of this through their estate planning attorney.

We find that each of these trusted advisors have normally provided great advice for accomplishing the objectives that existed at the time. However, objectives change. Situations change. Internal and external factors change. Most of the work I've done as a Business Continuity Attorney has come from those same trusted advisors who know that it's time to develop a new coordinated plan which takes on the new needs and objectives of their long time loyal clients.

> ## *Pioneer Mindset*
>
> ☑ *See It.* Have the passion and purpose to imagine and inspire a better, different future.

A Coordinated Process Is Needed

The purpose of the Fourth Quarter Game Plan is to provide a coordinated process and coordinated power tools to work in concert with a business owner and his or her trusted advisors to accomplish a successful, future Fourth Quarter.

Most business owners have become accustomed to seeing such a coordinated effort in other areas, such as computer system development, product research and development, marketing campaigns, building construction, and business site selection processes. No less level of professional collaboration is needed to plan for a successful business owner Fourth Quarter.

> ## *Pioneer Mindset*
>
> ☑ *Avoiding Train Wrecks.* Achieve "Results by Design". Not "Train Wrecks by Default".

Addressing The 4 Playbooks

The Fourth Quarter Game Plan addresses the 4 Playbooks detailed in this book that need to be addressed to help assure the successful future that you are looking for, whether this arises on account of your carefully laid out timetable or whether this occurs because of an unexpected mishap (death, disability, divorce, dispute or business down grade) or an unexpected opportunity (such as an early opportunity to sell).

Each of these 4 Playbooks contain a number of key business continuity, succession and transition strategies.

All Plans Are Firm Until Changed

In our firm, we operate on a simple principle that "All plans are firm … until changed." In the context of Fourth Quarter Planning, this means that while a Fourth Quarter Game Plan has been prepared, the plan needs to be adjusted and adapted as your objectives, and the facts which impact your objectives, change into the future.

Without a plan at all -- or with an insufficient plan -- there is no real basis for implementing the tools and steps which can help with a successful future. However, the intention is never to let the existence of the plan stifle the need to be flexible and adaptable going forward.

Fourth Quarter Game Plan Implementation

Once a Plan has been developed, it needs to be implemented. A great Fourth Quarter Game Plan is similar to architecting a building. The plans should include not only the design of what the building is going to look like, but also the specifics of who is going to do what in the timeline for accomplishing this.

Our Fourth Quarter System for business owners has been specifically designed to work with you and your other trusted advisors to accomplish all of your Four Quarters successfully.

Pioneer Mindset

☑ *Firm But Flexible. All plans are firm . . . until changed.*

Chapter
38

Achieving The Legacy You Had In Mind

As Stephen Covey has reminded us, we should "Begin with the end in mind." In the Fourth Quarter Planning context, we need to begin with an understanding of what you want to achieve and the legacy you want to leave. How do you want to be remembered by your family, your business and your community? What do you want to be able to look back upon as a particular accomplishment you achieved or as a particular good you provided for someone else?

Visualizing The Legacy You Want To Achieve

Whether you are just beginning or have been a long-time owner of your business, then the day-to-day operation of your business has been or will become a large part of your way of life. Like many Business Pioneers, you are probably largely known or identified with the business that you are building or have built and the success you have achieved in doing so.

In a very real sense, your business is or will become like a child to you. You will or you have nourished it and toiled through a lot of blood, sweat and tears with regard to it. You will or have seen it through the bad times and you've rejoiced during the good times. Although you've probably had more than your share of days when you've wanted to just walk out, lock up the doors and never return, for the most part, leaving (or thinking about leaving) your business can just be plain hard to want to do.

Your "Fourth Quarter" Is Not The End – It's Just The Beginning

Many business owners would probably be content to work until their dying day and be carried out boots up. It becomes necessary to consider whether that's the best result, whether for you, your spouse, your children, your key employees and the other constituencies affected by what you do through your eventual exit or non-exit from your business.

My Father, Ferd Niemann, was a good example of someone who loved his business and loved his family. I've mentioned some of his story earlier. He and my uncle owned and successfully exited from a number of businesses throughout their careers. This included the restaurant business, real estate development, retail merchandising, retail gasoline, horse ranching and poultry. However, their mainstay business was the supermarket business. This business began in 1917 as one corner grocery store owned by my grandfather and his brother. Over the years they added several corner grocery stores, before consolidating these into a couple of supermarkets in the 1940's. By the time of my grandfather's death in 1969, he was partners with my dad and my uncle. The Company owned and operated six supermarkets.

My dad and uncle spent the next quarter century after my grandfather's death continuing to grow and expand the supermarket operations. Retail, especially supermarket retail, involves a lot of work, long hours and very slim margins. It's a business which my Father loved, especially on account of the love and respect which he always held for his father and a clear mission in life to be able to hand the family business down to his children as his father had handed it down to him. However, while we all worked in the grocery business growing up, neither myself nor my other six brothers and sisters felt the supermarket business was our calling.

My Dad had always felt that he would never retire from the business he loved. However, as he approached age 65, he began to consider how this would impact his other passions in his life. He and my Mother loved to travel, but found it nearly impossible to do on a regular basis given the demands of helping to run a full-time retail supermarket operation. My Dad was a Korean war veteran, a former professional baseball player and an avid horseman. He remained active in professional baseball circles and Korean war veteran affairs throughout his life, as well as continuing to own and breed horses.

After a lot of thought and a lot of discussion with my Mother, they decided it was time to move on. He had accomplished more than most in his business career. It was finally time to have more fun with his other passions in life. So he did what he previously thought would be unthinkable – he sold his interest in the supermarket business to his brother, and he retired at age 70.

He hadn't regretted it for one moment. For ten years after his retirement, he and my Mother had opportunities to travel, to visit family and friends, to spend some time at their favorite destinations, to sleep in, to take drives through the countryside, even to travel across the country at their leisure on a train rather than trying to meet crammed travel deadlines.

Twelve years before this book went to print, my Father, the first Business Pioneer in my life, passed away unexpectedly. Two years ago my Mother passed away. No one was more thankful than they were that they made the move ten years before my Dad's death to retire and enjoy the time together that they have had.

My Father's real legacy, however, isn't the supermarket chain he helped build. His legacy was apparent to everyone he met, as illustrated in a story from several years ago. I was on a family trip almost a hundred miles from my hometown of Quincy, Illinois. Along the way I stopped in a restaurant for a quick lunch. We always kidded my Father how he could never leave a restaurant without first learning the life story of the waiter or waitress.

I must have inherited some of his genes, because in talking to the waitress that day, I learned she was the owner. I soon asked how she started the business. Before she knew my last name, she told the story how she had bought some used restaurant equipment from a man in Quincy, Illinois about twenty-five years earlier by the name of Ferd Niemann. She recalled that he had given her a fair deal, but mostly she recalled that "He was a man who loved people."

What is it most about a man's presence that would leave this memorable impression for twenty-five years. That's the legacy my seventy-hour per week working businessman Father left. I had seen this in my Father for years and this restaurant owner had summed it up. No matter how busy my Father was, he always found the time to talk to people – employees, customers, friends, business colleagues, family - for the simple reason that he loved people.

> ## *Pioneer Mindset*
>
> ☑ *Self Start.* *Act as if all depends on you. Pray as if all depends on God. And be grateful for every moment of success He brings you.*

You Absolutely Won't Achieve The Legacy You Don't Pursue

There's an old saying to the effect that no one on their deathbed ever wished that they had spent more time at the office. Our business is certainly a means to an end – it at a minimum provides us with a livelihood to support our families.

For many, our business may also be an end in itself as well. However, most Business Pioneers whom we know have a vision which extends beyond simply being known as a business owner.

Achieving Your Legacy

As we began this Fourth Quarter Planning discussion, we focused on your personal, business and financial objectives. If you keep the vision of those objectives in the forefront as you embark on the Fourth Quarter Planning process, your likelihood of successfully completing a successful Four Quarters will be substantially increased and your happiness with this process will be more thoroughly realized.

That's why the final strategy in the Fourth Quarter Planning process is to continue where we began – by continually looking forward to the end result you're trying to achieve and visualize the legacy you want to leave. Take the necessary steps, and then find the time to relax and, simply, enjoy the rest of the game.

"We expect to pass through this world but once. Any good therefore that we can do, or any kindness that we can show to any fellow creature, let us do it now. Let us not defer or neglect it. For we shall not pass this way again."

Author Unknown but
attributed to many

Information and Background

Dedication

This book is dedicated to:

My wife, Ann – the love of my life, a great wife and an amazing mother.

Our six children, Katie, Becky, Christine, David, Lisa and Tricia, and our seventeen grandchildren.

And to the first Family Business Pioneers in my life:

My grandfather
Ferd Niemann

My grandfather
Lawrence Jochem

My parents
Ferd and Rita Niemann

Our Story

When we work with Family Business Leaders, we ask about your story and the story of your family business. We get to see the heart and soul of America's family entrepreneurs, that is, America's new breed of Family Business Pioneers.

We get to see your passion and your excellence. We get to see the grit and determination which drive you. We get to see the love and respect you have for your colleagues and for those you serve.

In short, we get to see the pioneer spirit which drives you and your team. Just as it has driven me and our team.

The first two Family Business Pioneers I learned from were my father, Ferd, Jr. and my grandfather, Ferd, Sr. Starting at age 8, they began teaching me about the family business interests in restaurants, supermarkets, real estate, warehousing, ranching, farming, and retail merchandising.

Growing up on a small farm in Quincy, Illinois, and being a part of the Niemann family businesses, was the perfect setting to begin to learn the ins and outs of family business culture, leadership, spunk and drive.

Not all was rosy. Over the years a number of our family businesses faltered and failed, while others succeeded incredibly well. The family supermarket business which my grandfather started in 1917, and which my Dad and his brother carried forward, is now a 4th generation family business which continues to thrive today, serving thousands of families throughout the Midwest.

Throughout my life, I've seen firsthand the devastation that happens to a community and families when companies stall or fail and jobs are lost. The opportunity to do something about it is what attracted me to McGrath North in the early 1980s.

When a business succeeds, so do its employees and their families. This served as the mission for Ray McGrath and Jack North, who founded our firm in 1959. This continues to inspire me and my colleagues at McGrath North as we work with community leaders and Family Business Pioneers to help create jobs and help build industry–leading companies.

Now with over 70 attorneys deployed in over 80 practice areas, we are partnering with families, their businesses and their trusted advisors throughout the U.S. to create incredible, lasting value.

For my part, I enjoy learning from the many Family Business Pioneers I am blessed to work with as a Family Business Continuity Attorney. I met my wife, Ann, then a nursing student, 40 years ago while attending Creighton University's College of Business. We enjoy passing on these family business values to our six children and seventeen grandchildren, as the next generation of pioneers take on tomorrow's many challenges and opportunities.

Acknowledgements

We work with an ever increasing number of professional advisors as part of a number of Business Strategy, Continuity, Succession, Exit and Estate Planning teams to thoughtfully collaborate to achieve the objectives of business leaders, their families and their colleagues.

This includes Insurance Advisors, Financial Advisors, CPAs, merger and acquisition ("M&A") advisors, bankers, bonding professionals, corporate attorneys, business coaches, human resources specialists, strategic planners, estate planners, tax advisors, business mediators, investment bankers, transaction intermediaries, business brokers, management consultants, talent consultants, trust officers, business appraisers, compensation specialists, and peer group chairs.

These professionals all realize the benefits of Business Strategy, Continuity, Succession, Exit and Estate Planning, both to the business leaders they work with and to their own professional responsibilities.

I want to thank each of you for your input and ideas from each of your perspectives on how to serve Business Pioneers who are working towards remarkable success.

I also want to thank my partners at McGrath North, with whom I've worked for over 34 years, for the insights, creativity and strategies I've learned from you in working with Business Pioneers throughout the world.

A Quick "Fourth Quarter" Fitness Checkup

Profitable Growth

Family Business Leaders/Pioneers are telling us they want an effective way to overcome the rapidly accelerating "perfect storm" of business model, culture, demographic and technology changes affecting the business life and profits of all companies today.

Do you have a **Profit Plan** which deploys a carefully selected, well-informed, very active, decisive Profit Strategy Team that you are highly certain will keep your company in a growing, profitable business model?

Priority: ☐ Low ☐ Mid ☐ High

☐ Yes. Got It
☐ No. Not Yet
☐ Not Sure
☐ Look Into It

Wealth Protection

Family Business Leaders/Pioneers are telling us they want to protect and preserve their company and their personal wealth from owner and family disputes, lawsuits, loss of key personnel, divorce, bankruptcy, substance dependency and reckless spending issues.

Do you have a **Protection Plan** that you are highly certain will preserve and protect your personal, business and financial wealth for you and your loved ones?

Priority: ☐ Low ☐ Mid ☐ High

☐ Yes. Got It
☐ No. Not Yet
☐ Not Sure
☐ Look Into It

Lifestyle Continuity

Family Business Leaders/Pioneers are telling us they want more from their Estate Plan. They want lifestyle continuity for themselves and their families and business continuity for their family business.

Do you have an **Estate Plan** that you are highly certain will provide the lifestyle continuity, investment control and "bloodline" success you want for you and your loved ones?

Priority: ☐ Low ☐ Mid ☐ High

☐ Yes. Got It
☐ No. Not Yet
☐ Not Sure
☐ Look Into It

Personal Freedom

Family Business Leaders/Pioneers are telling us they want freedom on their terms. They are telling us they didn't go into business to run a business. They went into business to achieve freedom. And they want their advisors to know how to work together with them to achieve this.

Do you have a **Succession Plan** that you are highly certain will achieve the financial and personal freedom you want for you and your loved ones?

Priority: ☐ Low ☐ Mid ☐ High

☐ Yes. Got It
☐ No. Not Yet
☐ Not Sure
☐ Look Into It

Thank You

Thank you to many of the Business Pioneers I've learned from:

Jim Collins
Bestselling author of *Good To Great*, *Built To Last*, *How The Mighty Fall*, and *Great By Choice*.

John C. Maxwell
Ranked as the world's most influential leadership expert by Business Insider and Inc. Magazine.

Greg S. Reid
Founder and CEO of Secret Knock, ranked by Inc. Magazine as the #1 "Can't Miss" Business Program.

Berny Dohrmann
Founder and Chairman, CEO Space International, world's largest network for CEOs, entrepreneurs and visionary investors.

Kevin Harrington
Inventor of the Infomercial. Original Shark on ABC's Shark Tank and "As Seen on TV" Pioneer.

Randy Johnson
Family Business Advisor and Founder of Ash Johnson Company.

Andy Horowitz
First Vice President. Merrill Lynch – Bank of America Corporation.

Erin Saxton
Founder of eleven Communications. Led media strategy for "Chicken Soup For The Soul" series.

Les Brown
"World's Leading Motivational Speaker". National Speakers Association Hall of Fame.

Frank Schankwitz
Founder of Make - A - Wish Foundation.

Cathy Fitzhenry
Omaha Chair – Vistage International

Dave Anderson
Founder of "Famous Dave's BBQ" Restaurants.

Eryka Morehead
Founder and CEO of
Collaborative Planning Group.

Gene Landrum
Co-Creator and Founder of
Chuck E. Cheese.

Jeff O'Connell
Family Business Advisor,
Wealth Strategies Group.

Ron Klein
Inventor of the Credit Card
Magnetic Strip and the Bond
Quotation System for the New
York Stock Exchange.

Dina Dwyer-Owens
Co-Chair of the Dwyer Group.
Featured in CBS's Emmy-
winning hit reality show
"Undercover Boss".

**Dr. Gladys Taylor
McGarey**
Mother of Holistic Medicine.

Joe Theismann
NFL World Champion Quarterback, NFL Football TV
Commentator, Business Entrepreneur.

Brian Smith
Australian Entrepreneur and
Founder of UGG Boots.

David Houle
Renowned Global Futurist.
Author of *The Shift Age*.

Bob Arno
Criminologist and National
Geographic "Pickpocket King".

Scott Duffy
Founder of Smart Charter,
which he sold to Richard
Branson's Virgin Group.
Bestselling Author of Launch!

Ross Halleck
Pioneer in the World Wide
Web. Launched Netscape
website. Founder of Silicon
Valley creative service firm,
Halleck, Inc.

Dean Cardinale

Founder of World Wide Trekking. Avid mountain climber and guide. Founder of Human Outreach Project.

Dan Fleyshman

Founder of Who's Your Daddy, Inc., making him the youngest founder of a publicly traded company in history.

Sir Bruno Serato

Owner of Anaheim White Horse Italian Restaurant. Named a Top 10 Hero by CNN for his work as Founder of Caterina's Club.

David Freeman

Founder of Beyond Structure. Script development teacher to Pixar, Disney and BBC Executives.

Dr. Duc Vuong

Director of Bariatrics, Lovelace Health System. Empowerment Leader for the Beriatric patient.

Garth Watrous

The head of American Hat Makers, makers of exceptional artisan hats.

Evan Money

Bestselling author, Global Entrepreneur and Executive Producer of the groundbreaking film "Words of Art" starring Zig Zigler.

Steve Sims

Founder of Bluefish, an exclusive luxury concierge service that provides unique, once-in-a-lifetime experiences.

Mary Sarain

Founder and CEO of Pure Cupcakes. Winner of Food Network's 2013 "Cupcake Wars".

Sherry Watson

Coma survivor, one of the chief architects of the Americans with Disabilities Act. Co-Founder and CEO of The Power Of Purpose.

James Pham

Founder / CEO of Enligh Tea Holdings. National Best Selling Co-Author of "Initiative".

Josh Reynolds

Inventor of the Mood Ring & Thighmaster. R.J. Reynolds Tobacco Company heir.

Com Mirza

Runs the 45,000 member Dream Chasing Family community. Has launched over 3 dozen companies around the world.

Dave Farrow

Founder and President of Wizardtech, Inc., Creator of the Farrow Memory Method. Two Time Guinness World Record Holder for Greatest Memory.

Garrett Gunderson

Founder and Chief Wealth Architect of the Wealth Factory and New York Times bestselling author .

Steve Seroka

USAF Colonel, 30 year fighter pilot. Chief of Staff/Nellis AFB. Iraq war veteran.

Gene McNaughton

President of Elite Concepts Business Growth Consulting. Previously the leader of Tony Robbins' Global Salesforce.

Clarissa Burt

Producer Designer for QVC Italy. Founder and CEO of Clarissa International Motivational Media for Women.

David Corbin

Inventor of the touch screen patient interview system. Awarded the International Enterprise of the Year for Innovation.

Maria Kang

Founder and President of Fitness Without Borders Charity. Creator of "The No More Excuses Diet".

Rob Angel

Inventor of the popular word guessing game, Pictionary.

Ruben Gonzalez

Argentine Olympic Luger. First athlete to participate in four different Winter Olympics in four different decades.

Jonah White

Founder of the Billy Bob Teeth Company, which has manufactured over 20 million Billy Bob Teeth sold in over 185 countries.

Sharon Lechter

Co-Author of the international bestseller "Rich Dad Poor Dad". Bestselling author of "Think and Grow Rich - Three Feet From Gold".

John Brown
Founder and CEO of Business Enterprise Institute, one of the country's leading exit planning organizations.

Michael Houlihan
Co-Founder of Barefoot Wine, the world's largest wine brand, now owned by E & J Gallo.

Bonnie Harvey
Co-Founder of Barefoot Wine, the world's largest wine brand, now owned by E & J Gallo.

Nick Halik
Author of "The Thrillionaire". Founder and CEO of Financial Freedom Institute and Money Masters. Founder of Adventure Odyssey company.

Jerry Mathers
The Beaver in the popular "Leave It To Beaver" television show. A leading advocate for living with and dealing with Type 2 Diabetes.

Matt Elledge
U.S. Army Colonel. Founder of the "Heroes Corporate Fellowship Academy" and the "Shifting Gears" programs.

Aaron Scott Young
CEO of Laughlin Associates. Creator of "The Unshackled Owner".

Delia and Gabriel Richardson
Founders of Infinite Impact, LLC.

Curtis Sliwa
Founder of the New York City Guardian Angels Safety Patrol.

Wendy Hatton
CEO of Whi Consulting Group, an international CEO training organization.

Tony Bodoh
Customer experience analyst for startups to Fortune 500 companies and Founder of Tony Bodah International, LLC.

Hugh Ballou
Transformational Leadership Strategist. Founder of Syner-Vision International, Inc.

Mark Jones
Founder of the Sprowtt.com investor capital formation program and the Sprowttcf.com crowdfunding program.

Daniel Ruke
Founder of blink, which has helped launch hundreds of brands, products and companies.

Mario Andretti
Entrepreneur and Champion Race Car Driver. Winner Indianapolis 500, Daytona 500. Named Driver of the Century.

**George Campbell
(aka – Joe Malarkey)**
"The Worst Motivational Speaker in America!". Featured on the Hit TV Show "60 Minutes" and "To Tell The Truth".

Charles Van Kessler
Founder and CEO of Passion 4 Life Liquid Vitamins. Holocaust survivor.

Ed Bogle
Founder of IdeationEdge. Senior Faculty of CEO Space International.

Kevin Eastman
Vice President Basketball Operations LA Clippers.

Dr. Sudip Bose
Iraq War Bronze Star recipient, "CNN Hero", the ER Physician who treated the captured Saddam Hussein.

James Malinchak
Founder of James Malinchak International. Featured on ABC's Hit TV Show "Secret Millionaire".

Rev. Val Peter
Former Executive Director of Boys Town

Norman Hood
Founder of The Exit Plan Show.

Gerry Foster
Founder of Big Brand Formula. Known worldwide as "The Brand Master." Former Proctor & Gamble branding expert.

Conferences

Thank you to the companies and organizations, throughout the U.S. and Canada, who have had me present these topics at conferences to their customers, clients or members, including:

- American Society of Woman Accountants
- Arbor Bank
- Associated General Contractors
- Association of Corporate Growth
- Association of Language Travel Organisations
- American Association of Franchisees & Dealers
- Business Enterprise Institute
- Community Banks of Colorado
- Creighton University
- Council on State Taxation
- Domino's Franchisee Forum
- Estate Planning Council of Portland
- Financial Planning Association
- Great Plains Federal Tax Institute
- Greater Omaha Chamber of Commerce
- Home Instead Senior Care
- Iowa State Bar Association
- Land Improvement Contractors Association
- M Financial Group
- McDonalds (NBMOA)
- Management Recruiters International
- Merrill Lynch
- MOKAN Trust & Financial Services
- Mutual of Omaha
- National Advisors Trust
- National Association of Insurance & Financial Advisors
- National Business Institute
- Nebraska Association of Health Underwriters
- Nebraska Bankers Association
- Nebraska Bar Association
- Nebraska Chamber of Commerce
- Nebraska Farm Bureau
- Nebraska Society of CPAs
- New York Life Nautilus Group
- Northwestern Mutual
- Omaha Estate Planning Council
- Optimist International
- RETSO
- Secret Knock
- Strafford
- Society of Financial Service Professionals
- Tax Executive Institute
- Ted Rogers School of Management
- The Executive Committee (TEC)
- United Way
- University of Nebraska
- Vistage International

Testimonials

"Nick, it's important that I say THANK YOU. I know the work that goes into mastering something - and you are a master!"

> **Cathy Fitzhenry**, Omaha Chair, Vistage International, the world's leading CEO peer group organization.

"Nick Niemann takes E-Myth into the "super change markets" which dominate every business venture owner's thinking."

> **Berny Dohrmann**, Founder and Chairman, CEO Space International, the world's largest CEO network. Ranked by Forbes Magazine as the country's #1 "Can't Miss" entrepreneurs program.

"Nick, thank you for sharing your wisdom at our Secret Knock. Your energy, knowledge and insights were simply amazing."

> **Greg Reid**. Founder & CEO of Secret Knock. Ranked by Inc. Magazine as the country's #1 "Can't Miss" business program.

"Nick, your profit strategies and creative approach for business growth and success is a tremendous benefit offered to business leaders."

> **Ron Kline**, Inventor of the Credit Card Magnetic Strip and the Bond Quotation System for the New York Stock Exchange.

"Nick's approach is impactful, thought provoking, and critical to building a business platform that will stand the test of time."

> **Boyd Ober**, President & CEO Leadership Resources.

"Nick Niemann is an energetic and impactful speaker who has a riveting way of conveying fresh, powerful business concepts which are critical today for every business and profession, from the smallest firms to global giants."

> **G. Michael Beduze**, Managing Partner, DaVinci Global Consulting, LLC.

"Nick Niemann's inspiring approach to addressing the transformative forces which are shaping our future is a roadmap for game changers!"

> **Barbara Niven**, Hollywood's Top Business Media Expert.

"If you're ready to build your business so it will stand the test of time, then use the strategies by my friend, Nick Niemann!"

> **James Malinchak**. Featured on ABC's Hit TV Show "Secret Millionaire". Founder, www.BigMoneySpeaker.com. Co-Author of *Chicken Soup for the College Soul.*

"Nick Niemann does a masterful job of teaching us step by step how to build an organizational model that is able to survive and thrive in this competitive world today!"

> **John Formica**, Former Disney Leader, America's Customer Experience Coach, Author of *Making the Customer Experience Magical Now!*

"For every business leader looking for the next 'slight edge', Nick Niemann's business model myth program overdelivers."

> **Joe Theismann**, NFL World Champion Quarterback. NFL Football TV Commentator, Business Entrepreneur and Motivational Speaker. Featured in the Hit Movie, "The Blind Side".

"I appreciate Nick's unique understanding how leadership, company culture and Business Model connect and impact each other."

> **George Campbell** (aka Joe Malarkey), "The Worst Motivational Speaker in America!" Featured on the CBS Hit TV Show "60 Minutes". National Speakers Association Hall of Fame.

"Every business and profession is at risk for the commoditization trap. Nick Niemann's business model myth program shows us all a crystal clear formula for overcoming this."

> **Jonathan Sprinkles**, National Speaker of the Year (APCA), Marketer of the Year (JMI), Mentor of the Year (Disney), www.JSprinkles.com.

"Nick, you have done a great job in addressing one of the most important issues in business today. Congratulations! Keep up the good work!"

> **Brian Tracy**, Author of *The Way to Wealth*. Top selling author of over 65 books and legendary speaker who has addressed over 5,000,000 people in over 65 countries.

Business and Professional Sectors

The interest in the topics covered in this book runs throughout our nation's business and professional sectors. Business owners from a variety of small, middle-market and large companies and firms in various business and professional sectors have asked us to work with them to deploy the actions discussed in this book, including:

Business

Manufacturing	Distribution	Consumer Services
Business Services	Financial Services	Personal Services
Food & Beverage	Retail	Product Development
Construction	Human Resources	Technology
Health Care	Energy	Leasing
Agribusiness	Transportation	Management
Farm & Ranch	Franchise	Education
Real Estate	Security	Warehousing

Professional

CPAs	Investment Advisors	Architects
Financial Planners	Attorneys	Physicians
Insurance Advisors	Engineers	IT Professionals
Business Consultants	Environmental Specialists	Real Estate Developers

Locations

The interest in these topics stretches throughout the world. Nick has spoken to CEOs from over 40 countries about their Business Continuity and Succession Planning. Below are several of the locations where he has traveled to work with Family Business Pioneers and to speak at the request of the leaders of various companies and associations:

Alabama
Birmingham
Arizona
Phoenix
Scottsdale
California
Berkeley
Carlsbad
Cathedral City
Commerce
Downey
Glendora
Los Angeles
Menlo Park
Monterey
Oakland
Ontario
Palm Desert
Pomona
Salinas
San Diego
San Francisco
Santa Monica
Colorado
Colorado Springs
Denver
Greeley
Florida
Boca Raton
Ft. Lauderdale
Jacksonville
Orlando
Tampa
Georgia
Atlanta

Illinois
Chicago
Naperville
Quincy
Indiana
Indianapolis
Iowa
Ames
Cedar Falls
Cedar Rapids
Council Bluffs
Davenport
Des Moines
Ida Grove
Iowa City
Glenwood
Sioux City
Waterloo
Kansas
Kansas City
Manhattan
Topeka
Winfield
Kentucky
Louisville
Louisiana
Mandeville
Monroe
New Orleans
Maryland
Easton
Massachusetts
Boston
Michigan
Detroit
Lansing
Petoskey
Traverse City

Minnesota
Burnsville
Minneapolis
New Brighton
New Ulm
St. Paul
Missouri
Kansas City
St. Charles
St. Louis
Nebraska
Ashland
Bellevue
Columbus
Elkhorn
Grand Island
Gretna
Kearney
La Vista
Lincoln
Norfolk
Omaha
South Sioux City
York
Nevada
Las Vegas
New Jersey
Cranford
Morristown
New York
New York City
North Carolina
Charlotte
Greensboro
High Point
North Dakota
Bismarck

Ohio
Akron
Canton
Cincinnati
Cleveland
Columbus
Dalton
Oklahoma
Oklahoma City
Oregon
Portland
Pennsylvania
Harrisburg
Lancaster
Philadelphia
Pittsburgh
York
Zelienople
South Dakota
Pierre
Sioux Falls
Texas
Dallas
Houston
College Station
San Antonio
Utah
Alpine
Bountiful
Park City
Salt Lake City
Sandy
Wisconsin
Eau Claire
Madison
Milwaukee

Canada

Calgary, BC
Vancouver, BC

Winnipeg, MB
Burlington, ON

Markham, ON
Niagra Falls, ON

Ottawa, ON
Toronto, ON

Media

Nick Niemann has been featured discussing these topics in or on various media, including:

Inc. Magazine	Bloomberg Businessweek	The Wall Street Journal
Fox News	Midlands Business Journal	Financial Planning Magazine
Omaha World-Herald	Market Watch	The CW
ABC	NBC	CBS
Yahoo! Finance	Vistage International	Omaha Magazine
Atlanta Business Chronicle	Birmingham Business Journal	Portland Business Journal
Minneapolis St. Paul Business Journal	Chicago Business Journal	Denver Business Journal
Nashville Business Journal	Houston Business Journal	Memphis Business Journal
San Francisco Business Times	New York Business Journal	Los Angeles Business
The Kansas City Star Kansas City	St. Louis Business Journal	News Radio 1110 KFAB
StarTribune		Merrill Edge

* No claim is made here that these media companies have endorsed Nick Niemann, his program or his firm.

Background

For Your Profit Playbook

- Working with Family Business Leaders/Pioneers on their <u>Profit Plans</u> for 37+ years.
- Raised and worked in several Niemann family businesses starting at age 8.
- Served on the Board of Directors and as part owner of Niemann Foods, Inc.
- Taught the Business Model Profit protocol to over 100 business leader groups in the U.S. and Canada.
- Worked with over 900+ CEOs on their Business Model design and innovation and on how to set up their Profit Strategy Team.
- A graduate of CEO Space International.
- A graduate of the Business Model Strategyzer Program.
- Founder and President of Family Business Pioneer Institute LLC.
- Certified as a Leadership Coach by the John C. Maxwell Executive Leadership Program.
- Co-creator of the internationally acclaimed Business Model Generation program (introduced the world to the Business Model Canvas now being used by 5,000,000+ entrepreneurs and strategic planners).
- Designed Nebraska's business development platform (which has created over 100,000 new jobs and $30 billion capital investment in 850+ business expansions).
- Trained in the leadership and business decision making techniques of Vistage International (the world's leading CEO peer group and private advisory board organization).
- Vistage National Business Resource Speaker.

For Your Estate Playbook

- Working with Family Business Leaders/Pioneers on their <u>Estate Plans</u> for 37+ years.
- Member of the Family Firm Institute
- Wrote the book on Estate Planning: "The Next Move For Families".
- Member of the Omaha Estate Planning Council.
- Served as Adjunct Faculty teaching Estate Planning at Creighton University Law School.
- Selected to Best Lawyers in America® for Family Business Law, Tax Law and Trusts and Estates.

For Your Protection Playbook

- Working with Family Business Leaders/ Pioneers on their <u>Protection Plans</u> for 37+ years.
- Selected to Best Lawyers in America® for Closely Held Companies and Business Organzations.
- Awarded the AV Preeminent national ranking for attorneys by Martindale Hubbell.
- Member of the American Bar Association.
- Member of the American Institute of CPAs.
- Selected to the Trusted Advisor Board of the Omaha CEO Boards of Vistage International.

For Your Succession Playbook

- Working with Family Business Leaders/Pioneers on their <u>Succession and Exit Plans</u> for 37+ years.
- Member of the two leading Succession and Exit Planning Advisor Organizations in the U.S.: Business Enterprise Institute and Exit Planning Institute.
- Have taught Succession and Exit Planning to other attorneys, CPAs and financial advisors across the U.S. and to CEOs from 40+ countries.
- Lawyer of the Year – Tax Law (Omaha), Best Lawyers in America®.
- Wrote the book on Succession and Exit Planning: "The Next Move For Business Owners".
- Selected as the Face of Business Continuity and Succession Planning by Omaha Magazine.

The Family Business Continuity Attorney

Why Are Family Business Leaders Partnering With A Family Business Continuity Attorney?

Your Family Business Continuity Attorney should have the Training, Experience and Affiliations to handle what will be needed	Corporate Attorney	Estate Planning Attorney	Asset Protection Attorney	Tax Attorney	Executive Benefits Attorney	ESOP Attorney	Succession Planning Attorney	Exit Planning Attorney	M & A Attorney	Mediation Attorney	Family Business Continuity Attorney
Corporate Planning	✓										✓
Estate Planning		✓									✓
Asset Protection Planning			✓								✓
Tax Reduction Planning				✓							✓
Key Employee Retention					✓						✓
Group Employee Ownership						✓					✓
Succession Planning							✓				✓
Exit Planning								✓			✓
Company Sale									✓		✓
Dispute Resolution										✓	✓
Dispute Avoidance											✓
Leadership Development											✓
Key Employee Ownership											✓
Life Insurance Positioning											✓
Business Profit Strategy											✓
Business Valuation Protocol											✓
Family Business Dynamics											✓

Winning The Whole Game

The Right Team

The Right Plays

Starting Now

The Business Leaders/Pioneers we partner with have told us how they want us to work together with them and their team. So, that is how we work together:

1. Discover

Based on what you value most, we look into the future with you to <u>discover</u> the future you want for yourself, your family, your colleagues, your stakeholders, your customers, your business and your communities.

2. Decide

Together we <u>decide</u> what's really needed to reach that future.

3. Deploy

Together we move ahead with speed, clarity and purpose to carefully prioritize, design and <u>deploy</u> the Main Plays needed to "win the whole game".

This starts with making a decision that you will settle for nothing short of winning the whole game.

Next Step

To check Nick's availability to design and deploy a "Fourth Quarter" Game Plan with you, your spouse, your CEO, your President, your partner, your colleague, your mentor, your parent or your client, please contact him at:

(402) 633-1489
nniemann@McGrathNorth.com
www.FourthQuarterFirst.com

Legal Info

The Fourth Quarter Game Plan™ trademark is owned by Nicholas K. Niemann.

First Softcover Edition 2017
Second Softcover Edition 2018

ISBN 13: 978-0-9796195-9-5
LCCN: 2017933238

Printed in the United States of America
10 9 8 7 6 5 4 3

Published by:
Family Business Pioneer Institute LLC
1601 Dodge Street, Suite 3700
Omaha, NE 68102

The background in the cover photo is the Pioneer Courage Park in Omaha. The photo is from the edition of Omaha Magazine which named Nick Niemann as Omaha's Face of Business Continuity and Succession Planning.

Index